D1297492

A HISTORY
OF SOUTHERN BAPTIST
THEOLOGICAL SEMINARY

A HISTORY
OF
SOUTHERN BAPTIST
THEOLOGICAL
SEMINARY

William A. Mueller

BROADMAN PRESS
Nashville, Tennessee

Library of Congress catalog card number 59–9687

Printed in the United States of America
5.N58KSP

To
All the Alumni

Preface

THE DREAMS, devotion, and insight of James Petigru Boyce brought into focus the desires of Southern Baptists for a central theological institution and thus determined that a centennial history of the Southern Baptist Theological Seminary would have to be written at this time. It is appropriate, therefore, to let Dr. Boyce set the tone of this preface.

The Civil War had driven the Seminary from its original home in Greenville, South Carolina, to Louisville, Kentucky. On the occasion of the opening session in this new home, September 1, 1877, Dr. Boyce looked back over the first eighteen years of significant struggle and said:

I do not propose to recount the history of this enterprise. That history, so far as it ever can be written, must await the full fruition of all our hopes, and should come from one less intimately associated with it than I have been. It never can be written in full; it never ought to be thus written. It is only God's inspiration which dares speak of evils and faults and injuries and calumnies proceeding from men whom we know to be good. That inspired Word alone can make these simply the shadows which bring out more gloriously the brightness of the character of the good. Human prejudice and passion would make hideous deformity of all by the excesses which its pencillings would exhibit. Let all such evil be buried in the silence of forgetfulness. Let the history, when written, tell only of the toils and trials and sacrifices, and wisdom and prudence and foresight, and prayers and tears and faith, of the people of God to whom the institution will have owed its existence and its possibilities of blessing. And God grant that it may go down to succeeding ages to bless his cause and glorify his name when all of us here have been forgotten in this world forever! In the establishment and endowment of this Seminary we think we have solved a problem of interest, not to Baptists of the South alone, but to all who are interested in the ministry of Christ as an instrumentality for the salvation of souls and the edification of his saints.

The early days of the history of the Seminary, which were so close to Dr. Boyce, are now softened by the haze of distance. The people have become mere names. The agonizing struggles to plant a new venture in the life of Southern Baptists have become only memories. So, it is easy to tell the story of those early days but more difficult to appraise events which are still near.

Thus, as it is difficult to write the biography of a man while he lives, so it is always difficult to write the history of an institution which continues to make history even while the record is being written. Some future historian must provide the objective appraisal of the transitional times in which we now live.

It is significant that this history is written, as Dr. Boyce proposed, by one who is capable of objective evaluation of the past. Professor William Mueller has become a part of the life of the Seminary and of the Southern Baptist Convention only since World War II. He thus brings the perspective of a European scholar not only to the life of the institution but to the whole American scene. Yet he writes not as an outsider but as one who has chosen to belong to the heritage which he now records.

While an institution may want to highlight certain persons and events in its history, Professor Mueller has sought to maintain the true historian's balance to the end that the romantic story of the first hundred years of the Southern Baptist Theological Seminary may be understood, with its trials and its triumphs used as guideposts for all who live during this second century and beyond. Thus the good that men have done will not be interred, but we of this and future generations shall rise up to call them blessed who have invested their lives in this enterprise of theological education which is dedicated to the lordship of Christ.

DUKE K. McCALL, *President*
Southern Baptist Theological Seminary

Contents

1. Early Struggles for an Educated Ministry 1

2. James P. Boyce, Founder 16

3. James P. Boyce, Administrator and Treasurer . . . 33

4. The Faithful Four: the Original Faculty 52

5. Thoroughly Furnished unto All Good Works . . . 112

6. Crawford Howell Toy 135

7. William Heth Whitsitt, Church Historian 143

8. E. Y. Mullins, President 179

9. Sampey, Fuller, and McCall 211

Chronology 232

Abstract of Principles 238

Faculty 242

Bibliography 245

Index 251

Illustrations

facing page

The Original Faculty 100

Seminary Presidents 101

Prominent Members of the Faculty 116

Faculty, 1944–45 117

Faculty, 1949–50 148

Old Norton Hall 149

Buildings of the School of Church Music 164

Air View of the Seminary Campus in Louisville . . . 165

1

Early Struggles for an Educated Ministry

SOUTHERN BAPTIST THEOLOGICAL SEMINARY was founded in 1859, nine years after the mid-century milestone had been passed and two years before the War Between the States erupted with all its fury and devastation. The age into which the Seminary was born was characterized by numerous and often dangerous or contradictory currents of thought. It was the age of such Christian leaders as Charles Haddon Spurgeon, Dwight L. Moody, David Livingstone, Robert Moffat, R. H. Graves, and T. J. Bowen. But it was also the age of Karl Marx, Charles Darwin, and Herbert Spencer.

The Seminary was born in an awareness of the intellectual ferment of the age. Although never a Darwinian, James P. Boyce had a copy of *The Origin of Species* in his library within a year of its publication. He also had copies of such significant new works for biblical scholarship as Winer's *New Testament Grammar* and Tischendorf's *Novum Testamentum Graece*. Developments of the era would shape the history of the Seminary in various ways. On the one hand, the skepticism arising from evolution and biblical criticism would cause the loss of the brilliant Crawford H. Toy, the Seminary's "jewel of learning." On the other, fresh knowledge of New Testament Greek would enable A. T. Robertson to produce his monumental work, *A Grammar of the Greek New Testament in the Light of Historical Research*.

The immediate culture out of which Southern Seminary grew was that of the Old South. Culturally and economically, the peo-

1

ple of that era reveal interesting facets. On the one hand, there was an upper stratum of well-to-do planters with their large slave holdings, and on the other, hosts of middle-class artisans and struggling farmers. The majority of Baptists in the South around 1850 were rural people. They were simple, frugal, and hard-working folk, rugged of speech and manner and given to Jacksonian democracy. Slavery was taken for granted as an established fact in the cultural and economic life of the South.

The Seminary, as Dr. Duke K. McCall has well pointed out, "grew up alongside the Convention rather than inside it. Its roots are in Baptist individualism rather than Baptist organization. It rose not on the shoulders of the denomination but on the personal sacrifices of many individual donors."

In retrospect, the four noble men—Boyce, Broadus, Manly, and Williams—who constituted the first faculty of Southern Seminary were men of large vision and noble courage. Humanly speaking, they might well have staggered at the task of establishing a central theological seminary in a denomination so young and a world so torn by strife and perilous spiritual cross currents. But in spite of all odds, these men, aided by some far-sighted brethren in the Southern Baptist Convention, ventured forth and established their school of the prophets. To tell the story of this venture is the purpose of this book.

Southern Baptists were a rather small and divided group when serious interest in theological education first emerged among some of their leaders. It was Basil Manly, Sr., who in 1835 first entertained the idea of establishing a central theological seminary. When ten years later the Southern Baptist Convention was organized at Augusta, Georgia, the new denomination numbered hardly more than three hundred thousand members. Of these, one hundred thousand were slaves.[1]

The financial strength of the newly established body was also

---

[1] W. H. Whitsitt, "Historical Discourse at the 50th Anniversary of the Southern Baptist Convention," *Proceedings of the Southern Baptist Convention*, 1895, pp. 77–90.

comparatively weak. The Foreign Mission Board reported in 1846 receipts of $11,735.22. A year later, the Domestic Board of Missions for the Southern Baptist Convention had received only $9,594.60 for all its work.[2] In view of these conditions W. O. Carver has rightly said that "missions and theological education had to do their work of building a denomination in the face of retarding and opposing forces."[3]

The general simplicity of Baptist life and thought was one of the factors that tended to work against theological education. In the main, Baptists had grown by means of lay preaching. This was true in the colonial period and even in the early nineteenth century. They had profited perhaps most from the results of the Great Awakening, which so deeply affected the religious and political fortunes of colonial America. How, then, had the Baptists of America provided for their ministry?

Until the American Revolution, Baptists had secured their preachers from at least four sources. First, many ministers were immigrants from the British Isles, and some of them had received excellent theological training in their homelands or on the Continent. Roger Williams and John Clarke were of that group. Second, preachers from other communions, after accepting Baptist views, helped the ministerial cause. Third, schools like Hopewell Academy in New Jersey and the first Baptist college in colonial America, Brown University, established in 1764, were another source of the American Baptist ministry. These were still further aided by the founding of the Hamilton Literary and Theological Institute, later called Colgate University, in 1819, and Newton Theological Institution, the first distinctively theological school for Baptists in America, in 1825. Fourth, some Baptist preachers were privately tutored in the homes of older, experienced ministers. Perhaps most significant, local Baptist churches sometimes set aside men from their own ranks, often without benefit of training, as ministers of the gospel.

---

[2] *Ibid.*, p. 77.

[3] W. O. Carver, "The Southern Baptist Theological Seminary in the Growing of the Denomination," *Review and Expositor*, XLIII (April, 1946), 133.

Farmer-preachers abounded on America's frontier in the middle and southwestern states, nor were they wanting in some of the seaboard states. A. T. Robertson wrote in 1891:

The vast majority of our Southern Baptist ministers of the last century had little or no training in the schools. But there were few schools. They were self-educated men, often helped and taught by their wives. Those good men lacked education, not from choice, but from compulsion.[4]

Yet Dr. Robertson also made clear that although men like William Mason, Andrew Broaddus, David Barrow, and Jesse Mercer had little formal training, they literally thirsted for knowledge and were always friends of larger educational opportunities for their ministers.

Still another obstacle in the way of sound theological education lay in the sad memories of persecution that Baptists and their preachers had suffered at the hands of well-educated ministers of established churches in England and colonial America. This left an indelible mark on the minds of many Baptist people. Moreover, an educated ministry, these frontier Baptists argued, is set off from the common people both by learning and status. It is no wonder, therefore, that they were suspicious of the value of theological education. Older communions, established by law in at least nine areas of the American Colonies, could boast of ancient traditions and a learned ministry. But neither their antiquity nor the learning of their ministers prevented their casting Baptist preachers in jail in Virginia. These persecutors of Baptists and other free church people could boast of a superior education. They looked with utter contempt on these Baptist innovators and their often unlearned ministers. It took time and patience to overcome the prejudices of Baptist people against theological education which they, quite understandably, tended to identify with their detractors and persecutors.

Last, but not least, the common folk of evangelical and Baptist

---

[4] A. T. Robertson, "Southern Baptist Ministers of a Hundred Years Ago," *The Seminary Magazine*, IV (January, 1891), pp. 6–7.

churches in America and Europe have always had an instinctive aversion to theological education. They have felt that somehow theological reflection may lead either to spiritual pride or paralysis of faith.

The history of theological controversy is anything but pleasant reading. Melanchthon, the co-worker of Martin Luther, bitterly complained in his day about the *rabies theologorum*, the quarrelsomeness of theologians. John Macmurray, eminent British thinker, has in this century spoken of the "fall into theology" of the Christian movement. The perceptive reader may recall the warning of Soeren Kierkegaard against the perils of theological professors. Walther Koehler, a first-rate church historian, has discerningly pointed out that "theology always signifies an open door to reason, and the question is only how far that door may be opened." The bias, therefore, of many sincere Christian believers and of early American Baptists is understandable and is worthy of respect. The educated clergy had not made a favorable impression on these people.

However, there was a glimmer of hope. As early as 1788 the Baptists of Virginia had unanimously passed a resolution "that a committee of ten members, five persons from each side of the James River, be appointed to forward the business respecting a seminary of learning. This committee actually was organized, but abandoned its work eventually for lack of funds." [5] Oliver Hart of Charleston, South Carolina, had, even before this time, seen the need of organized effort and helped to form a society "to assist pious young men in obtaining an education for the public services of the Church." [6] Richard Furman, a leader among Southern Baptists, reported that the Charleston Association as early as 1790 maintained a theological library "for the education of pious young men new in divinity studies." [7] Education societies, established by far-sighted Baptist leaders, tried to dispel the prej-

---

[5] *Ibid.*, p. 1.
[6] *Ibid.*
[7] Charles A. McGlon, "Speech Education in Baptist Theological Seminaries, 1819–1943" (Doctoral dissertation, Columbia University, 1943) p. 15.

udices against theological education that were still lingering in the minds of Northern and Southern Baptists. [8]

But in every forward movement it is usually an individual leader with ideas who provokes reflection, stimulates action, and thus advances progress. Dr. Basil Manly, Sr., was such a leader. In 1835 he wrote an article in which he proposed a Southwide theological seminary for Southern Baptists. In this article he reviewed what had been done in the Carolinas and Georgia for theological education, revealed its inadequacy, and suggested that an individual state could not possibly meet the need for a Southwide theological training program. Manly, therefore, proposed that a "convention of the friends of this cause from the Carolinas and Georgia, and such other of the Southern and Western States as may be disposed to unite with them" be held in order "to deliberate and form some unified plan for the accomplishment of this great object." [9]

Manly's suggestion was welcomed by South Carolina but not by any of the other states. Three months later the editor of the journal that had published Manly's article confessed his dismay over the lack of response to the idea of a central theological school among the other Southern states:

It remains for the South Carolina Baptists to manage their own Institution in their own way. If we but carry forward our Institution, at any convenient site, with the energy and enlightened policy which the cause demands, we need not despair of union yet. The truth is, if we make but a good Institution, and hold out the substantial advantages which an intelligent student has a right to expect in an Institution of this kind, students will flock in from all quarters, either with or without the formality of union among the States.[10]

Was Manly's suggestion for a central theological school among Southern Baptists premature? Not necessarily so. Two years before his proposal Baptists in Cincinnati had convened in order to

---

[8] *Ibid.*, p. 19.

[9] *The Southern Baptist and General Intelligencer*, March 13, 1835, p. 172.

[10] *Ibid.*, July 31, 1835, pp. 72–73. Cf. W. W. Barnes, *The Southern Baptist Convention, 1845–1953* (Nashville: Broadman Press, 1954), p. 121.

project a theological seminary in that area. At this meeting in July, 1833, 102 delegates—74 from Ohio, 18 from Kentucky, 8 from Indiana, and 1 each from Illionis and the East—met as the Western Baptist Convention in order to promote theological education for the needy West.

Among the participants in this convention were Silas Mercer Nod, a Virginia lawyer who had become a preacher; Jonathan Going from Vermont, a Brown University graduate; Howard Malcolm, former missionary to Burma and past president of Georgetown College, Kentucky; Henry Jackson, trustee of Brown University and professor at Georgetown; J. Stevens, an Andover graduate and professor at Denison University; and finally, John Mason Peck, one of the founders of the American Baptist Triennial Convention in 1814 and pioneer in home mission work around St. Louis.

At the first session of the Cincinnati convention Dr. Peck proposed "that it is essential to the interests of Western Baptists that a theological institution be established in some central portion of the Mississippi Valley and that a committee be appointed to open correspondence on the subject, ascertain the view of the brethren, look out for a site for location, receive proposals for funds or donations, and report to the next Convention." [11]

Ezra Going was secured as agent, and a location at Covington, Kentucky, was considered for purchase, provided that friends in Kentucky would approve the plan and raise twenty thousand dollars. In January, 1835, Going and Stevens met with the Kentucky brethren and found them interested enough to pledge the sum of twenty-five thousand dollars. In June of that year, three hundred seventy acres of land were acquired at Covington for about thirty-three thousand dollars. However, during the first seven years of its existence the Western Education Society, which had proposed to build a theological seminary, received in cash the pitiful sum of only one hundred eighty-eight dollars and fifty cents.

---

[11] W. C. James, *A History of the Western Baptist Theological Seminary* (Louisville: Baptist World Publishing Co., 1905), p. 46.

Despite these difficulties, the Western Baptist Theological Institute at Covington, Kentucky, opened its doors in the fall of 1845. An able faculty, all of them Northerners, had been gathered, among them Ezekiel Gilman Robinson, graduate of Brown and Newton and a former chaplain of the University of Virginia; R. E. Pattison, who became president of the school; Asa Drury, a former pastor of the Covington Baptist Church; and Ebenezer Dodge, another Brown and Newton graduate.

Western Baptist Theological Institute operated for only three years. In its first session twenty-six students were enrolled, of which number seventeen came from Ohio, two from New York, one each from Indiana, Pennsylvania, Connecticut, and Maine, and only three from the South. During the session of 1847–48 no Southern students matriculated. When the American Baptist Missionary Union met in Cincinnati in 1847, the entire faculty of the Institute became its members. This led to the resignation of Dr. R. T. Dillard, a Kentucky trustee, and the withdrawal of his son, who was a student at the school. Several ministerial students from Georgetown College, instead of enrolling at nearby Western Theological Institute, preferred to go to Princeton Theological Seminary.

Due to the strained relationships between Northern and Southern Baptists over the slavery issue, as well as the fact that in the year of its founding Southern Baptists had broken away from their Northern brethren to establish their own convention, Western Theological Institute was doomed to extinction from the very start. However, despite its brief career, it had served its purpose. First, it had stimulated Southern Baptist leaders to pursue afresh and with greater vigor than ever before the dream of a central theological seminary for the training of its ministry. Second, its brief effort had not been in vain as far as its own graduates were concerned. Among the most distinguished alumni of Western Theological Institute were men like William Moore, who wrought mightily for the kingdom of God among the Karens in northern Burma. N. M. Wood, after initial labors in his native state of Maine, became a professor at Shurtleff College in Illinois.

And who has not heard of Rufus C. Burleson, a household word among Texas Baptists? On the day of his graduation from Western in June, 1847, he exclaimed, "This day I consecrate my life to Texas." [12] He kept his vow. Not only did he baptize Mrs. Dickenson, the heroine of the Alamo, and General Sam Houston, but he is remembered as the beloved and able leader who for many eventful years presided over the affairs of Baylor University. Still another famous graduate of Western Baptist Institute was William Ashmore, for more than fifty years a pioneer missionary in China. At the turn of the century Dr. Ashmore lectured to enthusiastic crowds at Southern Baptist Seminary.

The factors, favorable and unfavorable, surrounding the establishment of a central theological school for Southern Baptists finally worked out to its realization. The organization of the Southern Baptist Convention in 1845 had left the South without a theological seminary for its ministry. Hamilton Literary and Theological Institute and Rochester Theological Seminary in New York state as well as Newton Theological Institution near Boston were under Northern Baptist control. It was highly imperative, therefore, that Southern Baptists develop their own theological school.

The organizers of the Southern Baptist Convention had from the first discussed the question of establishing a seminary of their own. Yet many conflicting interests thwarted their efforts for a number of years, as W. O. Carver has indicated:

The State consciousness, pride and jealousy, the provincial claims of the colleges (at least seven) with theological departments, the vested interest and natural feeling of responsibility of the professors of these college departments to state sentiment, all unconsciously exploited the provincialism and unschooled conservatism of the people generally for delaying unity. There was lack of doctrinal and ecclesiastical unity. Disagreements in these matters became militant and worked along three most important lines: missions, ecclesiology, history; and continued to provide divisive issues for sixty years.[13]

---

[12] Barnes, *op. cit.*, p. 124 (footnote).
[13] Carver, *op. cit.*, p. 134.

However, the determination of several Southern Baptist leaders pushed the matter along. Men like R. B. C. Howell; A. M. Poindexter; James P. Boyce; Basil Manly, father and son; and others kept up the agitation for the sorely needed central theological school.

When the American Baptist Indian Mission Association met at Nashville, Tennessee, in October, 1847, Dr. Howell was able to convene a special meeting of men deeply concerned about such a theological school. Some one hundred and fifty people from eight states and two Indian nations gathered in this conference to discuss the question of a new central theological seminary. Dr. J. M. Pendleton of Kentucky presided at the meeting. As a result of the deliberations a rather large committee composed of Dr. Howell, P. S. Gayle, J. R. Graves, Adiel Sherwood, J. B. Taylor, R. Holman, T. W. Haynes, R. W. Elledge, J. L. Waller, S. Baker, and A. D. Sears was appointed to study the matter and make a report. Such a report concerning the proposed theological school was duly prepared, presented, and adopted on October 30, 1847:

Resolved, That to meet the wants of the South, a Theological School located in a central position, and in every respect thoroughly prepared to impart to its pupils a full and perfect knowledge of the word of God, and of all the branches of learning necessary to its correct exposition and to the effectual discharge of the pastoral office, is absolutely necessary.

Resolved, That the Churches in the whole South require at present but one such Seminary, and to secure it, it is necessary that we direct, in this behalf, all our energies to one point.

Resolved, That this subject be fully laid before our churches and brethren throughout the whole South, in such a manner as, if practicable, to unite them all in the good work, and to elicit their opinion and action in the premises.

Resolved, That to the brethren from all parts of the South, when assembled in Triennial Convention, at Nashville, in May, 1849, we submit the execution of this great work, and the question of the locality of the proposed Seminary.[14]

---

[14] Barnes, *op. cit.,* p. 126.

Exactly ten more years were to pass before this bold venture could be realized. Many difficulties were still to be overcome. Because of cholera raging in Nashville in May, 1849, the Educational Convention was adjourned to Charleston, South Carolina. There it gave one full evening to the discussion of the matter. Basil Manly, Jr., made an address on the subject of the proposed theological seminary. He expressed himself as heartily in favor of such a project "on the score of economy, efficiency, and practicability." [15]

Manly drove home the idea that in their Southern Baptist colleges seven theological professors were teaching only thirty students. In a central theological seminary the scattered efforts now exerted in these schools could be concentrated in one united effort. Moreover, a large number of students, he argued, gathered from various parts of the Southland in such a centralized theological seminary would help reduce sectional peculiarities and jealousies and thus contribute toward denominational cohesion and unity.

After considering various plans of getting such a common theological school under way, Manly advanced as the most feasible idea the establishment of an entirely new institution, with a new board of trustees, new funds, and possibly using the existing theological college departments as a foundation. The new board, Manly believed, ought to be selected from all the states of the Southern Convention. [16]

Dr. W. B. Johnson, president of the Southern Baptist Convention, also read an elaborate essay in favor of establishing a central theological seminary. Dr. A. M. Poindexter of Virginia then introduced a resolution to proceed seriously with the establishment of such an institution. Another Virginian, Rev. I. S. Tinsley, favored this resolution, while Dr. J. B. Jeter, also of Virginia, did not consider the project wise because of local state interests. Eventually, however, on May 28, 1849, Poindexter's resolution

---

[15] *Ibid.*, p. 128.
[16] John A. Broadus, *Memoir of James Petigru Boyce* (New York: A. C. Armstrong and Son, 1893), pp. 116–17.

was approved, and a committee of twenty, with Dr. Poindexter as chairman, was appointed and charged to place the matter before Southern Baptists.[17]

From this time onward, as Dr. W. W. Barnes has observed, the leadership in favor of a general and central theological seminary for Southern Baptists passed into the hands of the seaboard states. Progress was slow, since the advocates of a Southwide theological school were divided on several points. First, agreement regarding the location was hard to achieve. Some favored Nashville, Tennessee, while others pleaded for Greenville, South Carolina. A second difficulty turned on the relationship between the proposed school to the denomination. Dr. W. B. Johnson and Dr. R. B. C. Howell favored a denominationally controlled seminary, but others, like the editor of the *Religious Herald* of Virginia, were opposed to such a plan. The Southern Baptist Convention as such did not, at this juncture, concern itself officially with this question.

In the interval between 1849 and 1853 little was done with regard to the proposed seminary. Meanwhile, the Landmark movement had blown up into a storm under the leadership of James R. Graves of Nashville. This was a high-church movement among Southern Baptists, and its advocates claimed that only Baptist churches were true New Testament churches which could trace their history in unbroken succession to apostolic times. By now Dr. Graves was adamantly opposed to a Southwide seminary. But his opposition to the scheme played naturally into the hands of Southern Baptist leaders in Virginia and the Carolinas, all of whom ardently desired a central theological school.

It was in June, 1854, that the Baptist Education Society of Virginia re-opened the whole question. A committee was appointed and asked to report the following year. When, therefore, the Baptist General Association of Virginia met in the summer of 1855, this committee made a progress report on theological education in the South. It also informed the Virginia brethren of the re-

---

[17] Barnes, *op. cit.*, p. 128.

cent Educational Convention held in Montgomery, Alabama, in May, 1855.

A year later "the friends of theological education" met again at Augusta, Georgia, in April, 1856. Again serious difficulties arose. It was decided that still another conference be held, this time in Louisville, Kentucky, during May, 1857. A special committee, consisting of Basil Manly, Sr., A. M. Poindexter, and J. B. Jeter, was charged to continue the study of the matter and report at Louisville.

Meanwhile James P. Boyce of Furman University had been working behind the scenes and exerting a decisive influence in many quarters. When in July, 1856, the Baptists of South Carolina met in Greenville, South Carolina, Dr. Boyce induced his brethren to make a definite offer of the theological funds of Furman University to the proposed central theological seminary. South Carolina Baptists were asked to obligate themselves to increase existing funds of about thirty-thousand dollars in hand for theological education to one hundred thousand dollars, provided that the new seminary be located in Greenville and that all the other states raise an equal amount toward its endowment.

The next step in the unfolding drama of Southern Seminary's early history was the Educational Convention in Louisville, Kentucky, on May 7, 1857. Eighty-eight delegates from Maryland, the District of Columbia, Virginia, North and South Carolina, Georgia, Alabama, Mississippi, Louisiana, Arkansas, Tennessee, and Kentucky answered the roll call. Though some delegates were doubtful about the South Carolina offer, it was finally approved and unanimously accepted. Southern Baptist Theological Seminary had at last been launched.

Professor James P. Boyce of Furman University was asked to raise the needed seventy thousand dollars among South Carolina Baptists. Years later John A. Broadus, reminiscing on Boyce's heroic efforts to collect this large sum of money, wrote:

He probably had very little time for teaching in the course of the next session. We know that in his two-horse buggy, driven by a

13

servant, he travelled far and wide over South Carolina, visiting out-of-the-way churches, and planters on remote plantations, and throwing all the energies and resources of his being into what was then and there a very large and difficult undertaking. It was no doubt often with a sense of heavy sacrifice that the young husband and father left the bright home he loved so well, with the already rich store of choice books in which he so delighted, for these laborious and not always successful journeys. He no doubt cheered himself with the thought that all this would be only for part of one year.[18]

But Professor Boyce relentlessly pursued his goal. While busy raising the necessary funds, he found time to meet with the Committee on the Plan of Organization in Richmond, Virginia. To this committee belonged Basil Manly, Jr., then principal of Richmond Female Institute; John A. Broadus, chaplain and professor at the University of Virginia; and himself. Young Manly had drawn up an Abstract of Principles which each new professor of the seminary had to sign. Broadus, in turn, had prepared an outline of the plan of instruction.

The final stage in all this planning for the new theological seminary for Southern Baptists was the Educational Convention at Greenville, South Carolina, on May 1, 1858. For five days the salient points relating to curriculum, doctrinal standards, the proposed elective system of instruction, and its correlate, the establishment of separate schools, were discussed pro and con. At last agreement was reached on all moot points.

A faculty of four professors was elected at this Greenville Convention: James P. Boyce, John A. Broadus, Basil Manly, Jr., and E. T. Winkler. The latter at once declined the election, as did Broadus, who, however, later reconsidered and finally accepted. Due to the faculty's being incomplete, the opening of the new Southern Baptist Theological Seminary was postponed until the fall of 1859. Professor William Williams of Mercer University in Georgia was elected in E. T. Winkler's place when the newly appointed Board of Trustees of the Seminary met in Richmond, Virginia, in May, 1859.

---

[18] Broadus, *op. cit.*, pp. 149–50.

Meanwhile, Dr. Boyce had most of the seventy thousand dollars he had set out to raise in South Carolina. Having a large income himself, he was confident that fresh sources for needed income could be tapped. He also had secured rented premises for lodging the new school from the First Baptist Church in Greenville, South Carolina. Here the new Southern Seminary was to be located until 1877 when it was moved to Louisville, Kentucky.

Dr. Boyce was convinced that the new Seminary should not spend money on buildings until it had first secured sufficient endowment for its instructional task. John A. Broadus reports the remark of Rev. Thomas Curtis, D.D., principal of Limestone Female Institute, who in one of the deliberative assemblies had declaimed in sonorous English: "The requisites for an institution of learning are three *b's*,—bricks, books, brains. Our brethren usually begin at the wrong end of the three *b's;* they spend all their money for bricks, have nothing to buy books, and must take such brains as they can pick up. But our brethren ought to begin at the other end of the three *b's*." [19]

It was most fortunate that the new Seminary in Greenville did not encumber itself at first with expensive buildings, for two years after its opening the Civil War swept everything before it. When after the war the question of continuing the Seminary was up, "it was remembered with special gratitude that Boyce's plan had been adopted in regard to buildings; for even a few thousand dollars of debt [with the endowment lost] would have sunk the enterprise beyond redemption." [20]

Southern Baptist Theological Seminary opened its doors in Greenville, South Carolina, with four professors and twenty-six students in the fall of 1859.

[19] *Ibid.,* p. 153.
[20] *Ibid.*

2

James P. Boyce, Founder

JOHN HENRY NEWMAN is credited with saying that no great movement was ever begun or carried forward by a committee or a system. To substantiate his assertion the brilliant Oxford graduate and later cardinal of the Roman Catholic Church "pointed with strange audacity to Luther and the Reformation as an example."

Newman's observation applies to James P. Boyce, of whom Professor W. W. Barnes has fittingly said:

It is he who will ever remain in Baptist history as the founder of the Southern Baptist Theological Seminary. Others prepared the way, and great men labored with him, but his was the leadership that called the institution into being and gave it permanence. Under a sense of divine call, he held on through war, reconstruction, indifference, and even opposition from the brethren. When he was ordained, a member of the presbytery asked him if he proposed to give his life to preaching. He replied: "Yes, provided I do not become a professor of theology." That sense of vocation continued to abide with him to the end, culminating in victory.[1]

James P. Boyce was born January 11, 1827, at Charleston, South Carolina. He was the son of a wealthy cotton broker and banker, Ker Boyce. On both his father's and mother's sides Boyce came from sturdy Scotch-Irish stock. His ancestors had all been Presbyterians, and the first member of the clan, John Boyce, had landed in America in 1765. This John Boyce, about whom hair-raising escapades are reported, took an active part in the American Revolution. His son, Ker Boyce, born in 1787, in spite of a limited education and many adversities, climbed the ladder of

---

[1] Barnes, *op. cit.*, p. 129.

success until he became the wealthiest man in South Carolina. James P. Boyce was the first son born to his father's second wife, the former Amanda Jane Caroline Johnston. She was a delicate woman, attractive and full of charm. Under the preaching of Dr. Basil Manly, Sr., she was won to Baptist views in 1830, and she joined the First Baptist Church of Charleston, South Carolina, by baptism.

The childhood and youth of Jimmy Boyce, as he was called, were set in the most favorable circumstances. He received the finest education that Charleston could provide. At first he attended Professor Bailey's school, then the city high school.

Young Boyce was an omnivorous reader. At times he even neglected the prescribed studies in favor of his passion for reading. When, still in his teens, he refused to return to school, his resolute father made him go to work in a wholesale dry goods store in which he had a controlling interest. Each morning Jimmy had to get up at six o'clock and work as hard as the rest. After six months of this wholesome corrective, young Boyce was cured and gladly went back to school. When he graduated from Charleston High School, he received a silver medal for original work in algebra. Then followed two years of study at Charleston College, where Dr. W. T. Brantley, a Baptist preacher, was president. Boyce, who was full of pranks and mischief, was spotted one day by Dr. Brantley, who exclaimed, "There is Boyce, who will be a great man, if he does not become a devil." [2]

As a youth Boyce was not given much to sports except archery. But he seemed to excel at the waltz in dancing school, as John A. Broadus, his later colleague, has whimsically pointed out. Possibly his barrel-shaped figure inclined him to avoid the more exacting sports and explains his wide and often excessive reading in literature and history.

In 1845, at the age of eighteen, Boyce entered Brown University at Providence, Rhode Island. Here he studied under several rather excellent teachers, among them Alexis Caswell, in mathe-

---

[2] Broadus, *op. cit.*, p. 28.

matics; John L. Lincoln, the Latinist; and James R. Boise, professor of Greek language and literature. One of his classmates was George Park Fisher, who in 1854 became the first church history professor at Yale Divinity School—"a mellowed Puritan," as Roland H. Bainton has called him. Francis Wayland, Jr., son of the president of Brown, later distinguished himself as professor of law at Yale University. James Burrell Angell was for many years the head of the University of Michigan, while Benjamin Thomas became "the apostle to the Karens" in far-off Burma.

Boyce had gone to Brown without being a committed Christian. During the spring recess of 1846 he was converted under Richard Fuller's preaching in his home church. On April 22, 1846, he was baptized by the visiting preacher into the fellowship of the First Baptist Church of Charleston.

During his junior year Boyce concentrated on physics, chemistry, physiology, Greek and Latin poetry, French, logic, and history. The senior year was taken up with astronomy, geology, political science, intellectual and moral philosophy, Plato, the American Constitution, and Christian evidences.

At the Brown commencement in 1847 Boyce stood seventh in a class of thirty-five graduates. Just a few months before his graduation Boyce had announced to his parents his intention of becoming a gospel minister. This was quite a disappointment to his father, who had dreamed of his gifted son's becoming a lawyer, statesman, or manager of his large business interests. Ker Boyce was never a member of any church, although, strangely, he was for many years chairman of the board of trustees of the Charleston Baptist church to which his wife belonged. Eventually, however, like Martin Luther's father before him, he was reconciled to his son's desire to become a servant of God.

Brown University, its scholarship and spiritual atmosphere, and particularly President Francis Wayland, proved to be a decisive influence in the life of James P. Boyce. Wayland had come to the presidency of Brown in 1827 when things were at a low ebb, but conditions began to change for the better under his leadership.

Theologically a staunch conservative, Wayland was a preacher of merit, a fine teacher, and an administrator with original ideas. He had no use for lazy students or sleepy professors. His exploring, probing mind encouraged those whom he taught to think matters through to their very roots. His forte as a teacher lay in his careful analysis of facts and movements.[3]

Three things Boyce carried from his studies at Brown University into his work as a theological teacher: first, Wayland's method of analytical recitations in the classroom; second, the idea of the elective system of study; and third, certain views of theological education which Boyce developed in his inaugural address in July, 1856, as professor of theology at Furman University in Greenville, South Carolina.

In November, 1847, Boyce had been licensed to preach by his home church, and about a year later, on December 20, 1848, he married a charming young lady with whom he had fallen headlong in love at the wedding of a friend. Although she had at first repulsed him, his usual determination finally won her heart and hand. Boyce's wife was the daughter of Dr. Fielding Ficklen of Washington, Georgia. The good doctor, in addition to his medical practice, was also a successful planter and therefore in good financial circumstances. His daughter Lizzie had received a fine education in a private school in Washington. In this same city Jesse Mercer, first pastor of the local Baptist church, founded in 1833 *The Christian Index*, which is still the Baptist journal of Georgia Baptists.

Shortly before his marriage Boyce became editor of *The Southern Baptist*. Though only twenty-one at the time, he served in this capacity with considerable success. In the issue of March 28, 1849, there appeared "a leader of unusual length favoring the establishment of a 'Central Theological Institution' for all Baptists of the South." [4] This was a significant omen of Boyce's future career as Seminary teacher and administrator.

---

[3] Austen Kennedy de Blois, *Fighters for Freedom* (Philadelphia: Judson Press, 1929), pp. 412–13.

[4] Broadus, *op. cit.*, pp. 61–62.

The youthful editor had to engage at times in serious rebuttal of personal attacks made on him because of certain positions he had taken. But he came out of these ordeals unscathed and unembittered.

In the spring of 1848 James P. Boyce and his friend H. A. Tupper went to New York state to enrol at Madison University (now Colgate). But they learned to their dismay that three months of Hebrew had to be made up in about three weeks in order to qualify for entrance into the theological course. Boyce had to desist from his plan to enter, since his arduous studies at Brown had injured his eyes. He was at first at a loss as to what he should do next. Must he give up the ministry he so ardently coveted to pursue?

An ocean journey from New York to Charleston brought release to his eyes and restored him to full health. For a short time he acted as agent of the Southern Baptist Publication Society, whose secretary was the able Dr. A. M. Poindexter.[5]

Finally, in September, 1849, Boyce entered Princeton Theological Seminary, where he remained until 1851. Here he was deeply impressed by the scholarship, the full-orbed system, and the stern orthodoxy of Charles Hodge, then at the peak of his powers. Here, as at Brown, Boyce found congenial fellow students, most of them Presbyterians, who in later life made their mark in God's kingdom. Among the Southern Baptist students were men like Alfred Bagby; Andrew Fuller Davidson; James K. Mendenhall, Boyce's intimate friend; and Joseph W. Warder from Kentucky, who from 1875 to 1880 served as pastor of the Walnut Street Baptist Church of Louisville and then as state secretary of Kentucky Baptists.[6]

While a student at Princeton Seminary, Boyce worked according to a carefully laid out plan, since he had decided to finish the three years' course within two years' time. He left Princeton in May, 1851, before commencement and hence without receiving his diploma.

---

[5] *Ibid.*, pp. 57–58, 62.
[6] *Ibid.*, pp. 67 ff.

Boyce had thought of going to Germany for further study at Halle University if no sphere of service opened to him. In October of that year, however, a small Baptist congregation at Columbia, South Carolina, called him as its pastor.[7] Here in a city of only seven thousand people the young minister had a most happy pastorate. Diligently he visited his flock in their homes; carefully he prepared his sermons; and he also found time to continue his studies in theology. In the spring of 1852 Boyce was granted a three months' leave to raise funds for a new church edifice. During a vacation he went north to attend the annual class reunion of Brown University. At this time he secured the M.A. degree as the reward of his previous studies.

In 1854 Ker Boyce died, and James P. Boyce temporarily gave up his church duties in order to manage his father's large estates and business interests. He was then twenty-seven years of age. In the fall of that year Boyce became moderator of the Charleston Baptist Association, the second oldest in the United States. Meanwhile, Furman University tried to secure his services as professor of theology. Boyce, therefore, resigned from his church and accepted the Furman offer. His career as a theological teacher of which he had spoken at his ordination had begun.

Boyce, however, had served at Furman for only two years, 1855–57, when he became more deeply involved in the final stages of the founding of the Southern Baptist Theological Seminary. But before he relinquished his position at Furman University, in July, 1856, he delivered his famous inaugural address on "Three Changes in Theological Education." John A. Broadus in his *Memoir of James Petigru Boyce* devoted more than thirty pages to this address, which he called "epoch-making in the history of theological education among Southern Baptists."[8]

When Dr. John R. Sampey was inducted into his office as the fifth president of Southern Baptist Theological Seminary in the fall of 1929, he made the startling assertion that "before 1859 not

[7] *Ibid.*, pp. 84 ff.
[8] *Ibid.*, p. 142.

21

one of the twelve Apostles could have secured admittance as a regular student in any of the standard theological seminaries of our country." [9]

Briefly stated, in his inaugural address Professor Boyce proposed three significant changes in Baptist theological schools: (1) not only college graduates but men with less general education, even a common English education, should be offered such opportunities of theological study as they were prepared for and desired; (2) special courses should be provided so that the ablest and most aspiring students might be prepared for service as instructors and original authors; (3) there should be prepared an abstract of principles, or careful statement of theological belief, which every professor in such an institution must sign when inducted into office so as to guard against erroneous and injurious instruction.[10]

It is clear that Boyce was greatly influenced in his thinking, particularly on this first point, by the thinking of his former teacher, President Francis Wayland of Brown University. Perhaps the fullest expression of Wayland's views on ministerial education are contained in a disturbing message on "The Apostolic Ministry" which he delivered at Rochester, New York, in 1853, three years before Boyce's inaugural. A comparison of President Wayland's views with those Boyce expressed in his Furman inaugural shows at once how deeply the founder of Southern Seminary was influenced by his great teacher.

Since these suggested changes were incorporated in the basic articles of Southern Baptist Seminary, it is important that they be discussed in some detail at this point. Boyce, anticipating objections to his proposed changes, dealt with these objections in the spirit of fair play and critical acumen.

The first objection, of course, had to do with Boyce's proposal to admit both college and noncollege men to the seminary. Would this not contribute to lowering the standards of theologi-

---

[9] John R. Sampey, "The Future of the Seminary in the Light of Its Past," *Review and Expositor*, XXVI (October, 1929), 376.

[10] Broadus, *op. cit.*, pp. 119–21. Cf. Barnes, *op. cit.*, pp. 130–31.

cal education? Boyce believed it would not. Baptists, he argued, are and have been friends of education. They believe in an educated ministry.

I would see the means of theological education increased. I would have the facilities for pursuing its studies opened to all who would embrace them; I would lead the strong men of our ministry to feel that no position is equal in responsibility or usefulness to that of one devoted to this cause; and I would spread among our churches such an earnest desire for educated ministers as would make them willing so to increase the support of the ministry as to enable all of those who are now forced, from want of means, to enter without the fullest preparation upon the active duties of the work, so far to anticipate the support they will receive as to feel free to borrow the means by which their education may be completed.[11]

One reason that Boyce desired wider opportunities for theological education was his conviction that the existing Baptist seminaries—Madison University, Newton Theological Institution, and Rochester Theological Seminary—did not train a sufficient number of ministers to man the churches at home and abroad. With an unending stream of people pouring into the Middle and Far West, with immigrants from Europe flocking in large numbers to the United States, with doors opening in Africa and Asia, the sophistry of objection to the proposed scheme simply would not do. With "hydra-headed error" stalking through the land, increasing numbers of ministers needed to be trained to cope with the spirit of the age and herald the gospel everywhere.

Of course Boyce realized that it is God's providence that ever must call forth laborers into the vineyard. But the churches need to be spiritually quickened by God's Spirit if new volunteers for the ministry are to be recruited and sent out to preach. But, asked Boyce in this address, "Have we not disregarded the laws which the providence and word of God have laid down for us? And does he not now chastise us by suffering our schemes to work out their natural results, that we, being left to ourselves, may see

---

[11] James P. Boyce, "An Inaugural Address" (Greenville, S. C.: C. J. Elford, 1956), p. 6.

our folly, and return to him and to his ways, as the only means of strength?" [12]

Wayland, Boyce's teacher, believed in and defended a variety of ministries as well as means to utilize all the gifts that the Lord has promised to his people for the proclamation of the gospel among men. Boyce, like Wayland, considered it a mistaken idea

that the work of the ministry should be intrusted only to those who have been classically educated,—an assumption which, singularly enough, is made for no other profession. It is in vain to say that such is not the theory or the practice of our denomination. It is the theory and the practice of by far the larger portion of those who have controlled our institutions, and have succeeded in engrafting this idea upon them, contrary to the spirit which prevails among the churches. They have done this, without doubt, in the exercise of their best judgment, but have failed because they neglected the better plan pointed out by the providence and Word of God. [13]

Both Boyce and Wayland deplored the fact that the rigid standards of theological education diminished rather than increased the supply of preachers, pastors, evangelists, and missionaries needed in the churches at home and abroad. Boyce moreover recognized that the scriptural qualifications for the ministry do indeed require knowledge but that knowledge "is not of the sciences, nor of philosophy, nor of the languages, but of God and of His plan of salvation. He who has not this knowledge, though he be learned in all the learning of the schools, is incapable of preaching the Word of God."

Is it not true, asked Boyce, "that the mass of vineyard laborers have been from the ranks of fishermen and tax gathers, cobblers and tinkers, weavers and ploughmen, to whom God has not disdained to impart gifts, and whom He has qualified as His ambassadors by the presence of that Spirit by which, and not by might, wisdom or power, is the work of the Lord accomplished." [14]

[12] *Ibid.*, p. 11.
[13] *Ibid.*, pp. 13–14.
[14] *Ibid.*, p. 15.

As Wayland pointed to J. G. Oncken, the Baptist pioneer in Europe, so Boyce alluded to John Bunyan, the immortal tinker of Bedford, England, of seventeenth-century fame. Bunyan was ignorant in many respects and rough and rugged in speech. Yet he was a master of Holy Writ and an incomparable herald of God's grace. His *Pilgrim's Progress* has inspired and enthralled sinner and saint alike, and before his spiritual wisdom "the most learned scholars may sit silently and learn the wonders of the Word of God."

On the other hand, a man like Theodore Parker of Boston, who had "all the grace and polish of the finished scholar," was "so destitute of the knowledge of true Christianity, and of a genuine experience of the influence of the Holy Ghost, . . . and the religion of which he calls himself a minister, that the humblest Christian among our servants shall rise up in condemnation against him in the great day of accounts."

Boyce distinguished between the class of educated ministers and the ministry of educated men. The first might be represented by a Bunyan, the second by a Parker. But there need not really be a conflict between these two types of ministry. "The perfection of the ministry, it is gladly admitted, would consist in the just combination of the two; but it is not the business of the Church to establish a perfect, but an adequate ministry; and it is only of the latter that we hope for an abundant supply." [15]

Turning from Bunyan, Dr. Boyce mentioned names identified with the growth of Baptists in America. Were their early spiritual leaders men of education, of great eloquence or learning, or of intensive theological culture? By no means! Men like Hervey, Gano, Bennett, Semple, Broaddus, Armstrong, and Mercer were indeed bright and shining lights. And they did their best with the talents they had and advanced God's truth among men. But vastly more were needed in that day of peril and opportunity. Therefore, to fill this need of the churches and the country Boyce prayed for the churches to rise up in their strength and demand

---

[15] *Ibid.*, p. 14.

that theological institutions make due provision for the mass of their ministry.

Boyce's intention, it needs to be emphasized, was not to lower the requirements for the training of ministers but rather to widen the opportunities for a much larger number of would-be preachers, pastors, and missionaries. This goal, as the subsequent history of Southern Seminary has amply demonstrated, was more than realized.

What then, according to Boyce, is to be the nature of the theological training for "the illiterate, the educated minister," as he called the nonclassically trained applicant for seminary education? "Such a course, based on a plain English education, should include the Evidences of Christianity, Systematic and Polemic Theology, the Rules of Interpretation applied to the English Version; some knowledge of the principles of Rhetoric, extensive practice in the development from texts of subjects and skeletons of Sermons, and whatever amount of Composition may be expedient, and full instruction in the nature of Pastoral Duties." [16]

Lest anyone assume this scheme of studies to be nothing but an easy road into the ministry, Boyce concluded this part of his address on this note:

Let the studies of this course be so pursued as to train the mind to habits of reflection and analysis, to awaken it to conceptions of the truths of Scripture, to fill it with arguments from the Word of God in support of its doctrines, and to give it facility in constructing and presenting such arguments—and the work will be accomplished. [17]

The second change which Boyce advocated for theological education related to graduate or advanced studies in divinity. Its basic purpose ought to be the preparation of future theological teachers and original authors. Boyce believed that American theological schools had depended all too long on the scholarly productions of Europeans, especially the fertile and often dangerously speculative German scholars. He spoke of this condition as

---

[16] *Ibid.*, p. 18.
[17] *Ibid.*

a sore evil, "that we have been dependent in great part upon the criticism of Germany for all the more learned investigations in Biblical Criticism and Exegesis, and that in the study of the development of the doctrine of the Church, as well as of its outward progress, we have been compelled to depend upon works in which much of error has been mingled with truth, owing to the defective standpoint occupied by their authors." [18]

James P. Boyce in his Furman inaugural boldly challenged American theologians to emancipate themselves from the bondage of European and German scholarship. He looked forward to the rise of a truly American Christian scholarship. He hoped for such independence in this matter as would lead to the training of our "rising ministry . . . under the scholarship of the Anglo-Saxon mind, which, from its nature, as well as from the circumstances which surround it, is eminently fitted to weigh evidence, and to decide as to its appropriateness and its proper limitations." [19]

But Dr. Boyce had still a more potent reason for his advocacy of graduate studies in Baptist theological seminaries:

But the obligation resting on the Baptist denomination is far higher than this. It extends not merely to matters of detail, but to those of vital interest. The history of religious literature, and of Christian scholarship has been a history of Baptist wrongs. We have been overlooked, ridiculed, and defamed. Critics have committed the grossest perversions, violated the plainest rules of criticism, and omitted points which could not have been developed without benefit to us. Historians who have professed to write the history of the Church have either utterly ignored the presence of those of our faith, or classed them among fanatics and heretics; or, if forced to acknowledge the prevalence of our principles and practice among the earliest churches, have adopted such false theories as to church power, and the development and growth of the truth and principles of Scripture, that by all, save their most discerning readers, our pretensions to an early origin and a continuous existence have been rejected.[20]

[18] *Ibid.*, p. 28.
[19] *Ibid.*, p. 28.
[20] *Ibid.*, p. 29.

27

In this passage Boyce, whatever his own personal bias might have been, tried to stimulate his Southern Baptist brethren to undertake seriously the scholarly investigation of their own history and principles.

But how was all this to be accomplished? Most pastors, Boyce rightly avowed, have neither the books nor the leisure to engage in this quest. Therefore, the projected central theological seminary should have a library, "not only . . . filled with the gathered lore of the past, but also endowed with the means of annual increase. Without this, no institution can pursue extensive courses of study, or contribute anything directly to the advancement of learning." [21] Boyce spoke of an extended course of study of one or two years beyond the regular course of instruction. He also alluded to the writing of "an exegetical thesis" which would furnish the subjects for investigation and give more ample acquaintance with original texts or sources and the laws of their interpretation.

Being an eminently practical man, Boyce also underscored the value of the study of Arabic, especially for missionaries in Central Africa. He held the knowledge of the Koran in the original to be indispensable for Christian missionaries working among Moslems. Moreover, graduate studies would qualify, Boyce thought, prospective missionaries to become translators of the Bible and writers of religious and theological books. But he also realized that the evangelization of Africa and other countries must, in the main, be carried out by the nationals themselves.

Still another and distinct advantage of graduate training in the seminary would be to replenish the faculties of Baptist colleges with new professors. Other benefits, Boyce fervently hoped, his hearers would no doubt think about, but he was quite confident that with such ideas and schemes as he had projected in his address, "learning will abound among us, the world will be subdued to Christ, and the principles dear to our hearts will universally prevail."

[21] *Ibid.,* pp. 30–31.

Dr. Boyce's third proposed change in his inaugural of 1856 related to the demand for an abstract of principles or a statement of doctrinal beliefs which every professor of the contemplated seminary would be asked to sign. To Boyce, who knew the volatile temper of the age, the doctrinal instability of both ministers and laity, and the acids of modernity which at this juncture of Christian history had already eaten deeply into the fabric of evangelical convictions, the purpose of such an abstract of principles was quite obvious.

Boyce sincerely believed that without such an instrument the seminary might have to be abandoned. The reasons for his insistence upon this instrument were several: first, sound doctrine was much imperiled due to the Campbellite invasion and the distinctive principles of Arminianism which, Boyce maintained, "have also been engrafted upon many of our Churches; and even some of our Ministry have not hesitated publicly to avow them." [22]

Moreover, Boyce argued, "that sentiment, the inevitable precursor, or accompaniment of all heresy—that the doctrines of Theology are matters of mere speculation, and its distinctions only logomachies and technicalities, has obtained at least a limited prevalence. And the doctrinal sentiments of a large portion of the Ministry and membership of the Churches, are seen to be either very much unsettled, or radically wrong." [23]

Boyce, a shrewd observer of human nature, also realized that heresy usually becomes articulate first in an individual of strong influence and ability. Such a person is able to intrigue and seduce men's minds by his charm and eloquence and through his persuasiveness bring a blight on the church as a whole. One such man of large gifts was none other than Alexander Campbell.

Playing upon the prejudices of the weak and ignorant among our people, decrying creeds as an infringement upon the rights of conscience, making a deep impression by his extensive learning and

---

[22] *Ibid.*, p. 33.
[23] *Ibid.*, p. 34.

great ability, Alexander Campbell threatened at one time the total destruction of our faith. Had he occupied a chair in one of our theological institutions, that destruction might have been completed.[24]

If it be objected, said Boyce, that Scripture does not authorize such a test for churches and that Christians ought to be guided solely by Scripture precept and example, the objection may be granted. But a theological school is not a church. Its affairs are not a matter of scriptural regulation, but they are rather subject to such laws as human wisdom may devise so that the worthy designs of the founders be properly carried out.

Yet, according to Boyce, even in the light of Holy Writ creeds are not to be despised. New Testament churches were enjoined to contend earnestly for the faith once for all delivered to the saints. A heretic was to be cast out, in the early church, after the first and second admonitions. Truth must always be clearly distinguished from error. And it is wise to anticipate—better still, to prevent infection.

The time of trial is not the time for legislation. Too many evil passions are then awakened, too many unfounded prejudices then excited, to allow for freedom from bias necessary to justice, as well as to the purity of the Church of Christ, as to the orthodoxy of the member arraigned before it. Matters of doctrine then about which, if approached with prejudiced mind and excited feeling, there is such liability to mistake, must be arranged beforehand, when God can be approached in prayer, when His Word can be diligently studied, and when the mind is ready to receive the conclusions to which prayer and study may lead.[25]

As Dr. Boyce reviewed the evidence of the New Testament with regard to the demand for a public confession of faith, he found sufficient confirmation of the need of safeguarding the doctrinal standards of a theological school as he conceived it. The act of baptism, for instance, was in the early church a clear example of profession of doctrinal belief. Christ our Lord openly

---

[24] *Ibid.*, p. 36.
[25] *Ibid.*, p. 40.

appealed to his disciples for a declaration of their faith in his person.

Boyce, pointing to developments of the first three centuries, also referred to the confessions which the church fathers enunciated. And Baptists of all ages have had their confessions of faith. But, argued some of Boyce's friends, such creeds as Baptists formulated had only declarative force and not binding character. True, replied Boyce, the confessions which Smyth, Helwys, or the London Particular Baptists of 1644 put forth had a declarative purpose, denying, for instance, the right of the magistracy to coerce the Christian conscience. Who would deny that every act of baptism in the churches has a truly confessional character? The very spirituality of the church, as Baptists understand it, "impresses upon us the necessity of excluding those who have violated the simplicity which is in Christ." [26]

The three proposed changes in theological education—admission of noncollege men to theological studies, provision for advanced or graduate work, and the abstract of principles to be subscribed to by each new professor upon induction into office —Boyce was instrumental in having incorporated in the fundamental articles of the Southern Baptist Theological Seminary before it opened its doors in the fall of 1859.

On the whole, the founding fathers of Southern Seminary showed rare foresight and wisdom in following the lead of James P. Boyce. Students without a classical preparation mingled freely with the graduates of the best American universities and colleges. In the nineties graduate work got under way. Since that time hundreds of men have graduated from Southern with the Doctor of Theology degree, having been prepared for specialized ministries in teaching, writing, Christian education, student work, hospital chaplaincies, theological leadership, and the executive branches of Baptist institutions both North and South.

The Abstract of Principles is still in force. Dr. W. O. Carver has

---

[26] *Ibid.,* pp. 43-44.

suggested that if it were composed today, certain changes might be made in this instrument, but on the whole, even here James P. Boyce, Basil Manly, Jr., and the other leaders showed rare discretion and wisdom, for they excluded from this doctrinal statement with its mildly Calvinistic tenor those matters of belief on which Southern Baptists were in disagreement.[27]

---

[27] It is perhaps significant to point out that some of the new and vigorous seminaries in the American Baptist Convention, such as the Eastern Baptist Theological Seminary, founded in 1925 and patterned after Southern largely under the leadership of Dr. W. W. Adams, have a confession of faith to which professors voluntarily subscribe as they begin their work.

3

James P. Boyce, Administrator and Treasurer

W HEN IN 1859 James P. Boyce assumed the leadership of Southern as chairman of the faculty and treasurer of the new school, he was eminently fitted for this work. Though only thirty-two years of age, his practical experience as pastor, editor, professor, and administrator of his father's large estate had been quite extensive. He threw himself into the task of building the new seminary with determination, skill, and fervor.

It was both fortunate and providential that Boyce was a man of wealth and good breeding. When he began his work at Southern in 1859, he enjoyed robust health and possessed an exuberant vitality. From then on his family fortune and his mental and physical powers were at the disposal of the young institution he had helped bring into being. Boyce was a man whom a dream had possessed, and he labored without ceasing and with utter abandon at the task of making his dream come to full fruition.

Boyce owned a beautiful, spacious home located on a short outlying range of the Blue Ridge near Greenville, South Carolina, where the Seminary was established. This home with its large and airy rooms, its broad and spacious lawns, and its beautiful gardens and grand forest trees provided a respite from hard and often unpleasant labors. It was not often that young Boyce could enjoy the quiet of his lovely home, for when he was not busy teaching theology in the Seminary, he was traveling near and far to secure the school's financial well-being.

Little did Boyce and his three colleagues dream that before the second session of the Seminary had ended the nation would be on the verge of civil war. The first session of 1859–60 saw twenty-six students enrolled. The work was progressing nicely, but the second session of the school with thirty-two students in attendance was filled with the excitement of the presidential campaign of 1860. Abraham Lincoln was running for President. Soon the secession movement was under way in South Carolina and adjacent Southern states. Boyce at once tried to counteract this dangerous trend. He even ran as a candidate for the South Carolina legislature in opposition to secession, but he was overwhelmingly defeated by a secessionist politician. The fact that a fellow Baptist, President James C. Furman of Furman University, also ran on the secession ticket in the otherwise strongly Union district of Greenville added to the bitterness of his defeat at the polls.

It must be remembered, however, that Boyce, despite his anti-secessionist stand, was a proslavery man. To his friend and brother-in-law, H. A. Tupper, he expressed his convictions and apprehensions on the matter. He still wished and hoped for an intelligent compromise between the North and the South. Yet he also perceived that if the war between the contending parties were to come, it would mean the well-deserved end of slavery. Boyce strongly felt that the institution of Negro slavery in the South had been a curse for both masters and slaves. "I fear God is going to sweep it away, after having left it thus long to show us how great we might be, were we to act as we ought in this matter." [1]

Boyce was not alone in these sentiments against secession, but before many months had gone by, the Provisional Congress at Montgomery, Alabama, had elected Jefferson Davis president of the Southern Confederacy. By April 12, 1861, Fort Sumter had been captured, and the nation was in the throes of Civil War. Boyce's dream of preventing the fatal break of the Union was shattered. And with it, it seemed, went the dream of building a strong theological school for Southern Baptists!

When the second commencement of Southern seminary was

---

[1] Broadus, *op. cit.*, p. 185.

held on May 27, 1861, great excitement prevailed in the seminary family. But the speaker of the occasion, Dr. E. T. Winkler of Charleston, did not even utter a word about the peril of the hour. Instead he commended the Seminary's wise plans for the future and exalted the work of the ministry.

Three weeks before the close of the second session the Southern Baptist Convention met at Savannah, Georgia. Dr. Boyce and John A. Broadus were in attendance. When the messengers of the convention passed resolutions in favor of the Confederacy's cause, Dr. Boyce vigorously opposed what he considered meddling in politics by a religious body.

The third session of the Seminary, 1861–62, was overshadowed by the war that had meanwhile broken out. Only twenty students were in attendance, and before the year had ended, Dr. Boyce had become a chaplain of a volunteer regiment from the Greenville district. He counseled his colleagues to keep their connections with the Seminary and to make a living as best they knew how with farming and supply preaching. As a shrewd businessman, Boyce also advised them to lay in store supplies of groceries enough to last for years, for he anticipated a blockade of Southern ports and a long war. Boyce lent the professors money and said, "Some day you may find it very convenient to trade them off for other things." Few believed Boyce's predictions, but his wise counsel was heeded, much to the benefit and peace of mind of the harassed faculty and their families.

In May, 1862, Boyce resigned the chaplaincy in order to run again for public office. This time he won by a wide margin, being re-elected for two more years after his first term in the South Carolina legislature. When Boyce ran for the Confederate Congress in 1863, he lost. Interestingly enough, during the 1863 election campaign many of his Baptist friends voted against him since they were in principle opposed to a Christian minister's seeking public office.

While serving in the South Carolina legislature, Boyce's financial sagacity and know-how soon attracted the attention of his colleagues. When a Union general, early in the summer of 1862, ventured to predict that artillery would decide the war's issue, Boyce remarked to a friend, "Pshaw! The war will be decided by money; the side that manages its finances best will succeed." [2]

Having proposed that two hundred million dollars worth of Confederate bonds be raised throughout the Confederacy, Boyce soon was appointed special commissioner to the legislatures of the several Southern states "to secure the passage of Acts for State endorsement of Confederate bonds, similar to that which he carried through the Legislature of South Carolina." [3]

In an address before the Georgia legislature in April, 1863, Boyce warned, "But let our finances be ruined, let food and clothing continue to advance until our soldiers find their families are starving and naked, they will return to attend to that first of all duties,—to provide for their own households." [4]

John A. Broadus, commenting on Boyce's strategy with regard to Confederate financing of the war effort and the subsequent failure of that effort, wrote,

It was precisely this that reduced General Lee's army, during the winter of 1864–1865, to such small numbers that he was compelled to evacuate the Petersburg defences, and presently to surrender at Appomattox. When the soldier's monthly pay would buy scarcely half a bushel of corn, when word came from many a home that they were already suffering for lack of food, and hopeless as to raising a crop for the coming year, then many a husband and father did that which nothing else on earth could have induced him to do,— left his place in the ranks, and went home. As Boyce had said four years before, it was money that decided the war.[5]

From November, 1864, to the end of the war Boyce was aide-de-camp to Governor A. G. Magrath of his native state, with the rank of lieutenant-colonel. He was also a member of the Council of State and provost marshal of Columbia when that city was captured by General Sherman. Boyce retreated with the gover-

---

[2] *Ibid.*, p. 190.
[3] *Ibid.*, p. 193.
[4] *Ibid.*
[5] *Ibid.*, pp. 193–94.

nor to Charlotte, North Carolina, and from there made his way to Greenville—a hundred miles—by a roundabout way, on horseback and on foot.

A few weeks after his arrival in Greenville, Union troops invaded the city and descended upon many houses, eager for plunder. Under pretext of searching for firearms, these troops broke into many a home to secure the family jewelry. They naturally discovered the Boyce home and, pistols to the owner's head, furiously demanded what had become of his wife's diamonds and jewels. Quietly Dr. Boyce told them that upon hearing of the approach of the Union army, he had entrusted all his plate and other valuables to his brother, who had carried them away, he knew not where, in a wagon. The enraged soldiery threatened blood and thunder, but Boyce's calm finally disarmed their fury and greed, and they left, not without having first thoroughly ransacked the house and taken whatever was of value.

The holocaust of the war having ended, Dr. Boyce summoned his three colleagues to discuss the future of the Seminary. Years of hardship and uncertainty were to follow. Progress was slow, and prospects for the future were dim in view of the fact that most of the endowment, so painfully gathered prior to the conflict, had been swept away. A large part of this money had been paid in Confederate money and invested in Confederate bonds. With the failure of the Confederacy it was an utter loss.

Boyce himself made a contribution of a thousand dollars to the expenses of the first postwar session of 1865–66. Again and again he gave his own personal notes to the banks in order to pay the salaries of his colleagues. In April, 1866, he gave a note for seven thousand dollars for this very purpose, and this condition continued for many years to come.

The first session after the war, 1865–66, there were recorded but seven students in attendance. In his homiletics class Broadus had but one student, and he was blind. Yet the young professor did his work so carefully that from his lectures came five years later the classic *The Preparation and Delivery of Sermons*. It has appeared in numerous editions since.

With unabated zeal and against many obstacles Dr. Boyce continued his efforts, loyally seconded and aided by his colleagues, to secure new funds for the support of the school. At the Southern Baptist Convention held at Russellville, Kentucky, in 1866, his eloquent, passionate pleading secured the sum of $1,203.50. A visit to Baltimore yielded an additional $367.00, while Richmond, Virginia, contributed another $359.00. Boyce's heart rejoiced when Baptists in Missouri and Kentucky gave another $654.00. But, alas, the expenses for agents and travel cut deeply into these badly needed receipts. On July 1, 1867, Boyce sent out a lithographed appeal to various parts of the South, explaining the dire needs of the Seminary. In this letter he stated that during the previous year he had secured about fifty thousand dollars in bonds for five annual payments, but since the first payment on most of these bonds was not yet due, money was desperately needed at once. The securing of even this large amount of pledges was, considering the chaotic conditions of postwar days, remarkable. Many of these pledges, however, were never paid, and consequently the school had to discover new sources of income.

In 1868 the board of trustees requested Professor Basil Manly, Jr., to solicit funds for student aid among the brethren of the North. He succeeded in this effort, receiving liberal gifts in Philadelphia and New York City.[6] In this same year Dr. Boyce, the chairman of the faculty, was offered the position of president of the South Carolina Railway Company. It was a grave temptation for a man who was pressed as hard by financial embarrassments because of the Seminary as was James P. Boyce. But although the position offered him ten thousand dollars per year, an extremely large sum for those days, Boyce turned it down.[7] A man who owned a personal library of some five thousand books and a beautiful home might well have turned aside from the arduous task of keeping a struggling theological school alive. Had he done so, who could have blamed him? But he remained

---

[6] Broadus, *op. cit.*, p. 208. Cf. *Record of the Proceedings of the Board of Trustees of Southern Baptist Seminary*, book 1, p. 93.
[7] *Ibid.*

steadfast in his purpose and true to his vocation. On and on he struggled, and God honored his fidelity and stubborn resolution to see things through to a successful end.

From 1869 to 1877 valiant efforts were made toward raising an endowment of five hundred thousand dollars in order to secure the Seminary on a permanent basis. At the same time, the trustees and Seminary faculty decided to remove the school to a more strategic location. In pursuit of these plans Dr. Boyce, as treasurer and financial agent of the Seminary, traveled far and near, trying to enlist friends for the enterprise. He spent altogether five long years in and around Louisville, Kentucky, campaigning, pleading, and removing existing prejudices against seminary education; he finally saw his efforts crowned with considerable success.

In 1870 Furman University, which in 1856 had turned over its theological funds to the projected Southern Baptist Seminary, magnanimously released the Seminary from all claims upon it and thus cleared the way for action with regard to the removal of the school.[8] The president of Furman, James C. Furman, made it known that the trustees of the University would deplore the removal of the Seminary to another site, but the Seminary trustees resolved in their meeting at St. Louis in 1871 to find another location.

A number of cities vied with each other to attract the young Southern Seminary into their midst, among them Chattanooga, Atlanta, Nashville, Memphis, Murfreesboro in Tennessee, Russellville in Kentucky, and Louisville. President N. K. Davis of Bethel met with the Seminary trustees in 1872 at Raleigh, North Carolina, and presented an eloquent plea for removal of the Seminary to Russellville, uniting it with Bethel College and forming the Southern Baptist University. Dr. T. G. Jones made a strong case for Nashville as the most desirable location. Chattanooga had special attractions for Dr. Boyce since some of his father's estate was located in that city. But after careful considera-

---

[8] Robert Norman Daniel, *Furman University* (Greenville, South Carolina: Hiott Press, 1951), pp. 75–76. Cf. Broadus, *op. cit.*, pp. 221–22.

tion of all aspects of the matter, Louisville won out. It was by far the largest city among those eager to have the Seminary and contained a strong, vigorous Baptist constituency as well as a number of wealthy men who had been won by Boyce's skilful pleading. Thus during the summer of 1872, the final decision to remove the Seminary to Louisville, Kentucky, was made by the trustees.

The financial crisis of 1873 nearly wrecked the enterprise. In that same year, when the Southern Baptist Convention met in Mobile, Alabama, an influential Baptist leader from North Carolina tried to thwart the plan to remove the Seminary to Louisville. Dr. Boyce, then president of the Southern Baptist Convention, delivered a speech that electrified those who heard it. He spoke for a solid hour, and his earnestness gave wings to his imagination. He won the day for the venture of moving the Seminary to Louisville. Dr. John A. Broadus, who heard this speech, characterized it thus:

It was a lifetime concentrating itself upon one point; a great mind and a great heart surcharged with thought and feeling; a man of noble nature appealing to all that was noblest in his hearers; a Christian speaking in Christ's name to his brethren. Drs. J. C. Furman and J. O. B. Dargan, of South Carolina, then spoke in a spirit worthy of themselves and of their State. When the matter came to a vote, the Convention gave a most animated and cordial vote of approval; and the resolute and consistent brother from North Carolina, with his solitary "Nay," helped the matter by showing that it was in no sense a vote *nem. con.*[9]

Thus Dr. Boyce, in the face of financial crises and the opposition of some of his own brethren, pressed on with unconquerable fortitude, patient gentleness, and never-failing courtesy in the task of raising an endowment sufficient to establish the Seminary in Louisville.

By April, 1874, Dr. Boyce had about twenty-six thousand dollars worth of bonds in hand, and gifts and pledges amounting to a thousand dollars a day were gladdening his heart. By the time

---

[9] Broadus, *op. cit.*, pp. 237–38.

the Southern Baptist Convention met in Jefferson, Texas, some forty thousand dollars had been secured, but an additional sum of thirty thousand dollars was still needed. Again Boyce pleaded with his brethren, and the Texas friends pledged the required amount.[10]

With unrelenting persistence Dr. Boyce and the others kept at the task. Two weeks after the Texas meeting Dr. Broadus joined the Northern Baptist brethren at their anniversary gathering in Washington, D. C. There Dr. S. S. Cutting and Samuel Colgate approached Dr. Broadus with regard to his current efforts to secure funds for the Seminary. He was permitted to address the American Baptist Home Mission Society, and with the assistance of Dr. Richard Fuller, he received ten thousand dollars in pledges from the Northern brethren.

Dr. Broadus, who during his administration in the early nineties frequently journeyed northward to preach and also to collect funds for the Seminary, praised the generous Northern Baptist brethren in these telling words: "They paid it too, scarcely a dollar ever failing,—it is a way they have, to pay pledges they make in public meetings." [11]

Naturally, while living in Louisville between 1872 and 1877, Dr. Boyce spent most of his time soliciting in the state of Kentucky. Some of the leading men in the state feared for the continued welfare of their two colleges, Georgetown and Bethel. But Boyce knew how to overcome these fears. Patiently he labored. One such fearful and doubting Thomas was Nimrod Long of Russellville, where Bethel college was located. This good brother sincerely believed that bringing the Seminary from Greenville to Louisville would injure Bethel College, in which he had a large interest. Yet when Dr. Boyce announced his coming to Russellville, Brother Long invited him to his home and entertained him royally but assured him that it was out of the question for him to support the Seminary venture. However, Boyce's persuasive and patient manner conquered all difficulties. One

---

[10] *Ibid.*, p. 240.
[11] *Ibid.*, p. 241.

year later Nimrod Long gave five hundred dollars for current expenses and also pledged his support for the endowment.

Other noble men and women came to the rescue, among them George W. Norton and W. F. Norton. At this crucial juncture of the Seminary's history and in later years the Norton family have given liberally of their substance and their wise counsel to the Seminary's furtherance. Mrs. J. Lawrence Smith and Dr. Arthur Peter gave large and valuable tracts of land to the cause. Joe Werne, J. C. McFerran, J. B. McFerran, John S. Long, W. C. Hall, Theodore Harris, and C. W. Gheens gave five thousand dollars each, while twelve other people contributed one thousand dollars each. Among the latter were three donors who were not Baptists. Many others, both in Kentucky and in other Southern states, generously sent both small and large gifts. At last, after years of storm and stress the Seminary's fortunes seemed to turn for the better.

This state of affairs made it imperative that the school think seriously of effecting the final removal from Greenville to Louisville. In May, 1877, the trustees of the Seminary decided accordingly. Dr. Broadus, in a humorous vein, remarked about this removal operation: "It was physically no great task to remove the Seminary from Greenville to Louisville. There was nothing to move, except the library of a few thousand volumes, and three professors,—Broadus, Toy, and Whitsitt,—only one of whom had a family." [12]

Southern Baptist Seminary had been in Greenville, South Carolina, for eighteen eventful years. The faculty did not easily leave behind the charming city in the Blue Ridge. But the die had been cast, and subsequent developments proved the wisdom of going to Louisville. The Seminary at once surged forward in student attendance.

The plan to raise an adequate endowment of three hundred thousand dollars in Kentucky and two hundred thousand more in other areas of the South prior to the removal to Louisville was

---

[12] *Ibid.*, p. 251.

not fully realized. And although as in Greenville buildings were first rented in the new location, expenses were considerably higher than formerly.

It ought to be stated at this point that three years before the Seminary moved to Louisville, Dr. Boyce had seriously considered the wisdom of suspending the Seminary until the necessary endowment had been secured. The faculty minutes of January 30, 1874, record the following pathetic tale:

Dr. J. P. Boyce as Treasurer reported on the financial condition of the Seminary, and showed that the contributions of the churches had for the last year been very small, that the debt had been accumulating till it now is more than the value of our real estate in Greenville, that it is impossible to maintain the Seminary on the present system, and he accordingly stated that he would be forced to urge the Executive Committee to recommend to the Board of Trustees to suspend the Seminary at the end of the present session till such time as the completion of the endowment or other arrangements may enable us to resume exercises.[13]

The faculty, however, asked its chairman, Dr. Boyce, to desist from this proposal, and he bravely went on, borne up in prayer by his colleagues, the indomitable trustees, and a host of friends in the Southern Baptist Convention and elsewhere. Boyce might have given up the struggle for, again, as after the Civil War, tempting offers to leave Southern came to him. Both Brown University and Crozer Theological Seminary sought him as president, but he remained firm in his resolution to place the Seminary on a firm foundation so as to secure not only survival but continuous growth and effectiveness.

The seriousness of the Seminary's plight around 1874 is indicated by a moving letter that Dr. Boyce received a year earlier from his colleague, Dr. John Broadus:

I do not wonder that you sometimes feel discouraged, painfully. The task is difficult, and the kind of opposition encountered is very

[13] *Minutes of the Faculty of Southern Baptist Seminary, 1868–1894,* book 1, pp. 36–37.

depressing. But life is always a battle. My dear fellow, nobody but you can do it, and it will be, all things considered, one of the great achievements of our time. To have carried it through will be a comfort and a pleasure to you through life, a matter of joy and pride to the many who love and honor you, an occasion of thanksgiving through all eternity. Opposition—every good thing encounters opposition. Think of Paul, of Jesus!

Nay, nay, no such word as fail. Somehow, somehow, you are bound to succeed. The Seminary is a necessity. Our best brethren want it. God has blessed it thus far. It is your own offspring. You have kept it alive since the war,—fed it with almost your own heart's blood. It must succeed, somehow, and you are the man that must make it succeed.[14]

In his opening address on August 30, 1877, after the removal to Louisville had become an accomplished fact, Dr. Boyce said what had agitated his heart and mind through many hard and painful years of struggle and discouragement. At that time he laid bare his magnanimous spirit as he reviewed the trying years he and his colleagues had just passed through.

I do not propose to recount the history of this enterprise. That history, so far as it ever can be written, must await the full fruition of all our hopes, and should come from one less intimately associated with it than I have been. It never can be written in full; it never ought to be thus written. It is only God's inspiration which dare speak of evils and faults and injuries and calumnies proceeding from men whom we know to be good. That inspired Word alone can make these simply the shadows which bring out more gloriously the brightness of the character of the good. Human prejudice and passion would make hideous deformity of all by the excesses which its pencillings would exhibit. Let all such evil be buried in the silence of forgetfulness. Let the history, when written, tell only of the toils and trials and sacrifices, and wisdom and prudence and foresight, and prayers and tears and faith, of the people of God to whom the institution will have owed its existence and its possibilities of blessing.[15]

---

[14] A. T. Robertson, *Life and Letters of John Albert Broadus* (Philadelphia: American Baptist Publication Society, 1910), p. 289.

[15] Broadus, *op. cit.*, p. 252.

Dr. Boyce wisely surveyed the range and strength of Southern Baptists and the facilities of the strategic city that had opened its heart to the Seminary.

With its extensive railroad facilities we are put in immediate connection with all portions of the South. . . . Beginning with Maryland on the northeast, and extending to Missouri on the northwest, thence to Texas on the southwest, and to Florida on the southeast, . . . in connection with the Southern Baptist Convention there are one million one hundred thousand church-members, and five million five hundred thousand persons associated with Baptist congregations, seven thousand ministers, and thirteen thousand churches. From these we must expect large numbers. I have been accustomed to estimate the possibility of five hundred students in attendance after a lapse of years. I see no reason why this should not be so.[16]

Dr. Boyce's ardent hopes were fulfilled. During the first year in Louisville, 89 students were registered. The second session of 1878–79 brought the student body to 96, and before twenty years had passed, or only seven years after Dr. Boyce's death in 1888, Southern Seminary was able to welcome 316 students to its classes. By May, 1941, a few months before the Pearl Harbor disaster, the enrolment of the school stood at 520 students. Dr. Boyce had not dreamed nor prayed in vain!

As in his inaugural of 1856, Dr. Boyce in his opening address at Louisville in 1877 once more discussed and defended the type of curriculum Southern Seminary had developed. Baptist polity, he argued, made such a variety of ministry an existing fact. Among evangelicals, Baptists and Methodists, Boyce contended, "are the two who alone foster and rely upon men of such a variety of learning and ability." Between them they were in 1877 caring for twenty-five million people in the United States.

The removal of the Seminary to Louisville, as already previously stated, while enlisting a larger number of friends, did not solve all of its financial difficulties. When the third session began in 1879, Dr. Boyce discerned that the effort to secure the endow-

---

[16] *Ibid.*, p. 254.

ment would still have to go on with unabated vigor. Unless some donor would come forward with a large gift, there existed a real danger that funds already collected for endowment purposes might be dissipated for badly needed current expenses. Dr. Boyce, therefore, urged both colleagues and students to pray earnestly that "God would raise up someone able and willing to give the $50,000." But Boyce did not rely on prayer alone. He was ever willing to do his part to accomplish God's purpose. Constantly he talked to people about this need. By means of short articles in several state papers he informed the Baptist people of the South about the Seminary's plight. And once again his faith was vindicated. Dr. Broadus has beautifully written of how God answered his prayers:

It can never be forgotten with what a radiant and yet tearful face he came a few weeks later into a colleague's study, holding an open letter, and saying, "Here is the answer to our prayer." The letter was from Hon. Joseph E. Brown, of Georgia, Ex-Governor and United States Senator. It stated that he had for some time been considering the propriety of making a large gift to some institution of higher education. He had wished that one of his sons might feel called into the ministry; and as that apparently could not be, he felt all the more moved to help educate the sons of others for that work. He had seen Dr. Boyce's brief note in the "Index," and would be glad to have him arrange a visit to Atlanta at his expense, and explain the exact financial situation and prospects of the Seminary, so that he might decide whether it would be safe and wise to invest in its endowment.[17]

Dr. Boyce and the faculty were overjoyed. Dr. Boyce at once made his way to Atlanta, and he soon returned, happy as a king, with fifty thousand dollars in cash and first-class securities. The gift of Joseph E. Brown was made on February 11, 1880, forever a memorable day in the history of Southern Seminary. This was a gift of far-reaching consequences. It encouraged George W.

---

[17] *Ibid.*, p. 274. Cf. *Minutes of the Board of Trustees of Southern Baptist Seminary*, book 2, pp. 22, 28, for the record of the establishment of the John Emerson Brown Professorship in Systematic Theology.

Norton of Louisville to launch out on a new endeavor to secure additional gifts. The goal was set at two hundred thousand dollars.

The Norton brothers set a fine example by providing very large contributions. Dr. John A. Broadus, who by his preaching forays had made many friends around New York, was able to secure forty thousand dollars from Northern Baptist churches and individuals. And before ten years had elapsed, the endowment of two hundred thousand dollars was in hand.

The sagacious Mr. Norton, knowing the weaknesses of the flesh, suggested an amendment to the charter of the Seminary, "requiring that the principal of all contributions for endowment made since Feb. 1, 1880, be held forever sacred and inviolate, only the income to be expended,—and if any part of the principal were used for expenses, then the whole should revert to the donors." [18] He also proposed the creation of a financial board of five Louisville businessmen whose duty it would be to invest the principal in the wisest manner possible and turn over the income to the treasurer of the Seminary.

With the endowment thus secured, the next few years were given to establishing the Seminary in its own quarters. This was highly imperative because of the steady increase in the student body. It rose from 96 in 1878–79, the second year of the Seminary in Louisville, to 120 students in the session of 1882–83, and seven years later it had reached 164. Rented quarters no longer were adequate to house so many students. The need for erecting a student dormitory was the next major project to be accomplished.

When the faculty of the Seminary met on April 1, 1886, in the home of Dr. Broadus, it was moved "that the Chairman of the Faculty, Dr. Boyce, and Professor Manly be requested to push forward the enterprise of erecting as speedily as may be convenient the Students' Boarding Hall on the lot at the corner of Fifth and Broadway, the money having been subscribed in New York

---

[18] Broadus, *op. cit.*, p. 274.

City, and the lot having now been paid for by citizens of Louisville." [19]

The story of how the money for these lots was secured from Louisville citizens and how the needed funds for the student dormitory were secured by Dr. Broadus is dramatic indeed. The congenial Dr. Broadus has told this story with inimitable charm in his memoir of Dr. Boyce, but not without disguising his name and his part in it.

Strange are the ways of God. Dr. Edward Judson, the son of the famous Adoniram Judson of Burma, had been preaching at the Broadway Baptist Church in Louisville. It was natural that he should become acquainted while in the city with the Seminary's present struggles. Upon his return to New York City he spoke most warmly on the subject of the Seminary's patent needs to John D. Rockefeller. Mr. J. A. Bostwick, passing through Louisville in 1884, was shown the lots that the Seminary had purchased. While lingering in the city, he also discussed business affairs with Mr. G. W. Norton and spoke of his interest in the Seminary.

Dr. Boyce soon heard of the visit of these friends. He quickly dispatched Dr. Broadus to New York. Gathering funds was not at all as easy as it looked, even though Dr. Broadus was well known in and around New York City. But the Lord was with him. Mr. Bostwick, at Broadus' first visit, promised to give fifteen thousand dollars toward the new student dormitory. Mr. John D. Rockefeller, whom Dr. Broadus visited next, cheerfully promised to give twenty-five thousand dollars to the project. But more than half of this money had been given on condition that Dr. Boyce raise enough money to pay for the lots in full. The Nortons and Theodore Harris at once came to the rescue. But Dr. Broadus still had a hard furrow to plow. Somehow he had to raise an additional twenty thousand dollars for the building while in New York. Dr. Boyce kept sending telegrams to Broadus. He sent them night after night. "Don't think of coming back without

---

[19] *Faculty Minutes*, book 2, p. 151.

it. Nobody wants to see you here. Stay all winter, if necessary." [20] After three weeks of hard work Dr. Broadus was able to report victory. Sixty thousand dollars had been contributed by the Northern Baptist brethren for the erection of the student dormitory, which at its dedication was fittingly called New York Hall. When Senator Joseph E. Brown of Georgia heard the news, he gave an additional five thousand dollars for the building.

The total cost of New York Hall, furnishing dormitory space for about two hundred students, was around eighty thousand dollars. It also contained lecture rooms, professors' offices, and a lovely dining room. Building operations went on from September, 1886, till March, 1888. The Seminary magazine, established and published by the students of the Seminary, in its May issue of 1888 reported enthusiastically that New York Hall had finally been occupied.

At the Southern Baptist Convention in Richmond, Virginia, in May, 1888, Dr. Boyce was re-elected president of that body to succeed the late Dr. Mell. The trustees of the Seminary, at this same Convention, with the concurrence of the faculty, formally made Dr. Boyce president of the Southern Baptist Seminary. Until then he had been merely chairman of the faculty and treasurer and financial agent of the Seminary.

The committee, reporting on this matter, significantly reported to the board that

they have maturely considered the question submitted to them, and inasmuch as it does not appear that the name of the presiding officer of the Seminary is an essential part of the plan of the organization of the Seminary and as it is not proposed to enlarge the powers, or to increase the responsibilities of this Officer, but to leave the administration and government of the Seminary as heretofore in the hands of the Faculty with equality of rank and position; your Committee therefore recommend that the request of the Faculty be complied with and that the name of the presiding officer be changed from Chairman to President.[21]

---

[20] Broadus, *op. cit.*, p. 282.
[21] *Minutes of the Board of Trustees*, book 2.

This was an honor Dr. Boyce had highly deserved, but in view of the cited reservations, it was really an empty honor.

The late W. O. Carver has intimated that this matter of changing the title of chairman to that of president had been extensively discussed for two years, with strong differences of opinion expressed by the faculty. According to Dr. Carver, Dr. Broadus, as a graduate of the University of Virginia, was fully committed to the faculty method of administration. After Dr. Mullins' death in 1928 Mrs. Mullins told Dr. Carver that there was some jealousy and rivalry between Dr. Boyce and Dr. Broadus on this point. Moreover, the committee that had this matter under consideration for a whole year finally reported their inability to reach an agreement. Hence a new committee was appointed to pursue the matter further. They then were able to bring in the recommendation to change the title of the presiding officer of the Seminary from chairman to president.

Dr. Carver has interpreted the fact that the Seminary faculty, at the time when this recommendation was made, unanimously supported the recommended change as signifying that Dr. Broadus "had generously yielded the point." Dr. Carver surmised, without any precise evidence to substantiate his assumption, that the precarious condition of Dr. Boyce's health somehow influenced the faculty in supporting the trustees' recommendation.

Dr. Boyce's health had been undermined by his Herculean labors on behalf of the Seminary. In the summer of 1888 he undertook a journey to Europe to recover his health, if possible. Several members of his family accompanied him on this trip. They visited England, Scotland, and France. Dr. Boyce's condition improved somewhat, but then it again became critical. On Friday, December 28, 1888, James Petigru Boyce was called home to be with his Lord.

A few weeks later, on January 20, 1889, the mortal remains of the great soldier of the Lord were laid to rest in Cave Hill Cemetery in Louisville, Kentucky. Many of Dr. Boyce's friends from various parts of the country came to do him honor. Dr. Broadus, Judge Alexander P. Humphrey, and Dr. J. L. M. Curry, former

United States minister to Spain, made commemorative addresses. A hymn composed for the funeral by Professor Marcus B. Allmond was sung. When the Southern Baptist Convention met a few months later at Memphis, a memorial service was held on May 12, 1889, in honor of Dr. Boyce, who for seven years had been president of the Convention.

The faculty minutes of January 2, 1889, in the delicate handwriting of Dr. Whitsitt, record the sentiments of Dr. Boyce's colleagues regarding his departure. "We admired our departed brother as a man whom nature had cast in the largest mould, and rejoiced in his elevated character, his conscientious abilities, and his remarkable achievement. The fact that his powers were early sanctified by the Spirit of God, and throughout his career were consecrated to the highest uses will always render his memory a precious heritage." The members of the faculty also acknowledged "his merits as the foremost leader in the enterprise of establishing our Seminary for the higher education of the Christian ministry, to whose interests he gave many years of thought and exertion, and for which he made many sacrifices." [22]

The Board of Trustees in its first meeting after Dr. Boyce's homegoing expressed their sense of deep loss, calling him "the father of the great institution over which he presided. Identified with it from the beginning, he gave the whole of his noble life to it. Without his sagacious counsels, his heroic exertions and his sublime self-sacrifice the institution could not have survived its trials. The Seminary is his monument, and a blessed memorial of him is written in the hearts of the people of God." [23]

Rabbi Moses, speaking of Boyce, made this confession; "Before I came to Louisville, I knew Christianity only in books, and it was through such men as Boyce that I learned to know it as a living force. In that man I learned not only to comprehend, but to respect and reverence the spiritual power called Christianity." [24]

---

[22] *Faculty Minutes*, book 2, p. 171.
[23] *Minutes of the Board of Trustees*, book 2, p. 157.
[24] Broadus, *op. cit.*, p. 308.

4

The Faithful Four: the Original Faculty

SOUTHERN SEMINARY, established in 1859, began its work
with four professors and twenty-six students. The faithful
four—Boyce, Broadus, Manly, Jr., and Williams—who constituted Southern's original faculty were young men still in their
thirties, but men of rare ability and wisdom. Professor William
Barnes of Southwestern Baptist Theological Seminary has affirmed that "the first faculty . . . has never been surpassed, and
perhaps not equalled, by the first faculty in any seminary in
America. They had received the highest intellectual training that
America offered—the University of Virginia, Brown, Harvard,
Princeton Seminary, Newton Theological Institution. They set
a standard of high scholarship united with deep, genuine piety,
a standard carried on by their successors." [1]

The student generation of 1890, reflecting on the faithful four
of Southern's original faculty, warmly spoke of "the princely
Boyce, the able and sweetly spirited Manly, the safe guide and
unexcelled Williams, and the magnetic and scholarly Broadus." [2]
In this chapter it is our purpose to consider these men with regard to their abilities as theological teachers.

As we do so, it ought to be kept in mind that a school like
Southern, founded amidst many misgivings and after many obstacles had been partially removed, was from the start different in
outlook and motivation from a university-related seminary.
While it espoused from its inception what may be called the posi-

---

[1] Barnes, *op. cit.*, p. 133.
[2] *The Seminary Magazine*, III (October, 1890), 125.

tion of "progressive conservatism," its teachers were working within the context of an abstract of principles to which they subscribed upon induction into office. This was, as we have pointed out, a confessional statement of the basic convictions of the Southern Baptist denomination which they intended to serve. Southern, like Yale, was conservative before it was born. That fact, however, while suggestive of the determination to safeguard the rich tradition of the Christian faith, did not preclude the cultivation of an open mind toward all truth and its bearing on the faith.

JAMES P. BOYCE

Adolf Schlatter, the well-known New Testament scholar, once defined theology thus:

The area which theological labour must traverse extends as far as the revealing activity of God. This gives it direction towards the whole of reality. All of God's doing which grips and determines our consciousness demands our attention: nature as well as the Christ, the abnormal process as well as the normal one. In the idea of God the principle is involved that all being is related to God and that it makes manifest somehow his power and his will. Therefore for him who is confronted by the question concerning GOD, there is nothing that could be to him completely without meaning.[3]

The original professors of the Seminary might well have agreed with this rather broad definition of their task. In fact, James P. Boyce, who taught systematic theology, came close to this comprehensive definition of Schlatter. Theology, according to Boyce, as the science about God, is concerned with a thorough study of all the facts that bear on God, his nature and being, and on his relation with all that he has made, including man. Contrary to the opinion of some modern thinkers who would exclude theology from the sciences, Boyce was convinced that "theology is eminently worthy of that name, viz., science." Like other

---

[3] Adolf Schlatter, *Das christliche Dogma* (Stuttgart: Calver Verlag, 1923), p. 13.

sciences, theology is concerned with the investigation of facts. "It inquires into their existence, their relations to each other, their systematic arrangement, the laws which govern them, and the great principles which are the basis of this existence and of these relations." [4]

Boyce also avowed that in theology, as in other sciences,

there is much that is absolutely known, much beyond this that is little questioned, much that is still matter of speculation, and much as to which there is decided difference of opinion. New facts are constantly developing in this science, as in others, which enable us to verify . . . them when erroneous. New theories present themselves for the better explanation of facts already known, and are tested by these facts and by others subsequently discovered; and are received or rejected according to their ascertained correctness. The knowledge of the past is built upon for progression toward the future.[5]

Hence, while Boyce could speak with great assurance of God's supreme revelation in Christ Jesus, of his salvation and mercy, he seemed mindful of the counsel of Pastor Robinson to the Pilgrim Fathers of the Mayflower that "God has yet more truth to break fresh from his Word."

Boyce, good Calvinist that he was, had no scruples about natural theology. "According to the method of revelation, theology may be classified into natural and supernatural theology." Natural theology may be defined as that which "embraces what man may attain by the study of God in nature. This extends not only to what is beheld of him in the Heavens and the Earth, but also in the intellectual and spiritual nature of man himself." [6]

In the study of natural theology Boyce included the history of religions—the Vedas of Hinduism, the Zend-Avesta of the Persians, the Edda of the ancient Norsemen, mythology in general—and philosophy and all the sciences. He seems to have had a high appreciation of the philosophy of the ancient Greeks, for he said that no human mind can estimate the value of these contributions,

---

[4] James P. Boyce, *Abstract of Systematic Theology* (Philadelphia: American Baptist Publication Society, 1899), p. 3.

[5] *Ibid.*

[6] *Ibid.*, p. 4.

"Xenophon's 'Memorabilia of Socrates' and the works of Plato and Aristotle . . . nor the influence they have exerted even over those possessed of the Christian revelation." [7] Among the Latin writers Boyce thought highly of Cicero's *Concerning the Nature of the Gods.*

Supernatural theology, according to Boyce, addresses itself specifically to what is commonly called revelation. Here is the question of how God has made himself known. Boyce saw the heart of theology in soteriology. Every part of theology, whether systematics, eschatology, soteriology, or christology, ought to be biblically orientated. Boyce defined biblical theology thus: "Biblical theology consists in the facts of the Bible, harmonized by Scripture comparison, generalized by scriptural theories, crystallized into scriptural doctrines, and so systematized as to show the system of truth taught, to the full extent that it is a system, and no farther." [8]

Dr. Boyce had only a few works of Martin Luther, the reformer, in his large library. However, he very likely knew of Luther's remark that the Holy Scriptures are "the swaddling clothes in which the Christ child has been laid." Boyce knew something of the riches and the difficulties of biblical theology and hermeneutics, the art of interpretation, as did John A. Broadus, his able colleague in the field of New Testament.

But Dr. Boyce would safeguard the specific interests of the theological endeavor by keeping philosophy in its proper place lest it usurp absolute leadership:

These additions [by philosophy] are not necessarily non-scriptural, for they are often the embodiment of the very essence of Bible truth, though not of its formal utterances. They may be as much a part of Scripture as the theory of gravitation is of the revelation of nature. They should never be so far unscriptural as not to be either probable inferences from the word of God or natural explanations of its statements. The more perfectly they accord with that word, and the greater the proportion of its facts which they explain, the

[7] *Ibid.,* p. 2.
[8] *Ibid.,* p. 4.

more clearly do they establish their own truth and the more forcibly do they demand universal acceptance. Failure to explain all difficulties or to harmonize all facts does not deprive them of confidence, but only teaches the need of further investigation. Direct opposition, however, to any one scriptural truth is enough to prove the existence of error in any Christian dogmatic statement.[9]

Had Dr. Boyce been less entangled in the worries of finance and administration of the young seminary he came to lead, he may well have developed a creative apologetic of Christian truth. But enough has been cited to show that he knew that all theology is at best tentative, constantly in need of correction and restatement in the light of God's revelation in Jesus Christ and Holy Writ. In this world, he firmly believed, theology as an exact science is impossible, for full knowledge of the facts and ascertainment of all the doctrines, while desirable, "can never be looked for in this life." [10]

Suffice it here to say that Boyce's only major work in theology, *The Abstract of Systematic Theology*, is no mere logic-chopping treatise but is vibrant with an experiental faith centered in Jesus Christ as Lord and Saviour. While quite different in tone and texture from theological treatises written in our day, it is still a work of merit and worthy of serious study and analysis. It is significant that this book was translated into Spanish and has been effectively used at the Baptist seminary at Saltillo, now Torreon, Mexico.

It needs to be said that Boyce, of course, was indebted to the old Calvinism which was under serious attack at the time. Nor is it unfair to point out that his major theological work was deeply influenced by F. Turretin and Charles Hodge. Boyce himself never claimed to have made a contribution to theological science.[11] He conceived his work rather as a practical textbook designed for his own students and for pastors without the advantages of seminary training.

---

[9] *Ibid.*, pp. 4–5.
[10] *Ibid.*, p. 5.
[11] *Ibid.*, p. v.

Dr. Carver, in some of his unpublished notes, referred to Boyce in this fashion: "In the course of the years I heard many of the Alumni speak with great affection of Dr. Boyce. I have never heard much of any of these about his teaching. It was his prayers that impressed most of them deeply." [12] Dr. Carver evinced a high regard for Boyce's passion and capacity for work of the highest type in his field, but ventured to say that "his method was purely didactic, not creative or stimulating to original thought or research. He was training a ministry to pass on a theological tradition, not to independent experience and thought." [13]

Boyce, as Dr. Carver was aware, indicated in the Preface of his *The Abstract of Systematic Theology* the method he used in his classes. The student was required to prepare a brief but accurate analysis of each lesson, there being one hundred in all. Usually four or five pages had to be memorized—Carver says "literally"—and these memorized data were subsequently reproduced in class recitation. Outlines of the material covered were often put on the blackboard, and the students were held responsible for whatever assignments had been made. Students would usually stand up and recite, and then another student would "take it up at that point." "If by inattention or any other cause the student could not 'take it up' so much the worse for him. Down went a zero in the record book!" [14] Dr. Kerfoot continued this recitation method as did Dr. Mullins and Dr. Tribble, though in modified form.

Those who knew Dr. Carver, perhaps the most original thinker on the faculty of Southern at any time, need no assurance that he thought little of this method. It reflected an older educational theory of learning which, in Dr. Boyce's opinion, made for logical accuracy and arrangement of thought. Couple this with Boyce's conviction regarding the relevancy of Holy Scripture and his belief in "the perfect inspiration and absolute authority of divine revelation, and . . . that the best proof of any truth is

---

[12] W. O. Carver, "Unpublished Notes" (Southern Seminary Library), p. 18.
[13] *Ibid.,* p. 19.
[14] *Ibid.*

that it is there taught," [15] and one will understand the vigor and persuasiveness of his position despite its evident methodological limitations.

But again, we affirm, Boyce's high regard for textual criticism and his using the Canterbury Version of the Bible in his theological treatise "as furnishing the most accurate translation into English of the inspired originals" revealed his determination to be a responsible teacher of God's truth. He had an insight into the peculiar problematic of interpreting the Scriptures. Making mere statements about them is not enough. The peculiar *emphasis* matters greatly. He wrote:

Its true aspects are, like those of a country or continent, not to be measured only by lines and angles, but by elevations and depressions; or like the execution of a piece of music, which is not sufficiently accomplished by the striking of the correct notes, but by giving each its due length of time, its due emphasis of touch, with that expression which is only possible for one whose soul enters into the harmony of sound, and to whom the music speaks thought as distinctly as would written or spoken words. The possession of such soul-sympathy with the divine word and the power to feel and express with delicate exactness the true measure and weight of its emphasis of statement would give the system of theology in all the perfection which revelation affords. The lack of this is the great cause of difference of doctrinal sentiment among those who really revere and gladly receive the Scriptures as God's word. The tendency of Calvinists, for example, is to emphasize, perhaps too strongly, the sovereignty of God, and to receive only in a guarded manner the statements as to the freedom of the human will. That of Arminians is exactly the reverse. The differences between these are due not to any contrariety of teaching the word of God, but to human failure to emphasize correctly. It is not probable that this can ever be wholly avoided. But it is unquestioned wisdom and duty to approach as far as possible unto perfection.[16]

This attitude explains why Boyce could preach with equal fervor and grace in Baptist, Presbyterian, and Methodist churches.

---

[15] Boyce, *Systematic Theology*, p. vii.
[16] *Ibid.*, p. viii.

Surely there was nothing narrow in this Southern aristocrat who pioneered on behalf of wider opportunities in theological education for the best and the least prepared students. Has not someone in our own day declared that theological differences are but opportunities for deeper and more creative understanding? Boyce might have said that. This discussion of his theology and his method of instruction may be coucluded with still another word from the Preface of his *The Abstract of Systematic Theology:*

In order to secure unity Christians are often urged to ignore their differences and unite upon the great points of general agreement. But the better plan is to recognize these differences as starting-points for such investigations as shall result in greater nearness to the truth, and, therefore, in greater nearness to each other. To this end it is necessary that a system of theology should be mapped out before the human mind. The more correct the system the better it will be. But one had better have an incorrect system than none at all. To this every reading of the word of God, and indeed all study of divine truth, will contribute—to verify it, to correct it, to add to it, to take away from it, and to test and adjust its emphasis of statement. It is necessary only to remember always that the system in the mind is a survey of the truth, and not the truth itself. The worst map a surveyor can obtain is better than none at all, though it gives him only a starting-point. . . . As the land becomes more familiar the map can be made more perfect. The lines and angles having been fixed, the measurements of the elevations and depressions can be added, and the survey finally made as exact as the instruments will allow.[17]

The author expressed the wish that his book might induce others to study theology, the queen of the sciences, and that God, in answer to fervent prayer, might bless such study and the ends for the sake of which it would be pursued.

Dr. Boyce grappled honestly with some of the issues that agitated theologians, philosophers, and churches of his day. In his sermon entitled "The Place and Power of Prayer," Boyce revealed amazing capacity for dealing with the questions of the day.

---

[17] *Ibid.,* pp. viii–ix.

This sermon had been suggested to him by the proposition then familiarly known as Tyndall's Prayer Test. Tyndall, the scientist, had proposed that two patients suffering from the identical illness should be treated in the same hospital, with exactly the same remedies. While one of these patients should be made the subject of widespread prayer for his recovery, the other patient was not to be prayed for at all.[18]

The newspapers made a sensational story of this proposal. Although sincere Christians could not possibly join in thus testing their God, Dr. Boyce took up the challenge and thoroughly canvassed the whole question. Space forbids the detailed analysis of this sermon by Boyce. However, it shows depth of penetrating reflection, biblical knowledge, pastoral wisdom, and a faith tempered with common sense.

Dr. Boyce preached this sermon before Presbyterian, Methodist, and Baptist churches in South Carolina, Georgia, Virginia, Missouri, Illinois, Ohio, and Kentucky between the years of 1873 and 1885. In it he calmly refuted the dogmatism of materialistic, unbelieving, or skeptical scientists. He tried to steer clear between the Scylla of divine sovereignty and the Charybdis of human freedom. To many who heard this masterful sermon on the place and power of prayer, Dr. Boyce gave new assurance in the propriety and efficacy of belief-ful prayer.

Professor Winthrop S. Hudson has pointed out that the "new theology" of the latter nineteenth century had become primarily a culture religion, whose "most significant feature . . . was its lack of normative content." In the words of philosopher John Herman Randall, "the New Theology represented 'a pretty complete acceptance of the world, the flesh, and the devil,' and became largely 'an emotional force in support of the reigning secular social ideals' which offered 'no independent guidance and wisdom' to the Christian believer." [19]

---

[18] J. P. Boyce, "Unpublished Sermons" (Southern Seminary Library), MS 252, pp. 1–80.

[19] Winthrop S. Hudson, *The Great Tradition of the American Churches* (New York: Harper & Brothers, 1953), p. 161.

Whatever may have been the limitations of James P. Boyce's theological outlook, one fact seems clear: his thinking had not yet been eroded by the impact either of liberal or romanticizing tendencies of his age. Dr. Boyce's theology still had some of the "intellectual defenses of historic Puritanism" which, according to Dr. Hudson, had been dismantled by the work of men like Horace Bushnell, Mark Hopkins, and other neoromantic evangelicals.

JOHN ALBERT BROADUS: PASTOR, PREACHER, SCHOLAR

If James P. Boyce was the head of the Seminary, John A. Broadus was its heart. This is not to say that Boyce was only a heartless wizard of finance and administration. On the contrary, these two personalities superbly complemented each other. Together they formed a perfect team bent on building a strong theological school.

"No Baptist of his generation surpassed Broadus in his influence among Southern Baptists" was the opinion of the late W. O. Carver. Few would contest this judgment, and to this very day Broadus is still spoken of in glowing terms. The eulogies expressed at Broadus' funeral in March of 1895 bespoke the high esteem in which John A. Broadus was held by his colleagues, the trustees, the students and the alumni of the Seminary, and by friends all over the world.

Broadus hailed from Culpeper County, Virginia. He was the fourth son of Major Edmund Broadus and Nancy Simms Broadus. His early education was received in his own home under private tutors. It was in Culpeper County that Baptist preachers like James Ireland, Elijah Craig, Nathaniel Saunders, and others had sat behind prison bars in the eighteenth century. And for what crimes? Simply because they had proclaimed the crown rights of King Jesus! This part of Virginia, situated in the middle west of that day, "is sacred soil for all lovers of religious freedom." [20] It was the cradle of rugged tillers of the soil and bold heralds of God's love. Here young Broadus learned to plow,

---

[20] Robertson, *op. cit.*, p. 12.

mow, bind wheat, and rake hay before he plowed a deep furrow for God and his kingdom.

In 1846 John A. Broadus matriculated in the University of Virginia, studying under such eminent teachers as Gessner Harrison, W. B. Rogers, J. L. Cabell, R. E. Rogers, E. H. Courtenay, M. Schele de Vere, W. H. McGuffey, John B. Minor, and John Staige Davis. The University of Virginia was still a young school when Broadus entered, but it had a corps of exceedingly able teachers.

Among these teachers Professor G. Harrison made perhaps the deepest impression on Broadus. Though trained for medicine, Harrison had turned to classics and comparative philology as a career. Influenced by the researches of German philologists, Harrison did much to advance scholarship at the University. Broadus became one of his star pupils, and when Gessner Harrison died in 1873, it was John A. Broadus who pronounced a noble panegyric on this able teacher.

Though the University of Virginia had only 150 students in 1846, it attracted men from various parts of the country. Among the fellow students of Broadus were men like Roger A. Pryor of New York, later a general and lawyer; C. A. Briggs, for many years a distinguished professor in Union Theological Seminary of the same city; and others who made their mark in law, medicine, theology, and other fields of endeavor.

In 1850 John A. Broadus graduated, receiving the Master of Arts degree. He had established an excellent record both in the classics and the sciences. Although committed to the Christian ministry, Broadus spent a year as tutor in the home of General J. H. Cocke in Fluvanna County, Virginia. This, as it were, was his Arabia. Here he found leisure to continue his studies so as to better prepare himself for his life's work.

In 1851 Broadus became pastor of the Charlottesville Baptist Church and also assistant professor of classics at the University. For a time he also served as chaplain to the University of Virginia. Each task committed to his hands he carried out with utter abandon and faithfulness. In this endeavor he seriously endangered his health. But when he closed his work in 1859 in order to become a professor in the newly established Southern Baptist Theological Seminary, Broadus could look back upon a work well done. During the eight years of his ministry as pastor, professor, and chaplain, some 241 people, of whom 112 were Negroes, had been baptized by Dr. Broadus upon confession of their faith in the Lord Jesus Christ and added to the church.

When Broadus was first asked in 1858 to become professor in the new Seminary in Greenville, South Carolina, he declined the offer. Crawford H. Toy, a Virginian and fellow student at the University, was among those who petitioned the Baptist brethren not to rob Charlottesville of their able pastor. But finally in 1859 Broadus did accept the call, leaving behind him the security of his pastorate and a promising teaching career at his beloved University. From now on he was God's pilgrim in a new and precarious venture of faith.

It may be safely said that in his day John A. Broadus achieved more recognition beyond his own denomination than any of his brethren. Interestingly enough, his first sermon was preached in 1849 at Mount Eagle Presbyterian Church in Albemarle County, Virginia. Though ever a staunch Baptist and firm evangelical, Broadus was a welcome preacher in many communions. Large congregations, North and South, vied with each other to secure Broadus as their pastor. When Southern Seminary was struggling for its very survival in the early seventies, the old University of Chicago sought Broadus as its head. Later Vassar, Brown University, and Crozer Theological Seminary were eager to call him as president. Newton Theological Institution wanted Broadus in 1878 as professor of New Testament and homiletics. One influential congregation offered him ten thousand dollars per year as its pastor. But Broadus stuck to his post.

In January, 1889, Yale University honored Dr. Broadus by asking him to deliver the Lyman Beecher Lectures on preaching. He discharged his duties with distinction. Broadus was also widely in demand as a lecturer at Chautauqua in western New York. The Northfield conferences, inaugurated by Dwight L. Moody, claimed his ministry again and again. In 1891 Broadus gave four lectures at Dr. William Harper's Institute at the University of Chicago. That same year Broadus spoke on "Christ's Teaching on the Old Testament" at the University of Virginia. The latter had sought him in 1873 as successor of the great Dr. McGuffey, one of his most admired teachers in student days.

Prior to these events, in 1876 and 1884, Dr. Broadus lectured at Newton (now Andover-Newton) on "The History of Preaching" and "Textual Criticism of the New Testament." In 1890 Broadus delivered the opening lectures on the Eugene Levering Foundation before the YMCA at Johns Hopkins University. These lectures were heard by a large appreciative audience and appeared in book form under the title *Jesus of Nazareth* in the same year they were first given.

As a member of the Slater Fund for Education, Dr. Broadus, succeeding Dr. James P. Boyce, rendered significant service. His cultural breadth lent dignity to all he did and in whatever field he labored.

Broadus corresponded with the leading scholars of the Western world. Among them were men like Professors W. F. Moulton and J. B. Lightfoot of Cambridge University, England; Bishop B. F. Westcott, the famous textual critic; Professor J. H. Thayer of Andover and Harvard; Professor B. B. Warfield of Princeton; and many others. Broadus was a friend of Philip Schaff, and he never broke friendship with Professor C. H. Toy, his former colleague and after 1880 a distinguished professor at Harvard University.

Dr. Broadus was a man of many gifts. His experiences were large and enriching. He baptized Lottie Moon, famous Southern Baptist missionary in China. He also preached before General Robert E. Lee, whom Dr. John R. Sampey, his colleague, came to admire so much. During the dark days of the Civil War, Broadus toiled in a humble country church, twenty-one miles from Greenville, for the pittance of two hundred dollars per year. Later he preached in America's greatest pulpits before cultured congregations.

Broadus was a bridge builder and a peacemaker in the life of Southern Baptists, though he never held the office of president of that body. Yet on at least two occasions it was the gentle, persuasive Broadus who in the midst of the stormy sessions of the Southern Baptist Convention saved it from possible disaster.[21]

Broadus was also an active member of the International Sunday School Lesson Committee. The Baptist Young People's Union found in Broadus one of its most ardent supporters.

In view of these achievements President Eliot invited Dr. Broadus to participate in the two hundred and fiftieth anniversary of Harvard University and conferred on Dr. Broadus an honorary doctor's degree on that occasion.

Broadus was loved among Northern Baptists. Their churches in Chicago, Detroit, North Orange, New York, and Boston often invited him for extended supply preaching. During a ministry at Woodward Avenue Baptist Church in Detroit in the early nineties Broadus' last remark to a close friend of his, Mr. C. C. Bowen, was, "Don't let Kalamazoo College go down!" When Mr. C. C. Bowen died in 1900, he left fifty thousand dollars to Kalamazoo College for the endowment of the John A. Broadus Chair in Greek Language and Literature.

It was no surprise to those who knew Dr. Broadus that when Dr. James P. Boyce passed away in 1888, he was the logical successor in the presidency of the Seminary with which he had been connected since its beginning. He was elected in May, 1889, and served until his death in 1895.

Broadus was not as prolific a writer as his successor, Professor A. T. Robertson. In view of his frail health and his years of administrative involvements, Broadus' achievements in the realm of scholarship are nevertheless considerable.

In order of their appearance Dr. Broadus' works are as follows:

A Treatise on the Preparation and Delivery of Sermons, 1870.

---

[21] For details consult P. E. Burroughs, *Fifty Fruitful Years* (Nashville: Sunday School Board of the Southern Baptist Convention, 1941), pp. 33–34, 40–44, 64–65.

Lange Commentary on 1 and 2 Samuel, translated from the German together with C. H. Toy, 1874.

Lectures on the History of Preaching, 1876.

Sermons and Addresses, 1886.

Commentary on the Gospel of Matthew, 1886.

St. Chrysostom's Homilies on Philippians, Colossians, and Thessalonians (Nicene Library; revision of the Oxford Translation with Preface and Critical Restoration of the Text), 1889.

Jesus of Nazareth, 1890.

Memoir of James Petigru Boyce, 1893.

A Harmony of the Gospels, 1893.

These larger works, some of them running beyond five hundred pages, were supplemented by extensive monographs dealing with a variety of subjects.

Moreover, Dr. Broadus also wrote a large number of articles for *Kind Words for the Sunday School Children,* issued by the first Sunday School Board of Southern Baptists. Broadus and Basil Manly, Jr., brought this board into being in 1863. This series of Sunday school lessons appeared for many years prior to the establishment of the present Sunday School Board. In addition to these contributions, Broadus published numerous articles in many denominational and other journals.

The content and quality of these works is important, but even more important is the staying quality of one of Dr. Broadus' books. Here he excelled. Had he only written his *The Preparation and Delivery of Sermons,* Broadus would have made a signal contribution in the field of scholarship.

In January of 1870 Broadus wrote to Dr. J. L. M. Curry, then United States Minister to Spain, telling him of the writing of *The Preparation and Delivery of Sermons:*

Last summer I went to work at a treatise on the "Preparation and Delivery of Sermons," hoping to make a text-book for Manly, and at the same time meet the wants of young ministers who have no course of instruction in homiletics, and give some useful hints to older ministers. I worked at it all summer, but have not yet completed it. Such books do not get a wide sale, and no publisher is willing to take one from an unknown Southern author. So I am arranging to publish at my own expense, through Smith & English. A generous contribution from unknown persons in Richmond, lately received through Wm. B. Isaacs & Co., came when I was quite despondent about the prospect of commanding the means to publish, and will be a very important help to me.[22]

That "no other work in the field of homiletics has had so wide and extended a use in the history of theological education" is the judgment of Dr. W. O. Carver. Slightly revised first by Dr. Edwin C. Dargan, the book was completely recast and revised by Dr. Jesse B. Weatherspoon in the late thirties. It is a classic in homiletics and is still selling well. This work, with its more than five hundred pages, has been translated into Japanese, Chinese, Portuguese, and Spanish.

Dr. Broadus, so W. O. Carver believed, was rightly credited with changing the ideal of the Southern Baptist ministry from eloquence and flashy oratory to the conversational and expository style of preaching. In fact, in his youth Carver remembered hearing a Virginia pastor, given to the grandiloquent method of preaching, charge Dr. Broadus with having ruined Southern Baptist preaching.

Dr. A. T. Robertson once made this provocative remark: "It has been my fortune to hear Beecher and Phillips Brooks, Maclaren, Joseph Parker and Spurgeon, John Hall and Moody, John Clifford and David Lloyd George. At his best and in a congenial atmosphere Broadus was the equal of any man I have ever heard." [23] Lest the reader discern a bit of bias on the part of the late Professor Robertson, the successor of Broadus, we cite an outsider, Professor W. C. Wilkinson, of the University of Chicago, who ten years after Broadus' death wrote:

I have named in my title a man with every natural endowment, every acquired accomplishment, except, perhaps plentitude of phys-

---

[22] Robertson, *op. cit.*, pp. 233–34.
[23] William Cleaver Wilkinson, *Modern Masters of Pulpit Discourse*, quoted by V. L. Stanfield, "Elements of Strength in the Preaching of John A. Broadus," *Review and Expositor*, XLVIII (October, 1951), 379–80.

ical power, to have become, had he been only a preacher, a preacher hardly second to any in the world.

. . . . His preaching work has been incidental, rather than principal in his career. He presents a conspicuous example . . . . of a man who, notwithstanding that this must be said of him, yet enjoys, and justly enjoys. . . . a national reputation as a preacher.[24]

Among the elements of strength in the preaching and the teaching of John A. Broadus, Professor Vernon L. Stanfield has noted the following: (1) His high concept of the preacher's office. This was inspired to a large extent by his early training and family background. (2) His own call to preach and its continuing impact on the concept of his task. Broadus had originally planned to be a medical doctor. After an intense struggle that lasted three years, Broadus was persuaded to become a preacher by a sermon of Dr. A. M. Poindexter. (3) His deep devotion to God's redemptive message in Jesus Christ and to God's Word. (4) The simplicity of his preaching. While pastor at Charlottesville, Virginia, Broadus learned the art of preaching effectively to an audience composed of business people, university professors, students, country folk, and a large group of slaves. (5) "His conscious purpose to lead his hearers to some spiritual decision." He preached for a verdict, i.e., for conversion, commitment, and decisive Christian living. (6) His careful preparation and delivery of his sermons. Though he did not generally write out his sermons in full, he meticulously studied the text and the context, drawing on a rich store of knowledge for illustration. (7) "All these elements were reinforced by his greatest element of strength—depth of Christian character. His preaching was simply an expression of his life in Christ. . . . It was Broadus, the man—the man in Christ—which contributed most to Dr. Broadus, the preacher." [25]

---

[24] *Ibid.*, p. 379.
[25] *Ibid.*, pp. 383–403. One of the best and most scholarly analyses of Dr. John A. Broadus' homiletical art may be found in Charles A. McGlon's unpublished doctoral dissertation, "Speech Education in Baptist Theological Seminaries in the United States, 1819–1943" (Columbia University, 1943).

But Dr. Broadus was not only eminent in the field of homiletics and preaching, for he also excelled as a competent interpreter of the New Testament. For twenty years he labored, beginning during the harrowing days of the Civil War, on his *Commentary on the Gospel of Matthew.*

This large and scholarly work appeared in 1886, and it was at once enthusiastically received. Crawford H. Toy of Harvard had through the years encouraged Dr. Broadus to complete it. When it appeared, Professor J. H. Thayer of Andover Seminary called it "probably the best commentary in English on that Gospel." [26] Alvah Hovey, president of Newton Theological Institution and editor of the *American Commentary on the New Testament* of which Broadus' work was the first to be published, wrote, "No doubt it will prove to be *the Commentary* of the whole series. Had I read it before writing mine [on John's Gospel], I could have improved the style and substance of my work in several particulars." [27]

Dr. Broadus' *Commentary on Matthew* of 610 pages, while written for persons unfamiliar with the Greek New Testament, contains valuable text-critical notes scattered through the text itself and in the margin. Broadus carefully weighed the external and internal evidence as to the reliability of certain text traditions. He distinguished between *intrinsic* probabilities (as to what the author wrote) and *extrinsic* probabilities (as to changes likely to have been made by well-meaning copyists and students). [28]

Although Broadus had the highest respect for the Westcott-Hort text-critical approaches, he "in a number of cases . . . felt bound to dissent, and to give the reasons as fully and strongly as the character and limits of this work allowed. Hence arises a certain polemical attitude towards writers to whom I feel indebted

---

[26] J. H. Thayer, *Books and Their Uses*, quoted by Robertson, *op. cit.*, p. 357.
[27] *Ibid.*, p. 350.
[28] John A. Broadus, *Commentary on the Gospel of Matthew* ("An American Commentary on the New Testament Series," ed. Alvah Hovey [Philadelphia: American Baptist Publication Society, 1886]), p. xlix. Today scholars usually speak here of transcriptional errors.

and cordially grateful." [29] Significantly, in this context Broadus indicated that while "it may be well to state in a general way, that Westcott and Hort appear to me substantially right in their theory as to a 'Syrian' and a 'Western' type of Greek text," he affirmed that "their supposed 'Neutral' type is by no means disentangled from the 'Alexandrian.' And while they have nobly rehabilitated internal evidence, building their system originally upon that basis, they seem to err in some particular judgments by following a small group of documents in opposition to internal evidence which others cannot but regard as decisive." [30]

The homiletical and practical comments appended to Broadus' exegetical work on particular passages of Holy Writ are extremely helpful and suggestive. He draws on a wide range of sources. The Church Fathers—Origen, Jerome, Athanasius, Chrysostom, Augustine—are mentioned most often. Broadus also refers to Cyprian and Tertullian, cites the Epistle to Diognetes, alludes to Philo and Josephus, and does not overlook ancient non-Christian writers like Plutarch, Plautus, and Cicero. Even Terrence, the comic writer, comes into view, as does also the slave and philosopher Epictetus and Hillel, the learned rabbi.

The Talmud is frequently mentioned, and so are the Targums. Catholic exegetes like the able Romanist commentator Arnoldi are aptly cited to refute Roman Catholic interpretations.[31]

St. Bernard, the passionate lover of the crucified Saviour, receives due attention. And so does Thomas Aquinas, the angelic doctor of the Middle Ages. The Reformers are, of course, summoned to throw light on scriptural truths, with Luther and Calvin being most often quoted. Grotius, the Dutch scholar, and Bengel, the eighteenth-century text critic, as well as John Bunyan, John Milton, and Bishop Hall, must pay their tribute in Broadus' work. Among more recent scholars Neander, Tholuck, Bleek, Keim, Bernhard Weiss, Godet, and Lightfoot often are cited.

Dr. Broadus also uses the chief New Testament codices such as

---

[29] *Ibid.*, (footnote).
[30] *Ibid.*
[31] *Ibid.*, p. 89 (footnote).

Vaticanus, Sinaiticus, and Beza with competence and discrimination. He is likewise conversant with the ancient versions—Egyptian, Syrian, Ethiopic, Gothic, Old Latin—and later versions such as those by Wycliffe, Luther, and Tyndale, and the Great Bible, the Geneva Bible, the King James Version, and the nineteenth-century English and American Revised versions of the Scriptures. He also made use of the translation of John Nelson Darby, the founder of the Plymouth Brethren of the British Isles.

Dr. Broadus likewise cites David Friedrich Strauss and Ernest Renan, the extremely speculative interpreters of the New Testament in the last century. The great grammarians of his day—Buttmann, Winer, Gesenius, and Cremer—often are drawn into the exegesis, and with all his erudition Dr. Broadus plowed a straight line, avoiding forced interpretations and dealing fairly with those with whom he differed.

Broadus, of course, was fully aware how easily some sincere yet ill-informed Bible readers are upset when some critical scholar questions the chronology of the life of our Lord as recorded in the Synoptic Gospels. Yet despite this realization, Broadus could still say that while "the common and probable reckoning of our Lord's public ministry occupied about three years and a half," it may be concluded on the basis of evidence that Jesus' ministry in Galilee lasted less than two years.

He was also cognizant of the fact that the several Gospel writers had been *selective* in their accounts of the life and work of Jesus. Matthew, Mark, and Luke report, for instance, that Jesus began his ministry *after* John the Baptist had closed his labors. The writer of the Gospel of John, on the other hand, "records a number of intervening events, embracing the testimony of John the Baptist to Jesus, after his baptism . . . ; the gaining of disciples, the marriage at Cana, and the brief residence at Capernaum . . . ; the first Passover of our Lord's public ministry, with the expulsion of the traders and the conversation with Nicodemus." [32] Broadus solves this apparent discrepancy between the

---

[32] *Ibid.*, p. 71.

Synoptic writers and the Fourth Gospel in a forthright yet guarded tone: "What were the reasons for omitting one thing and inserting another, we may not in all cases be able to perceive. But the concurrence of the three first Evangelists in beginning their account of Christ's public ministry just after that of the forerunner closed, suggests (Ewald, Alexander), that the work of Christ then assumed in some sense a different character." [33]

Still another problem refers to the time of the birth of our Lord. Broadus held that this event took place at least four years before the commencement of the Christian era. "Most books of history and tables of chronology," he wrote, "still fail to give these dates correctly, probably from fear of confusing the popular mind. There can however be no danger of such confusion, if the simple facts, as just stated, receive the slightest attention." [34]

Here it can be seen that Broadus as an honest interpreter of the New Testament was neither fearful of adverse criticism of well-meaning but uninformed Christian believers nor easily frightened by radical critics, provided that he knew truth to be on his side.

Broadus considered it as "one of the excellencies of the Scriptures, that the form of the revelation is constantly in accordance with the modes of conception natural to man, and even sometimes conformed to the peculiar way of thinking of the people chosen to receive it." [35] Interestingly enough, this latter reference deals with the passage in Matthew 3:17 (the voice from heaven heard after Jesus' baptism) and the parallel passage in Mark 1:11.

The Matthean passage reads, "This *is* my beloved Son, in whom I am well pleased," while the Markan reading says, "Thou *art* my beloved Son, in whom I am well pleased." Dr. Broadus did not try to evade the issue or cover it up with a devotional tour de force. He wrote:

Of course, it cannot be that both of these are the words actually spoken. As to the authenticity of the narrative, such slight and

---

[33] *Ibid.*
[34] *Ibid.*, p. 25 (footnote).
[35] *Ibid.*, p. 58.

72

wholly unimportant variations really confirm it, being precisely such as always occur in the independent testimony of different witnesses. As to the complete inspiration of the Scriptures, we must accept it as one of the facts of the case that the inspired writers not infrequently report merely the substance of what was said, without aiming to give the exact words.[36]

In this context Broadus alluded to the institution of the Lord's Supper (26:26 ff.), Jesus' experience in Gethsemane (26:39 ff.), the inscription on the cross (27:37), and then continued thus:

While such facts as these should make us cautious in theorizing as to verbal inspiration, they do not require us to lay aside the belief that the inspiration of Scripture is complete, that the inspired writers have everywhere told us just what God would have us know.[37]

It is highly illuminating to observe how Dr. Broadus was careful not to read Pauline ideas back into the Synoptic Gospels. At least four passages in the Gospels dealing with the idea of righteousness (Matt. 3:15–16; 5:6; 5:20; 6:33) come under Broadus' critical review. In all these passages he rightly held that the idea of *imputed righteousness*, so evident in Paul's writings, is absent.

In the instance of Jesus' baptism by John "the simple and natural view, for all who do not insist on carrying back the Pauline doctrine of imputed righteousness, is . . . [that] it was proper for all devout Jews to be baptized; therefore it was proper for Jesus." [38]

The hunger and thirst for righteousness in 5:6 means personal righteousness, as even Martin Luther admitted, i.e., "the being and doing what is right." [39] Likewise, the disciples are to manifest a righteousness exceeding that of the Pharisees as Jesus enjoined in 5:20, one that is more spiritual and free, "and a more complete righteousness." [40]

---

[36] *Ibid.*
[37] *Ibid.*
[38] *Ibid.*, p. 56.
[39] *Ibid.*, p. 90.
[40] *Ibid.*, p. 101.

Broadus summed up his view by saying that "it is very doubtful whether the Pauline idea of imputed righteousness occurs anywhere in the Gospels, not even in John 16:10." [41]

A number of times Broadus warned in his *Commentary on Matthew* against mystical and allegorical exegesis. Though he cited Origen, a strong advocate of allegorical interpretation of Scripture, in various places, Broadus was most critical of his spiritualizing the petition in the Lord's Prayer, "Give us this day our daily bread." [42] In fact, while appreciative of the Church Fathers, Broadus held them to have been guilty of spiritualizing "well-nigh everything in Scripture."

Speaking to the condition of his contemporaries, enamored as many were by the immutable laws of nature which scientists were proclaiming, Broadus wrote, "In the present age, it is especially important to urge that men shall pray for temporal good, since so many think that the recognized presence of law in all temporal things puts them beyond the sphere of prayer; as if that would not exclude God from his universe; and as if there were not law in spiritual things also." [43]

But had not some scholars intimated that the Lord's Prayer lacked originality, that its basic teachings were already known to the rabbis of Israel? Dr. Broadus knew that both Jewish and rationalist Christian writers were in his day trying to discredit this prayer on that account. Patiently and without rancor he explored the matter. He had no qualms in admitting certain resemblances, even citing Max Müller's intimation of the word "father" in the Vedas. But Dr. Broadus was not perturbed in the least by such comparisons with ancient lore. "The heathen, too," he argued, "were not wholly unfamiliar with the thought," i.e., of God viewed as Father. And the Jews, of course, as well as the learned rabbis in Jewry, had certainly some awareness of God's fatherhood. Wisely, Dr. Broadus came to the conclusion that the Lord's Prayer need not be considered original.

[41] *Ibid.*, p. 90.
[42] *Ibid.*, p. 135.
[43] *Ibid.*

What then is the amount of the charge that the prayer is not original? Some of its petitions have no parallel in Jewish literature, and others only partial parallels. And as to the resemblances, exact or partial, a little reflection shows that nothing else would have been natural. Is it reasonable to suppose that the Great Teacher would give as a model of prayer to his followers a series of petitions that were throughout such as nobody had ever thought of or felt the need of? A wise teacher links new instruction to what is already known and felt. And our Lord's ethical and devotional instructions would have been really less efficient if they had been marked by the startling originality which some have unwisely claimed for them.[44]

We must refrain from further elaboration of Dr. Broadus' exegetical method. It was honest, critical in the best sense, and reverent. Broadus knew of the awesomeness of Holy Writ and God's revelation. In his exegesis of the Christmas story, Broadus concluded one section with these words:

The Incarnation, as to its nature, is of necessity unfathomably mysterious; but as a fact, it is unspeakably glorious, and, with the Atonement and Intercession, it furnishes a divinely simple and beautiful solution of the otherwise insoluble problem of human salvation. Many things the world accepts and uses as vitally important facts, concerning the nature of which there may yet be questions it is impossible to answer.[45]

And what shall we say of his *Jesus of Nazareth*, a simple but beautiful treatise, first delivered as lectures at Johns Hopkins University YMCA in 1890? In this work of small compass Broadus painted with bold strokes the picture of him who is the very heartbeat of the Christian believer, the head of the church, and the desire of the nations. Here, as in his *Commentary on Matthew*, Dr. Broadus firmly yet modestly stated the case for Jesus the Christ, Son of man and Son of God. The language he employed was chaste and simple. And how eager he was to understand the opponents of the Christian faith! How untroubled when

---

[44] *Ibid.*, p. 133.
[45] *Ibid.*, p. 14.

critics pointed out parallels of the Golden Rule of our Lord in rabbinic lore or even the Analects of ancient China!

Broadus trembled at the thought of drawing the portrait of Jesus, one so unique and so universally reverenced, yet so utterly like ourselves. Our spirits are hushed when we read:

The effort is fore-doomed to failure. It must be disappointing to taste and unsatisfying to devotion. No painter among all the great names has made a picture of Jesus which a loving reader of the gospels can feel to be adequate. How can we depict his character in words? But if one undertakes the task, of all things he must beware of high-wrought expressions. The most inadequate language is less unworthy of Jesus than inflated language.[46]

Was Dr. Broadus cognizant of those who in his day took offense at Jesus of Nazareth? Most certainly. He came to grips with John Stuart Mill, the philosopher, and Henrik Ibsen, the Norwegian dramatist. He was not unaware of Count Tolstoy, the naive dreamer, or of David Friedrich Strauss, the iconoclastic New Testament scholar. Broadus also recognized much of beauty in authentic Buddhism. But as he scanned the horizons of the world's great ethnic religions and their leaders, he found nowhere the empowering spirit that would help men to the full stature of spiritual, ethical, and moral achievement.

To those who would live by the Sermon on the Mount while ignoring Christ's teachings regarding the need of divine pardon and atonement or newness of life and thinking, Broadus simply said, "You deceive yourselves! For Jesus Christ stands before men not only as an ethical and religious teacher, but also as Lord and Saviour!"

The last lecture of *Jesus of Nazareth* puts in sharpest focus the supernatural works of the Master. Here, too, Dr. Broadus confronted the agnosticism of Professor Huxley, the wistful doubt of Matthew Arnold, the pathetic loss of all relish for poetry in Charles Darwin, and the bold speculative theories of Ferdinand Christian Baur.

---

[46] John A. Broadus, *Jesus of Nazareth* (New York: A. C. Armstrong & Son, 1890), p. 10.

Broadus surveyed with considerable detachment the agonizing doubts of his contemporaries; he acknowledged their brilliance and pitied them for their little faith or unbelief. Even in 1890 Broadus painfully realized men's preoccupation with a "sensate culture," as Pitirim Sorokin, the Harvard sociologist, has called it. He felt that the multiplication of facts and inquiries had somehow atrophied men's capacity for appreciating the data of the spiritual world. At the same time, Broadus grieved and sometimes became angry as he observed how theologians and preachers were "undertaking to pass judgment upon any and every question in the exact sciences, and appearing to think that their views on these subjects carry the authority which attaches to the religious and moral lessons they draw from revelation." [47]

But Broadus was equally disturbed when men "who have given their whole lives to matters of physical observation and mathematics, and in those directions have gained deserved reputation, to take it for granted that they are equally qualified to pass judgment off-hand upon questions of general philosophy, or upon the validity of historical testimony." [48]

Dr. Broadus would cultivate such breadth of knowledge, such sympathy for the work of his fellow investigators, whatever their field, such humility before the facts, scientific or religious, philosophical or sociological, so as to overcome the myopic tendencies of the age and to encourage a *whole* response to truth, beauty, and goodness.

It needs no special emphasis that to Dr. Broadus Jesus Christ was a supernatural being who wrought supernatural works, notwithstanding his having been fully human.

Tear out all the supernatural elements from the gospels, and the remainder will be no history at all, but a mass of shattered and broken matters worse than the ruins of so many noble buildings which the other day I left shapely and useful in the city where I dwell. Jesus himself speaks of his miracles as real. In several instances he prom-

---

[47] *Ibid.*, p. 82.
[48] *Ibid.*

ises beforehand, as in regard to Lazarus, and especially in regard to his own resurrection. In other cases he points back to his past miraculous work. Take the gospels as they stand, in all their beauty and simplicity, their pathos and power, and if Jesus of Nazareth did not perform supernatural works, he many times spoke falsely. The very suggestion is painful, even to many who altogether deny the supernatural.[49]

Dr. Broadus was convinced that Christ's person and his miracles formed one redeeming whole. Like the opposite parts of an arch they uphold each other. Either Jesus was what he claimed and what believers through the centuries have experienced of his grace and power, or he was an impostor and a blind leader of the blind.

The resurrection of Jesus Christ from the dead, Broadus firmly believed, is absolutely basic to genuine Christian faith and victorious Christian living. Citing F. C. Baur, the founder of the Tübingen school of higher criticism, Broadus referred to the great scholar's admission of the authenticity of at least three of Paul's chief epistles, that is, Romans, Corinthians, and Galatians. These letters, Broadus pointedly affirmed, unambiguously declare the resurrection of Jesus Christ from the dead. And while Baur declared the book of Acts to be spurious, Dr. Broadus could refer to Ernest Renan, "who is surely skeptical enough for ordinary demands," as believing Luke and Acts to be from the hands of Paul's companion, even Luke the physician. Yet F. C. Baur himself had admitted, as did Keim in his three volume *Geschichte Jesu v. Nazara* (1867–72), that the early church remains an enigma without its firm belief in Christ's resurrection.[50]

Dr. Broadus, of course, knew quite well that it required scholarly competence to determine the reliability of Holy Scripture in terms of external evidence. But this does not mean then that for our certitude of faith in God's truth we are utterly dependent

---

[49] *Ibid.*, p. 72.
[50] *Ibid.*, pp. 88–89. Cf. F. C. Baur, *Geschichte der christlichen Kirche* (Tübingen: Verlag L. Fr. Fues, 1863), I, 39–40. "Only the miracle of the resurrection could scatter the doubts which seemed to plunge faith itself into the eternal night of death."

on the theological or critical expert. Not at all, for Dr. Broadus knew of still another dimension of the problem:

As regards the *internal* evidences, every thoughtful reader can largely judge for himself. And if only men would thoughtfully read the gospels, coming near in historical imagination to the person they exhibit, and listening with simple candor to his words of wisdom and love, many who are skeptical now would feel all that is best in them drawn toward him in living sympathy and devotion. The Scriptures in general, and the four gospels in particular, carry credentials of their own on every page.[51]

At this point of the inquiry Dr. Broadus was close to the conviction of the Reformers, Luther and Calvin, with regard to the self-authenticating nature of Holy Writ. But he took issue with men like Baur and Keim who, while affirming that the early church's *faith* in Christ's resurrection is beyond question, yet argued that since historical science is bound within the limits of "material perception and the natural order of the world," the historian can therefore say nothing with regard to the intrinsic truth or reliability of the facts on which the faith of first-century Christians was based. Broadus seriously questioned the propriety of thus limiting the scope of historical science. Why must we, he asked, limit historical science to material perception and the sphere of the natural order?

On the basis of the New Testament evidence, which to Broadus was cumulative in force and reach, he was satisfied that even on rational grounds modern Christians may have full assurance with regard to the pivotal fact of Christ's resurrection from the dead. However, he also admitted that in the last resort there is more to the centralities of the Christian faith than any external proofs men might muster. For Dr. Broadus concluded his delineation of Christ's supernatural works with these words:

Let us remember too that believing in Jesus Christ and his religion is not like believing in some mathematical formula, or some metaphysical conclusion, or some ascertainment of general history. If

---

[51] *Ibid.*, p. 94.

Christianity be true, it is gloriously true—yea, and tremendously true. Remember furthermore; Christianity is not only a system of ethics, or a system of doctrines, it is embodied in a *person*. Egotism is often ridiculous; but take one step upward, and behold it is a sublime egotism when Jesus Christ says, "I am the way, and the truth, and the life. No one cometh unto the Father but through me." Through him, then, let us draw near, on him let us personally rely. It may be that differences of doctrinal conception are at present unavoidable, but why shall we not all trust and lovingly obey the personal Saviour? Nor must we forget that to hold aloof from Christianity is not simply rejecting some creed, or system of opinion, it is rejecting Jesus Christ himself, the Son of God, the Saviour of men. Cannot each one of us say at least so much as this, "Lord, I believe, help thou mine unbelief?" Behold, he who one day said that to Jesus was heard and blessed.[52]

Dr. Broadus had a simple faith in the reality of God revealed in the face of Jesus. He was ever a growing Christian. Diligently he enlarged his opportunities for service. Patiently he deepened his insights through study and prayer. Always he was conscious of his own limitations and of God's larger truths beyond human grasp.

Broadus was a man of ecumenical breadth and taste. He loved all of God's children, whatever their communion. "After all, there are but few passages of the Gospel in regard to which evangelical opinion is seriously at variance." His high regard for the Bible prevented Broadus from wresting the truth in the interest of partisan interpretations. Yet he was a fully convinced Baptist and ever a winsome herald of the gospel.

Broadus believed that the Bible did not merely contain but *is* the Word of God. "Wherever the Bible undertakes to teach, its teachings are true. It does not attempt to teach on all subjects. It uses popular language which must be interpreted accordingly. But whatever it intends to teach, that is paramount in authority." [53]

---

[52] *Ibid.*, pp. 104–105.

[53] Broadus, "The Paramount and Permanent Authority of the Bible," in *Address, Essays, and Lectures* (Philadelphia: American Baptist Publication Society, 1883), p. 8.

But—and this is a most significant point—Broadus also made it clear that while the Word of God is true, "it does not follow that our interpretations are infallible." [54] Dr. Broadus affirmed himself to be an advocate of progressive orthodoxy. But let the Christian theologian and exegete beware lest he forsake or add to the teachings of God's truth. Men are but interpreters, exegetes, and witnesses of God's truth revealed in his Word, and supremely in the Word made flesh, Jesus Christ.

Is there then progress in our understanding of God's truth? Broadus answered with a firm yes. "There was progress in giving revelation, in adding to, modifying, completing the earlier by the later revelation." [55] Thus the findings of archeology in the Nile Valley and Mesopotamia, modern scientific syntax of the philologists, and social and political changes "have also prepared us to interpret the Bible more wisely." [56]

Professor William H. Whitsitt, the successor of John A. Broadus in the presidency of Southern Seminary after 1895, delivered in 1907 a Founders' Day address on his former teacher, colleague, and friend. In this address Whitsitt acknowledged the superior qualities of Broadus as a teacher and research scholar. He credited him with a striking power of co-ordinating his own treasures of learning with the results of all other research. Whitsitt spoke of Broadus' possessing "a sort of a faculty of divination, an extraordinary scientific and historical imagination. Of all the teachers I have encountered on this side of the water, Broadus laid the most distinct emphasis upon the duty of original research." [57]

Dr. Whitsitt also alluded to Broadus' easy mastery of the German language. Together with Dr. C. H. Toy he had translated from the German 1 and 2 Samuel in Lange's famous commentary. Daily he made use of German in his private studies, keeping up with German periodicals and currents of thought. In

---

[54] *Ibid.*

[55] *Ibid.*, p. 7.

[56] *Ibid.*

[57] W. H. Whitsitt, "John Albert Broadus, Founders' Day Address," *Review and Expositor,* IV (July, 1907), 348.

the classroom Broadus would often refer his students to these researches.

Again, while the friends of Whitsitt encouraged him to attend a Scottish rather than a German university after his graduation from Southern Seminary, John A. Broadus said to him, "In my opinion you ought to go to Germany and do the best work that is in you, and afterward to return in the fullness of the blessing of the Gospel of Christ." [58]

While in Dr. Whitsitt's estimate John A. Broadus excelled in scholarship both as a teacher and writer, his "foremost asset was a royal character. He was a product of Virginia, and always displayed Virginian thoroughness, Virginian system, and the Virginian sense of duty. A portrait of him holds a place among the Virginia immortals who are collected in the Gallery of the Virginia State Library." [59]

This verdict of the mature Dr. Whitsitt blends perfectly with the judgment of Dr. William O. Carver, who upon the death of Dr. Broadus wrote these words:

When asked to name that in Dr. Broadus which most impressed him one is confused amid many characteristics, each claiming, for the instant, pre-eminence. This is equivalent to saying that he was a complete man—scholar, teacher, Christian. He was perfect in the sense of the Greek *teleios,* so often expounded by him. You ask for a man; behold, he is before you. You ask for varied scholarship, comprehending and always emphasizing the fundamental principles of every subject, and yet always insisting, for himself and for others, on minute accuracy of detail; Dr. Broadus was most remarkable for this rare combination. Name any important qualification for a great teacher; Dr. Broadus exemplified it. Name any serious defect of a great teacher; in vain you look in him to find it. As a Christian he was "all things to all men," but something—much—to everyone.

It is because of his completeness that whatever the peculiarity of our natures there was in him a characteristic by which he made us all desire and determine, by the grace of God, to be all that is noblest and best. [60]

---

[58] *Ibid.,* p. 350.
[59] *Ibid.,* p. 342.
[60] W. O. Carver, *The Seminary Magazine,* VIII (April, 1895), 422.

In the classroom Dr. Broadus was exacting. He tried to inculcate into the minds of his students the high standards of scholarship he had set for himself. While he was compelling and often fascinating in his lectures, he could be stern in his reproofs and sometimes even cruelly sarcastic. On one occasion while Dr. Broadus was lecturing with wonderful skill and enthusiasm on Saul of Tarsus as he sat at the feet of Gamaliel, an impulsive youth from Missouri, a very fine student, broke into the lecture and said, "Dr. Broadus, you remind me of Gamaliel!" In a curt manner Broadus retorted, "Well, Mr. Johnson, do you want me to say that you are like Saul at my feet?"

Dr. Broadus realized at once that he had been too severe. At the close of the class session, he asked the student to come to his desk. Soon Mr. Johnson emerged, and joining his fellow students outside the classroom, he said with husky voice and moist eyes to a friend, "You know that great man begged my pardon." [61]

Dr. Broadus died on March 16, 1895. In a memorial address at Chautauqua, New York, President William Harper of the University of Chicago summed up his impression of Dr. Broadus in these words:

No man ever heard him preach but understood every sentence; no one ever heard him preach who did not feel the truth of God sink deep down into his heart. He was one of the best known preachers, not only in the South, but in the North as well. As a teacher of the New Testament, as well as of the department of homiletics in the theological seminary, it is perhaps not too much to say that he had no superior in this country. Year after year his work went on, and judging by the influence which he exerted upon those around him, we must confess that Dr. Broadus was one of the great men of our Christian world of the present generation. There is no town or city in all the Southland, and but few towns and cities in the North, in which his voice has not been heard, and in which he was not known and remembered. The purity of his diction and the purity of his thought commanded attention. Chautauqua has lost this year, in Dr. Broadus, one of her greatest teachers, and the Christian world has lost one of its greatest men. [62]

[61] David M. Ramsay, "Founders' Day Address," January 11, 1941. (Southern Seminary Library).

[62] William R. Harper, *The Seminary Magazine*, IX (February, 1896), 289.

BASIL MANLY, JR., CO-FOUNDER OF THE SEMINARY

Basil Manly, Jr., son of Basil Manly, Sr., and Sarah Murray Rudolph Manly, was born December 19, 1825, in Edgefield County, South Carolina, the first of six children. In his blood mingled Irish, Welsh, English, and German strains. While not as great a scholar as John A. Broadus, he deserves a high place of honor in the esteem of our denomination as one of the pioneers in theological education. As Dr. Joseph P. Cox has pointed out in his excellent dissertation on Dr. Manly, the latter advocated the establishment of a central theological seminary for Southern Baptists even earlier than James P. Boyce.[63]

Basil Manly, Jr., grew up in Charleston, South Carolina, where his father was pastor of the First Baptist Church from 1826 till 1837. Young Manly grew up in a rich cultural milieu. His education was of the very best. His earliest schooling was under J. T. Lee, the principal of the German Friendly School Society's Academy, which he entered in 1832. Here discipline was strict, and on occasion a recalcitrant pupil would be thoroughly whipped. But the students absorbed the rudiments of knowledge despite this discipline.

The instruction in school was carefully supplemented by the atmosphere of a lovely Christian home. Here the mother exerted an especially deep influence on her children. Though the father was often preoccupied by his studies and pastoral work, he took an active interest in his son's upbringing. Many prominent Baptist leaders visited the home, contributing to widening the horizons of young Manly.

Quite early a fine friendship developed with James P. Boyce, also of Charleston. It lasted until Dr. Boyce's death. Boyce's mother, a woman of much ability, came to accept Christ as Lord and Master under the ministry of Basil Manly, Sr. Both Boyce

---

[63] James Powhatan Cox, "A Study of the Life and Work of Basil Manly, Jr." (Doctoral dissertation, Southern Baptist Theological Seminary, 1954), pp. 139–40. In this section of the Seminary history the writer is indebted to Dr. Cox's research on Manly.

and Manly, Jr., though equally enamored with books and reading, were gay young blades, ever ready to indulge in mischief like other normal boys. Young Manly, for instance, experimented with the smoking of his first cigar before he was ten years old, while Boyce was always up to tricks and innocent pranks.

Another influence for good was the Sunday school class led by Charles H. Lanneau, Sr., a man of parts and Christian character. In this class Boyce, Manly, William Royal, J. L. Reynolds, and William J. Ward received valuable lessons for their Christian life. Manly, Sr., encouraged his son to listen most carefully to his sermons in order to report on them in detail after the service, a wholesome discipline indeed.

Fearing that throat trouble might eventually end his pastoral ministry, Manly, Sr., accepted in 1837 the presidency of the University of Alabama. He served that institution with distinction until 1855. His son continued his education in a private school at Tuscaloosa for about two years and then entered the University of Alabama in January, 1840, at the precocious age of fourteen. The diary of the elder Manly revealed his anxiety at committing his son so early "to the great and trying responsibilities of college life." [64] But not knowing how to employ the lad's time in other suitable affairs, his father expressed the hope that "God may preserve and succeed him."

When he graduated in December, 1843, young Manly ranked first in his class with an academic average of ninety-eight.[65] Being the son of the president of the university, Manly, Jr., worked the harder to merit his standing in his class.

Soon after entering the University of Alabama, that is, in April of 1840, while reading the *Life of Jonathan Edwards*, Manly, Jr., received, to use a word of Friedrich W. Schleiermacher, "the impetus to an eternal movement." He was converted to a living faith in God. The college freshman, only fourteen years old, was "brought to such a loathing of [myself] for the ingratitude and

---

[64] *Ibid.*, p. 32. Cf. "Diary of Basil Manly, Sr.," (1834–46), p. 173. (Amelia Gayle Gorgas Library, University of Alabama).

[65] *Ibid.*, p. 35.

neglect, and meanness, as it seemed to me, of disregarding the Saviour, and to such an admiration of holiness that I came deliberately and solemnly to the conclusion, that I would try to become a Christian; that as I had tried before, and failed apparently, I would now begin with the purpose of trying till I died." [66]

It is rather remarkable that a fourteen-year-old youth could thus describe his initiation into the mysteries of the Christian faith. How seriously Manly, Jr., took his profession concerning God's awful holiness may be discerned from a remark attributed to him by one of his students. Said Manly in a class at the Southern Seminary in 1891, "The idea that God is too good to punish the evil doer is the half-way house to infidelity." [67]

It was but natural that soon after accepting Jesus Christ as Lord and Saviour young Manly would share his new-found joy with his friends and the members of his home church. Thus on October 12, 1840, he confessed his faith before his father's congregation in Tuscaloosa, and a week later, October 18, 1840, he was baptized by his father in the Black Warrior River.

Basil Manly, Sr., spoke warmly of his "dear son whom I committed . . . to God—, so far as belongs to me, wholly and unreservedly hoping the Lord may like him and use him for his glory." [68] Four years later, on May 13, 1844, the First Baptist Church of Tuscaloosa authorized Basil Manly, Jr., to preach the gospel of Jesus Christ. On June 23, 1844, the young minister preached his first sermon on 2 Peter 3:10. In it he confessed having heard God "calling him to a walk of unutterable responsibility, from which he shrank in trembling insufficiency." [69]

The choice of where to further his ministerial education was now upon Basil Manly. Should he attend one of the college-related theological departments like that of Mercer University? The able Dr. J. L. Dagg taught at that school, but he advised Manly to go elsewhere. Finally, the choice fell on Newton

---

[66] *Ibid.*, pp. 36–37.
[67] *The Seminary Magazine*, IV (May, 1891), 125.
[68] Cox, *op. cit.*, p. 37. Cf. "Diary of Basil Manly, Sr.," p. 202.
[69] *Ibid.*, p. 40.

Theological Institution near Boston, Massachusetts. Imagine the youthful Manly starting out on July 2, 1844, on horseback, for the long journey from Alabama to New England! En route to Newton Centre Manly preached in various churches, visited old friends, and while at Raleigh, North Carolina, heard a raucus revivalist preacher who by his mercenary spirit and manner of preaching filled the young man with deep disgust.

Newton Theological Institution appealed to Basil Manly. It had a faculty of renown—Barnas Sears, president and professor of theology; the able Ira Chase in church history; Dr. H. B. Hackett in biblical literature; and Dr. H. J. Ripley in sacred rhetoric and pastoral duties. Professor Hackett, whose Baconian or inductive method of teaching found many imitators and admirers, was, in the words of the late President Everett C. Herrick, "one of the most brilliant students that Moses Stuart [of Andover Seminary] ever trained." [70] It was Dr. Hackett who apparently made the deepest impression on Basil Manly, Jr.

That the serious Manly also possessed a lighter vein in his make-up may be seen in his reaction to a forthcoming examination:

I have nothing particular to do today, and after strumming my fiddle awhile to keep me awake, I thought of that infallible anti-soporific—a letter to Alabama. . . . Well, to-morrow is examination day. . . . Well, I hope I may survive the shock . . . I wonder if there won't be some dreadful meteor or horrific prodigy tonight to show to the admiring world, and to the citizens of Boston also, that tomorrow is examination day. . . . Hang it on the horns of the moon —stick it on the tail of a comet, and give him a bell and let him go ringing through the vast expanse to let the gentlefolks of Jupiter and Saturn and Mars know they must put on their sundry clothes and come here. . . . cause tomorrow is examination day. [71]

In time Manly developed into a solid though often overly cautious conservative without, however, ever being bereft of his

---

[70] Everett Carlton Herrick, *Turns Again Home* (Boston: Pilgrim Press, 1949), p. 30.

[71] Cox, *op. cit.*, p. 48.

critical faculties. Although while in Raleigh he had been repelled by the excessive emotionalism of a self-seeking revivalist, New England Baptists seemed to him to be all too formal in their worship. Rev. Samuel F. Smith, pastor of First Baptist Church, Newton Centre, Massachusetts, it seemed to Manly, was "a good little man, and preaches his best; but the man has no life in him, and he can throw none of it, therefore, into his sermons—they are good, sound, sensible, but tiresome." [72]

President Francis Wayland fared ill at young Manly's hands. When he first met the president of Brown University in the spring of 1845, Manly sought his advice as to the wisdom of leaving Newton. Just then the slavery issue was warmly debated by both Northern and Southern Baptists. But when Manly met the famous Dr. Wayland, it was a disappointing experience for the young man from Alabama. He wrote to his father:

You have heard of the proverb—Never think you can tell how a frog will jump by his looks. I never was more completely astonished in my life at any man's appearance. You will laugh, but the prominent idea as I came out was—That Dr. Wayland! Why he looks like a rowdy! This was really the notion. . . . The Dr. was in a hurry, but kind, and polite. . . . Still with his kindness he treated me more like a boy than I altogether liked, called me Manly, etc., ... I don't care what he calls me but I'll try and make him *respect* me before I'm through. . . . I never saw anybody I could not make way with yet, and I'll see if I can't get the weather gauge of Dr. Wayland.[73]

The quick succession of events—the Northern Baptist mission boards' solemnly demanding that all Southern Baptist slave-owning missionaries abandon the practice of slavery or forfeit reappointment and that in the future no slaveholders could possibly expect appointment to missionary service, either on the home fields or abroad—made Manly decide to leave Newton in order to enrol in May, 1845, at Princeton Theological Seminary.

---

[72] *Ibid.*, p. 49. Cf. "Letter to Basil Manly, Sr.," November 5, 1845. (Southern Seminary Library).
[73] *Ibid.*, pp. 58–59.

The summer of that year he worked in the libraries of Princeton Seminary and the university, studying advanced Hebrew, church history, and philosophy.

Manly spent two happy and fruitful years at Princeton. He relished his studies under such able and stalwart Calvinists as Dr. Archibald Alexander, Dr. Samuel Miller, and Dr. Charles Hodge. Dr. W. H. Green, later to become one of the foremost Old Testament scholars of America, was already on the scene, being an instructor in Hebrew. On May 17, 1847, young Manly received his diploma as a Princeton Seminary graduate. In later years he always looked back with deep gratitude to his studies at Princeton, remembering the unfailing Christian courtesy shown him and other Baptist students in that famous community of learning.

Well equipped by a full university and theological course, Manly, Jr., spent the next twelve years in varied activities. He became active in denominational affairs; was pastor of both small and large churches; edited, together with his father, *The Baptist Psalmody* with its 1,295 well-chosen hymns, nine being from the pen of Manly, Jr.; and, from 1854 till 1859, was principal of Richmond Female Institute.

For the period of one year, 1856–57, Manly was also editor and owner of *The American Baptist Memorial*. In this capacity he showed journalistic verve, bravely engaged in controversial issues, and soon was elected a member of the Southern Baptist Foreign Mission Board in Richmond, Virginia. He also helped forge a new constitution for Virginia Baptists, changing their pattern from the society to the denominational form of organization.

Manly helped edit still another hymnal, this one *The Baptist Chorals*, which he issued with A. B. Everett in 1859. Finally, together with his father and James P. Boyce he became deeply concerned about the establishment of a central theological school for Southern Baptists during the fifties of the last century. As a member of the Committee on the Plan of Organization, Manly was asked to work out the "Abstract of Principles" which was designed to safeguard the doctrinal stability of the new seminary.

When Basil Manly, Jr., was called in 1858 as professor of the Southern Baptist Theological Seminary, he accepted the call with much trepidation of heart. In the end he gladly gave up his already enviable position of leadership in Virginia in order to assist in the birth and ongoing of the new institution. Since he was to teach Old Testament and Hebrew, he was a bit fearful as to how things would work out. Until then he had been pastor, editor, academy principal, hymn writer, and Sunday school promoter. Though he had taught the more advanced collegiate subjects in the school of which he was president, his Hebrew was rusty. In this predicament he wrote to his father:

I am woefully ignorant of Hebrew. It will take a good deal of hard work between now and October to prevent the classes which I am to undertake, from finding it out. There is one advantage, however, which a teacher has, if he understands his business. He can enlarge on the points he knows, and pass with extreme censoriness over what he does not know.[74]

Dr. Basil Manly, Jr., made a contribution to the first thirty years of Southern Seminary that was far from negligible. It was definitely not in the realm of scholarship that he gained acclaim. But as a helpful teacher of Old Testament and biblical introduction, as a versatile and cultured rather than a deeply thoughtful scholar Manly made his mark. He was mighty in his influence for godliness and righteousness, a fine counselor of students, and a promoter of popular Christian education.

From the catalogue of the first session of the Seminary may be gathered the exact plan of study which Professor Manly pursued in teaching biblical introduction, Old Testament introduction, and Hebrew grammar. Under biblical introduction were listed five subdisciplines: (1) biblical criticism; (2) the canon of Scripture; (3) inspiration, its nature and extent; (4) biblical archeology; and (5) special introduction to each book of the Old Testament as to date, author, design, circumstances under which it was written, "as far as known."

---

[74] *Ibid.*, p. 158.

Old Testament interpretation was divided into two divisions: (1) the English class, which studied select portions of the Old Testament in chronological order, giving an idea of the passage's connection with Bible history as such, of the Old with the New Testament, and of the parts of the Old Testament with each other. The history of topology and leading systems of expositions were likewise to be investigated. (2) The Hebrew class had as its aim the study of the rudiments of the language so as to produce ability to study the Old Testament "with some degree of well-founded confidence at independent results." [75]

The textbooks used in Manly's courses were, among others, Angus' *Bible Handbook*, Gaussen's *Origin and Inspiration of the Bible*, Davidson's treatise on *Biblical Criticism*, Hackett's *Hebrew Exercises*, Rigg's *Chaldee Manual*, Bush's *Notes on the Pentateuch*, and Gesenius' *Hebrew Grammar and Lexicon*. The whole tenor of this arrangement is indicative of times and seasons, of spirit and intention, of outlook and purpose.

When in the eighties of the last century the American Standard Revised Version of the Bible appeared, many Christians became alarmed as they did in 1946 and 1952 when the Revised Standard Version was first published. Dr. Manly patiently defended the revised version of his day, saying, among other things, "There is not a name famous in the whole study of Text Criticism which is not subsequent to 1611." [76] Hence, no serious student of the Bible should ignore this work.

It is also to be noted that such a brilliant student as Crawford H. Toy found much delight in Professor Manly's Hebrew class, for he felt "as if he were one of his companions in study," [77] a testimony that speaks for the young professor's skill and inherent humility.

From the very start of its existence Basil Manly was secretary of the faculty of Southern Seminary. His neat entries grace the

---

[75] *Ibid.*

[76] Basil Manly, Jr., "The Advantages of the Revised Bible," *The Seminary Magazine*, IV (January, 1891), 24.

[77] Cox, *op. cit.*, p. 168.

minutes of the faculty meetings until August 31, 1871, when Manly resigned in order to accept the presidency of Georgetown College at Georgetown, Kentucky.

Before the first session of the Seminary had ended, James P. Boyce, chairman and treasurer of the school, asked Manly to compose a Seminary hymn. This hymn, "Soldiers of Christ, in Truth Arrayed," set to a lovely German tune, was sung during the first commencement exercises near the end of May, 1860. At that time Basil Manly, Sr., first president of the Board of Trustees, delivered the main address on the theme, "I have set watchmen upon the walls."

This hymn by Basil Manly, Jr., has since been sung at every subsequent commencement of Southern Seminary. Though one hundred years have passed since Basil Manly, Jr., wrote it, its simple truth and beauty continue to appeal to heart and mind.

> Soldiers of Christ in truth arrayed
> A world in ruins needs your aid:
> A world by sin destroyed and dead;
> A world for which the Saviour bled.
>
> His Gospel to the world proclaim,
> Good news for all in Jesus' name;
> Let light upon the darkness break
> That sinners from their death may wake.
>
> Morning and evening sow the seed
> God's grace the effort shall succeed.
> Seed times of tears have oft been found
> With sheaves of joy and plenty crowned.
>
> We meet to part, but part to meet,
> When earthly labors are complete,
> To join in yet more blest employ,
> In an eternal world of joy.

In May, 1863, Manly was elected president of the first Southern Baptist Sunday School Board. Together with John A.

Broadus, its first corresponding secretary, he had helped bring this board into being. Faithfully Manly advocated the evangelization of the Negro slaves. He also championed the cause of orphans and their education. The war had increased their number and their plight, and through Manly's efforts, linked with that of his brethren, he induced South Carolina Baptists to aid these unfortunate victims of man's folly.

As president of the new Sunday School Board, Manly, Jr., agitated on behalf of establishing Sunday schools in every state of the Southern Baptist Convention. Interest lagged and there was, of course, opposition in many quarters. But since the South was now severed from the American Baptist Publication Society in Philadelphia, the ministry of this new Sunday School Board was sorely needed.

To supply this lack, Manly wrote, and the Sunday School Board distributed, "two excellent little Sunday School question books, 'Little Lessons for Little People' and 'Child's Question Book on the Four Gospels.' " [78] These had a wide distribution. Manly was also instrumental in beginning the publication of *Kind Words*. He became its editor and often contributed to it. Before the year 1867 had come and gone, the Sunday School Board, so ably led by Basil Manly, Jr., and his associates, John A. Broadus and C. J. Elford, could report a monthly distribution of twenty-five thousand copies of *Kind Words* in the churches of the Southern Baptist Convention.

Thus as farmer, preacher, hymnwriter, religious educator, and theological professor Basil Manly filled the time of war and the postwar years brimful with meaning and godly service. No ivory tower saint was this man of many talents, tender heart, and strong convictions!

When in 1869 C. H. Toy was elected as the fifth professor at Southern Seminary, Manly was asked to teach polemics and homiletics so as to relieve both Boyce and Broadus who had until

---

[78] Louise Manly, compiler. *The Manly Family* (Greenville, South Carolina: n.p., 1930), p. 209.

then taught these two subjects. Manly would have preferred teaching New Testament while John A. Broadus was abroad for the sake of his impaired health in 1870–71. But that could not be arranged.

One other task entrusted to Manly in May, 1868, was the management of the Student Aid Fund. While all the professors had through the years helped in raising funds, the major duty of providing student aid funds fell now upon Manly. When first appointed by the trustees, Manly was asked to secure badly needed funds in the North. He did not particularly relish begging for funds among his Northern brethren.

As early as September, 1868, however, only three months after his appointment to this task, Manly had secured $964.24 in Missouri, but begging for funds in the North was a hard pill to swallow in view of Manly's sentiments toward those who still were in occupation of the Southland. He also feared that the Northern brethren might expect special favors or concessions in return for money they might provide for the struggling Seminary and its impoverished students. But Manly, despite his misgivings and fears, went North and obtained liberal donations in Philadelphia and New York. Everywhere he was cordially welcomed by the Baptist brotherhood.

Other honors came to him. While his colleagues Boyce and Broadus served on the Slater Foundation, Manly became a commissioner of the George F. Peabody Fund for the Advancement of Education among both Negro and white people. The fund's first agent was his former professor and president of Newton Theological Institution, Dr. Barnas Sears.

No one's life is without its sadness. It was so in Manly's case. Between 1866 and 1868 two infants had died in rapid succession. Consumption ended his wife's life at the age of thirty-five in the summer of 1867. Manly was left to care for eight children. Two years later he found a new companion in Miss Hattie Summers Hair of Newberry, S. C. She was a woman of many advantages and of fine cultural background. But the responsibilities of his large family, the uncertainties of the times, and the "corruption and the degradation of this negro government in South Carolina," made Manly yearn for a "white man's country," that is, Kentucky, where Georgetown College had offered him the presidency in the summer of 1871.

Manly remained at Georgetown College for eight years. Although he received a thousand dollars more salary than at the Seminary, Manly's troubles and anxieties were also increased. The financial situation was not as rosy as it had been painted to him prior to the call. Discipline was at a low ebb, and the faculty of six was too small for the one hundred twenty-five students of the college.

It was but natural that the trustees of Georgetown expected the new president to raise an adequate endowment. This was to be done in connection with the centennial of Kentucky Baptists in 1876. The situation was further complicated because of Dr. Boyce's efforts to move the Southern Seminary from Greenville to Louisville. What should Manly do in that situation? His heart was at first divided on the matter. His realism told him that two campaigns for funds, going on simultaneously in Kentucky and surrounding states, would ruin the prospects for both schools. As a way out Manly offered the funds of the Western Theological Seminary, now in possession of Georgetown College, to Southern Seminary if it would remove to Georgetown. For a time he favored Russellville as the future location of the Seminary. In the end Manly worked enthusiastically with Dr. Boyce for the removal of the Seminary to Louisville. This event took place in 1877. Manly unselfishly allowed his own financial campaign to lag so as to give Southern a chance to secure needed endowment and to settle in the new location.

Understandably, Manly fared ill with some of the leaders of Kentucky Baptists who were fearful of the coming of Southern Seminary to Louisville. They anticipated loss of income for the two existing colleges, Bethel and Georgetown. But Manly bravely faced the opposition and the unfounded fears of his brethren.

The misgivings of Dr. Manly as a college administrator found rather sharp expression in a letter to his friend John A. Broadus:

The three pillars on which a Western Baptist College nowadays must be supported are *Brag, Beg, and Grab;* and all these devices in their turn must be resorted to, or all together in order to win students, or else you are stigmatized as "inefficient." If you hear of anybody that has a son (or daughter) and is able to send him from home . . . and do not hunt him out, and track him down, boast to him of superior advantages, outrun the thronging advocates of other institutions, and clutch the aspiring heir—Why—you are an 'old fogy'— behind the age, slow. I acknowledge I sometimes feel a big disgust at things of this kind.[79]

Yet, despite these feelings, Manly brought about certain changes at Georgetown College. He introduced the elective system of studies, enlarged the faculty, saw an alumni professorship established, and provided for the enlargement of Pawling Hall. When one considers that while being president of Georgetown College, Dr. Manly ministered at various intervals to several churches in the Elkhorn Association, wrote a number of extensive essays in Baptist history in the South, and furthered the interests both of his own school and of Southern Seminary, his achievements may be said to have been fairly remarkable.

When in 1879 Professor Crawford Howell Toy resigned his professorship in Old Testament interpretation and literature because his advanced critical views of the Bible were no longer acceptable, his leaving caused deep sorrow and left a great void in the Seminary's life. Basil Manly was asked to return to the Seminary, since the faculty and trustees did not dare to call some inexperienced and unknown person.[80]

Professor Manly was painfully conscious of the predicament he would face as the successor to the brilliant Dr. Toy:

In some respects my position will be one of special delicacy, and difficulty, not only as coming after a man of unusual scholarship, power and attractiveness, but as having to meet doubtless in his students and attached friends the very questions and discussions, the difficulties and arguments, which have been brought up by him to them,

---

[79] Cox, *op. cit.* p. 268. Cf. letter to J. A. Broadus, Sept. 28, 1878.
[80] Professor Manly so interpreted his being called back to Southern.

and which in fact lie on the very front of the subjects I will have to teach. . . . If I agree with him, I shall be censured for unsoundness, if I differ, I shall be thought to be actuated by prejudice or narrow views, clinging to orthodoxy rather than the truth. . . . There is nothing for it but just to go ahead and try to do right, for folks will talk.[81]

Upon his return to the Seminary Professor Manly gave the introductory lecture on "Why and How to Study the Bible." This was on September 1, 1879, eight years after he left the Seminary for Georgetown College. In this address Manly expressed his joy at returning to the school with whose early struggles he had been so closely associated. He then outlined as the main objective of theological education "a practical knowledge of the Scriptures." Lest, however, his audience carry away the wrong impression he underscored his remarks as follows:

Every school and department of the Seminary is mainly valuable as it promotes the elucidation of the Word of God, and the practical application of its teachings. Nor do we fear being charged with Bibliolatry in giving the Bible the central, dominant place in our system and in our affections. From the doubt or denial of God's book, the road is short to doubt and denial of God;—and after that comes the abyss, where all knowledge is not only lost but scoffed at except that which the brute might enjoy as well.[82]

Dr. Manly strongly urged the study of the Bible in the original languages. He bewailed the fact that all too few in "our Southern Zion" are able to appreciate and independently weigh an elaborate critical argument upon questions of New Testament philology. And conditions, he held, were even worse with regard to the Old Testament. He concluded by saying, "If we are to be mighty in God's work, we must be mighty in God's Word."

Due to the widespread discussion in denominational papers of the doctrine of the inspiration of Holy Scripture, Manly felt impelled to deal with that issue and soon published a book on the

---

[81] Cox, *op. cit.*, p. 283.
[82] *Ibid.*, p. 291.

subject.[83] Dr. Carver has called this work a "rather skillful summarizing of the traditional positions and of the arguments in their support in behalf of a rather rigid and literal theory of verbal inspiration. He labors a distinction between revelation and inspiration which a later generation has come to regard as at best superficial. His entire course in Biblical Introduction, while fitting well into the curriculum of that day, was for thoughtful students, not very comprehensive nor very profound." [84] In the main, Dr. Manly's views of inspiration reflected those of the fierce Hengstenberg, the erudite Keil, and the gentle but learned Delitzsch.

While some would not necessarily agree with all of Manly's views concerning theology and Holy Writ, no one who has studied his life can well deny that he bore his burdens and sorrows like a Christian man. When in 1880 three of his children died, one of them, Basil R., taking his own life during a fit of mental aberration, Professor Manly, though deeply shaken, resigned himself to the strange ways of God.

In his declining years Dr. Manly received several well-deserved honors. The Southern Baptist Convention in 1886 elected him vice-president in view of his many services to the fellowship.

During the academic session of 1886–87, Manly was still alert enough to teach a class in Assyrian and engage in other useful activities. He broke up his old family home in downtown Louisville and moved to the Crescent Hill section where he and his children boarded with Mr. and Mrs. F. K. Walker. Then near tragedy overtook the man who had carried many heavy burdens through the years. One afternoon, December 15, 1888, while walking home with Mr. Walker from the afternoon train, both men were knocked down by an assailant. Manly, summoning what strength remained, dragged himself to his nearby house and collapsed. His doctor discovered a leak in the mitral valve of the heart. He advised a long rest and convalescence. Manly from now on would have to slacken his pace.

---

[83] Basil Manly, *The Bible Doctrine of Inspiration* (New York: A. C. Armstrong and Son, 1888).
[84] Carver, "Unpublished Notes," p. 22.

Dr. James P. Boyce, as previously pointed out, had passed away in Pau, France, a few days after Manly's accident, on December 28. And although as always there were many aspirants for the office of president of the Seminary, it was Dr. Basil Manly who at once suggested Dr. John A. Broadus as the best qualified person to assume the presidency. Dr. Manly's wise counsel prevailed.

After still another period of rest near Mobile, Alabama, Dr. Manly returned to his duties at the Seminary. However, the heart trouble which was added to his other afflictions forced a greatly reduced teaching schedule. By May, 1888, Manly had resigned as treasurer of the Student Aid Fund, thus being released from an often burdensome task. Dr. William H. Whitsitt took up this work. Yet, at the end of the session of 1889–90 Dr. Manly felt honored that he could deliver the commencement address, exactly thirty years after his father, Basil Manly, Sr., had given the first graduation address in 1860. When the session of 1891–92 opened, Professor Manly was still on hand to deliver the introductory lecture on "The Old Testament in the Twentieth Century." [85]

Manly, in this address, first of all impressed his hearers with the need of a careful and reverent study of the inspired Old Testament Scriptures. "Those sacred hymns and devotional breathings of ancient piety have not diminished in their fitness for kindling anew, as in every age past, the ardor of pious souls," he argued. He made clear, furthermore, that the revelations of truth contained in the Old Testament "are unchanged in their accuracy, in their interest, and in their importance." [86]

The decades between 1890 and 1910 have been called "the golden age of Old Testament study." [87] Professor Manly, the successor of Dr. C. H. Toy, at this time at Harvard University, could not help being aware of what was going on in this field.

---

[85] Cox, *op. cit.*, p. 316. Cf. *The Seminary Magazine*, V, (October, 1891), 1–12.

[86] *Ibid.*

[87] Arnold S. Nash, ed., *Protestant Thought in the Twentieth Century; Whence and Whither* (New York: The Macmillan Company, 1951), p. 20.

Quite naturally he was led to speak of the critical studies in Old Testament science:

At present what is termed the Higher Criticism is busying itself specially with minute discussions as to its authorship, antiquity and history. Let the inquiry proceed. The book is in no danger. Investigation has brought to view important facts that had been too much overlooked. It may present still more discoveries. But it may be candidly asserted that none of the *proved results* of criticism have diminished in the slightest degree that just claim of this book to the confidence and reverence of mankind. Hundreds of thousands of students, a few with suspicion and dislike, many more with eager love, have examined it from end to end with microscopic minuteness and unwearying diligence; have explored every field of kindred study that was likely to yield confirmation or contradiction. And out of this the book has come not only unscathed, but more firmly established than ever.[88]

Here we have a fair statement on current Old Testament criticism by one who without evasion affirmed the plenary inspiration of the Scriptures. Manly's book *The Bible Doctrine of Inspiration* had outlined his view of the matter with simple force and what seemed to him sound and cogent arguments. In this address Professor Manly did not oppose critical study as such, for he spoke of the proved results of such labor. At the same time he sensed the inherent perils of much speculative, critical endeavor in the field of biblical studies.

It is perhaps also significant that when Professor Manly in May of 1891 spoke before the alumni of Newton Theological Institution, he chose as his subject "Free Research and Firm Faith."

Less than a year after his Newton address Professor Manly died on January 31, 1892. At the funeral Dr. John A. Broadus, Dr. W. H. Whitsitt, Pastor T. T. Eaton, and R. S. Dudley spoke words of comfort and praise on behalf of the departed teacher and friend.

---

[88] Cox, *op. cit.*, p. 317.

James P. Boyce
Chairman of the Faculty, 1859–88
President, 1888

John A. Broadus
Professor, 1859–95
President, 1889–95

Basil Manly, Jr.
Professor, 1859–71, 1879–92

William Williams
Professor, 1859–77

William H. Whitsitt
Professor, 1872–99
President, 1895–99

John R. Sampey
Professor, 1887–1942
President, 1929–42

Edgar Y. Mullins
President, 1899–1928

Ellis A. Fuller
President, 1942–50

Duke K. McCall
President, 1951–

When Manly's son, George Whitefield, entered Southern Seminary in the fall of 1878, his father wrote him a letter which sheds much light on honest, saintly Professor Manly. As he looked back on his life, it seemed filled with many shortcomings. "Much that I had planned, I have never attempted—much that I have attempted has only partially succeeded. With the dying Grotius, I feel much like exclaiming—'*Eheu, vitam perdidi laboriose, nihil agenda.*' [I have spent my life laboriously doing nothing.] As far as I can, I would like to guard you against my mistakes." [89]

The letter itself is a simple, personal revelation of the faults that Manly saw in himself. Professor Manly's failures were those common to the whole of mankind; his comparison was of himself with the perfect man. The final word of Dr. Manly's letter to his son contains advice that is worthy of being read and heeded by any theological student anywhere and at any time:

Most of all, dear George, *watch your heart*—not with a brooding, morose, remorseful disgust, that discourages rather than corrects or guards,—but with an honest cheerful desire to avoid the occasions of evils which have ensnared you, and to fight manfully against the impulses, which you have found to draw you downward and away from God. To me a theological course was not a temptation but a spiritual experience, especially after I went to Princeton. I think I grew in grace by it. God grant it may be so with you.[90]

There is no evidence that Manly ever intended such a confession of his academic and spiritual pilgrimage to become known. This being so, it honors him the more as a man of integrity of mind and unimpeachable honesty, justifying the appraisal of Dr. W. O. Carver, who had known him, though for but a very brief period: "He made an impression upon students, as he did upon people who knew him in other relations, of extraordinary saintliness of character, purity of life, and of gentle strength." [91]

---

[89] *Ibid.,* p. 275.
[90] *Ibid.,* p. 277.
[91] Carver, "Unpublished Notes," p. 21.

WILLIAM WILLIAMS: THE SAFE GUIDE

The fourth member of the original faculty of Southern Seminary was Professor William Williams. A student once described this man as "the safe guide and unexcelled Williams."

Born in Georgia, Williams graduated from the University of Georgia. Later he went to Harvard University, studying law under competent teachers. After graduating from Harvard Law School, Williams for a while practiced law, then became a pastor and served churches in Alabama and Georgia. In 1856 he became professor of theology at Mercer University, then located at Penfield, Georgia.

When the movement toward establishing a central theological seminary for Southern Baptists got under way, Williams, together with James P. Boyce, John A. Broadus, Basil Manly, Jr., and E. T. Winkler, became a member of the Plan of Organization Committee.

E. T. Winkler was first elected to become a teacher in the new school, but when he declined, Dr. William Williams was chosen in his place. In the fall of 1859 Professor Williams was asked to teach ecclesiastical history, church government, and pastoral duties—a formidable assignment—for the Seminary's first session. He was thirty-eight years old at that time.

Something of Professor Williams' character may be divined from a letter he wrote to John A. Broadus shortly after he had been elected to the faculty of Southern. He said:

My appointment by the Board at Richmond took me by surprise. I had not expected or thought of it. I have taken up some time in making inquiries. I now take the first opportunity to inform you of my acceptance. My mind is not so clear, however, as I would like it to be, and as it always heretofore has been, in settling any important question of duty. I hope I may not have erred. If a man may ever be sure of the honesty and sincerity of his feelings and desires, I think I may say it has been my wish to act just as God would have me act, without reference to self. Perhaps longer time might make the matter plainer. I do not know that this would be the case, however, and it is due to others that I decide, as well as due to myself.

I thank you for your kind letter and assure you that I reciprocate all its kind and friendly expressions.[92]

It seems that with the exception of James P. Boyce the other three elected members of the first faculty of Southern all entered upon this venture with considerable hesitations. Did they anticipate possible failure? Yet they followed through, walking by faith. But a sense of duty and call from God led both Broadus and Manly to surrender whatever security they had already achieved professionally and to dare, in the name of God, to possess new land for his kingdom.

Professor Williams would have preferred teaching systematic theology as he had done at Mercer, for this subject was his first love. But church history, together with church government and pastoral duties, became his chief responsibilities. Williams entered upon his teaching in Greenville with zeal and zest, soon acquiring the reputation of being one of the finest lecturers both in the classroom and on the public platform.

As a winsome preacher Dr. Williams was gladly heard in Baptist and other churches. During one period he was permitted to teach systematic theology, taking the place of James P. Boyce, who had temporarily left the Seminary to join a Confederate regiment as chaplain and later to serve in the South Carolina legislature. In a letter to John A. Broadus, Boyce expressed his gratitude to his colleagues and especially to Dr. Williams for his labors with his class. "I shall have the comfort of knowing that at least one class ought to understand theology if they do not. What would I not give for his wonderful power to put things clearly before those he addresses." [93]

After Dr. Manly left for Georgetown in 1871, a reorganization of the curriculum added homiletics to the duties Williams was to perform. But for this task he felt entirely unsuited. He definitely did not want to teach in the field of homiletics. When James P. Boyce, the chairman of the faculty, insisted that he take

---

[92] Robertson, *op. cit.*, pp. 160–61.
[93] *Ibid.*, p. 192.

on this discipline, there was a sharp contention at first. But the difficulty was eventually composed, and Dr. Boyce took homiletics himself, Dr. Broadus being then in the poorest of health.

Dr. Broadus, commenting on the temporary sharp dissension between Boyce and Williams, later wrote, "This was the only time in the Seminary's history that there ever arose the slightest unpleasantness between professors; and this was gone the next day." [94] This contention at least was amiably settled, much for the good of the Seminary and the parties concerned. Professor Williams taught systematic theology during Dr. Boyce's prolonged absence from the Seminary while he was trying to raise a new endowment for the Seminary in Kentucky in preparation for its removal to Louisville. But since Williams also had to continue teaching church history, a subject which he disliked, as well as the other classes, he was soon overworked and became ill.

Williams' health had always been frail. Even in the fall of 1872 Dr. Broadus, writing to Professor Manly, expressed concern for Williams' condition.[95] It was also at this time that Williams came under attack by the Landmarkers because of his advocacy of alien immersion. Dr. Williams sincerely held that those who had been immersed upon confession of their faith in Jesus Christ by Pedobaptists or even Campbellites might be properly received into a local Baptist church without being rebaptized by a Baptist minister. The Landmarkers, and other Baptists in the South who did not subscribe to all of the Landmark tenets, denied the validity of baptism performed by other than properly ordained Baptist preachers.

It was a delicate situation in the life and teaching of the young, struggling Seminary. In view of the attacks upon Dr. Williams, Dr. Boyce, desirous of avoiding unnecessary controversy and eager to attract all sorts of students, regardless of party, again made a remarkable sacrifice. He took Dr. Williams' class in

---

[94] Broadus, *Memoir of James Petigru Boyce,* p. 224.
[95] Robertson, *op. cit.,* p. 287.

church government, hoping in this way to allay the fears of the opponents of his colleague.

Southern Seminary had enough difficulties and problems to contend with at this time without becoming involved in a bitter controversy about alien immersion. This is borne out by a letter that Dr. Boyce sent to John A. Broadus, his yokefellow in the Lord, a year after Dr. Williams first came under fire by some of the brethren in the Southern Baptist Convention. He wrote:

I have now seventy-eight thousand dollars and over. My prospect of reporting one hundred thousand dollars tolerable. The fact is that my Louisville subscription of one hundred and fifty thousand dollars is now to my mind certain. But time, time; I hope to see many of you at the Convention. But I am anxious for Williams to go to Mississippi. If they should treat him badly I shall be sorry on his account and theirs, but it will help us. Soul liberty is worth more than alien immersion, even with Landmarkers.[96]

This liberal attitude of Dr. Boyce is the more remarkable in view of his own personal convictions in the matter. Suffice it to say that Dr. Boyce acted honorably toward his colleague and was unwilling to sacrifice the principle of soul liberty over an issue on which Southern Baptists have never been agreed.

In the few years that remained to Williams' life, he lectured with enthusiasm and brilliance in the field of theology and the other subjects which duty and the exigencies of the situation thrust upon him. His colleague, John A. Broadus, thought most highly of his gifts and ability. "He had extraordinary power of terse, comprehensive, and clear statement of truth. After two or three years of experience, his lectures in Systematic Theology must have been of an excellence rarely equalled. . . ; they were highly valued by the students."[97]

But due to the enforced absence of Dr. Boyce, whose work Dr. Williams had assumed in addition to his own, Williams' health finally broke down. Though the trustees granted him a leave of

---

[96] *Ibid.,* p. 290.
[97] Broadus, *op. cit.,* p. 227.

absence in 1876, the ravages of tuberculosis laid him low at last, and on February 20, 1877, Professor William Williams died at Aiken, South Carolina, at less than fifty-six years of age. Dr. John A. Broadus preached the funeral service on a text that Williams himself had chosen from Psalms: "My times are in thy hand!"

Dr. Williams did not write much. That which survives of his sporadic efforts encourages the belief that had he been less overburdened with work and in better health, he might have produced some serious works.

Professor Williams delivered an address in the form of the annual sermon at the Southern Baptist Convention in St. Louis in May, 1871. This address reviewed the twenty-five-year history of the convention, which had been established in May, 1845, at Augusta, Georgia. It is a comprehensive statement on the mooted origins of the Southern Baptist Convention. As Dr. Williams pointed out, the Convention conceived itself to be "the real and proper successor and continuator of that body [the late General Convention of the Baptist Denomination of the United States formed in 1814 at Philadelphia], which at a special meeting held in New York, November 19, 1845, was 'dissolved,' and the American Bible Missionary Union, with an entirely new constitution and a different basis of membership, organized in its stead." [98]

Williams expressed the conviction that

the formation of a Convention by the Southern Baptist churches, holding its meetings within their precincts, with Boards for Foreign and Domestic Missions located in their midst, had the effect, as was anticipated by the Baptist Register [of New York, April, 1845], to quicken their sense of responsibility, and to develop their resources and energies to an extent which had not been done, and probably could not have been done, by a Convention generally meeting in a distant section of the country, and by a Board located very far from them.[99]

---

[98] *Proceedings of the Sixteenth Meeting of the Southern Baptist Convention held in the Third Baptist Church, St. Louis, Missouri*, Appendix D, p. 5.

[99] *Ibid.*, p. 6. Cf. Robert A. Baker, *Relations Between Northern and Southern Baptists* (n.p., 1948), pp. 7–42.

The proof for his assertion of enlarged opportunities of service and responsibility Dr. Williams found in a comparison of the contributions of the churches to domestic missions for the first thirteen years of the Southern Baptist Convention with their gifts to the same cause for the thirteen years of their connection with the American Baptist Home Mission Society.

The total sum contributed by them to this Society from 1832 to 1845, as is shown in the report of our Domestic Board for 1859, was $38,656 in round numbers. The total sum contributed by them to the Board in Marion from 1846 to 1859, was in round numbers $204,-715, besides contributions to Indian Missions of $61,614, making a total of $266,356 against $38,656. As examples of progress in individual States, the contributions of Virginia from 1832 to 1845, were $9,182. The contributions of the same State from 1846 to 1859, were $40,472. The contributions of Georgia from 1832 to 1845, were $9,529; from 1846 to 1859, $42,461. The contributions of Alabama from 1832 to 1845, were $493; from 1846 to 1859, $44,259.[100]

Dr. Williams was unable to present a similar comparison with regard to gifts to the Foreign Mission Board, but he was assured that even in this respect comparative progress had been made since the Southern Baptist Convention was organized.

He appealed to the then 750,000 Southern Baptists to lengthen the cords and to strengthen every endeavor undertaken in their midst. Referring to the trying postwar times, Williams stated that

our Boards are showing a steady progress; and as our people learn to adjust themselves with equanimity to the new position—which they are doing as rapidly as amazing misrule and plunder will admit—and as they rise from the pressure that is upon them, may we not fairly expect that in no very distant years, more will be done by them than has ever yet been done for the spread of the Gospel at home and abroad, and for all the enterprises both of moral and mental culture which should enlist a Christian's prayer and beneficence? We have no real ground for discouragement, but much for encouragement and thankfulness.[101]

[100] *Ibid.*, p. 6.
[101] *Ibid.*, p. 7.

This annual address of Professor Williams, delivered six years before his lamented death, is indicative of his perceptive mind, his love for God's people, and his firm hope that the Lord would continue to further the work of Southern Baptists in years to come.

Another index of Dr. Williams' insight is a brief monograph, written with scholarly acumen, on "Apostolical Church Polity." It is part of a larger work published by the American Baptist Publication Society under the title *Baptist Pamphlets*.[102] This monograph of seventy-one pages confirms the judgment of those who knew Dr. Williams with regard to the clarity of his ideas and the manner in which he expressed them.

Williams seemed to be at home in the best literature bearing on the subject of church polity. He argued his points with discretion; cited the Church Fathers such as Cyprian, Clement of Rome, Chrysostom, and Theodoret; deftly used Anglican and Presbyterian divines to buttress his case in favor of Baptist congregational polity; and even referred to the erudite Roman Catholic Church historian Döllinger to confirm his position.

Williams argued that the term "church" was not "probably applied to Jewish Christians with any technical meaning until after the Gentiles are received, and the fact becomes developed by the subsequent controversy growing out of their conception, that Christianity is not supplemented Judaism." [103]

Episcopacy, according to Williams, entailed "a radical change in the apostolic organization." However, historically its development is understandable. The absence for some time of a normative New Testament Scripture, the presence and example of a centralized pattern of political government, the emergence of heresies in the churches, and the stimulus of carnal ambition and the love of rank and power—all these factors contributed toward developing out of a plurality of elders, originally equal in rank, the idea of the Catholic bishop with distinctive prerogatives and an indelible character.

---

[102] Philadelphia: American Baptist Publication Society (no date).
[103] *Ibid.*, pp. 5–6.

Williams, moreover, did not contend "that full and minute directions are given as to the *incidentals* and *circumstantials* of church government" in the New Testament. All that could be expected were "the great leading, essential principles." [104]

In his conclusion of the matter Dr. Williams sanely summed up the advantages of congregational church polity. He wrote:

There are obvious excellencies belonging to this form of polity which would lead us to believe that our Saviour *did* intend it. Among others, its ministerial parity offers less temptation than any other to ministerial rivalries and jealousies, and a carnal ambition. Its elective franchise offers less opportunity than any other to a priestly lording over God's heritage. Its congregational form begets, more than any other, a sense of individual responsibility, an active interest in church matters, and the exercise of private judgment. Its cardinal principle of a converted church membership tends more than any other to maintain the purity of the church. Its independent form guards better than any other against schism. Indeed, when this independence is faithfully observed, there cannot be a schism to which a great confederated church is liable.[105]

But what of its actuality in our midst? How true are we to the heritage of the fathers and the New Testament? Evidence abounds that the actual situation is far from the ideal.

But we would end this chapter on Dr. Williams on a happier note, for he terminated his essay on "The Apostolic Church Polity" by raising the sights of his listeners. He said:

Let us hope that the day may not be so distant as the present divisions among Christians would indicate, when the word of God shall be accepted by the people of God as the only authority in all matters of religious belief and practice, and when our Savior's prayer that his people "may all be one" will be completely answered.[106]

The faculty minutes, under date of February 23, 1877, with Professors Boyce, Broadus, Whitsitt, and Toy being present,

---

[104] *Ibid.,* p. 60.
[105] *Ibid.,* pp. 70–71.
[106] *Ibid.,* p. 71.

have recorded their sentiments with regard to their departed colleague, Dr. William Williams, in these words:

> The Faculty of the Southern Baptist Theological Seminary desire to place on record an expression of their sentiments in regard to the death of their friend and colleague, the Reverend William Williams, which took place on Tuesday, the 20th inst. at Aiken, S. C.
>
> He was of the number that were present at the foundation of the Institution, and was chosen almost at the start as a member of the corps of instructors. After nearly eighteen years of unremitted toil he has fallen just at the period when his powers and usefulness had attained their completest development. During all these years so full of vicissitudes for our Seminary, we have enjoyed abundant opportunities of learning his worth.
>
> The sweetness and openness of his temper, his abundance and genuineness of his sympathy, and the transparency and solidness of his character rendered him always a charming and most desirable friend.
>
> It is extremely gratifying to our feeling to be able to record the fact that during eighteen years of almost daily intercourse in which we were called on to discuss and decide innumerable questions, frequently of great importance and difficulty, the cordiality of our relations was never for a moment disturbed.
>
> He possessed great fitness for and achieved great usefulness in the position he occupied as Theological instructor. The breadth and clearness of his views, the terseness of his expression, his probity, his force, the depth and fervour of his piety were acknowledged and valued by all his pupils. Few men could have been more successful in acquiring their admiration and affection, and in impressing them for good.
>
> As a preacher, though he was seldom equal to himself on distinguished occasions, and always shrank from them, those who enjoyed his ordinary pulpit ministrations cannot lose the impression of his massive power and engaging clearness and simplicity.[107]

These words were ordered to be printed in the Greenville, South Carolina, newspapers and the denominational journals of the

---

[107] *Faculty Minutes*, book 1, pp. 57–59.

South. C. H. Toy, the secretary of the faculty, signed this expression of esteem for the departed Dr. William Williams.

THE FAITHFUL FOUR: SUMMARY

This concludes the narrative concerning the first and original members of the faculty of Southern Seminary—James P. Boyce, John A. Broadus, Basil Manly, Jr., and William Williams. The last was the first to go, followed by Boyce in 1888 and Manly in 1892. Three years later, in 1895, John A. Broadus was called to his reward.

Two of these stalwart men of God, Boyce and Broadus, served both as professors and as chairmen and presidents of the faculty. All of them sacrificed much of time and talent—of their very lives—in order to make Southern Baptist Seminary a reality and a true school of the prophets. Though children of their time, they rose again and again above its strife and clamor, steering under God an even course amidst the turbulent currents of the age. Their eyes had beheld a vision of service in God's kingdom, and they rendered this service with firm resolution and holy zeal. They were, one and all, men of depth, breadth, and large horizons in thinking and living.

Ere these founding fathers of Southern Seminary passed off this mundane sphere, the dream that had possessed them had been realized, the Seminary firmly established, and its usefulness widely acknowledged among their brethren in the Southern Baptist Convention and even beyond its boundaries.

The memories of John A. Broadus and Basil Manly, the pioneers of Sunday school work among Southern Baptists, are being perpetuated in the name of the publishing house of the denomination, the Broadman Press, located in Nashville, Tennessee. On the campus of Southern Seminary, Broadus Hall, Manly Hall, and Williams Hall are constant reminders to students, old and new, of the teachers who once taught in its halls of learning and who magnified the name of Christ through Southern Seminary.

5

Thoroughly Furnished unto All Good Works

THE PREVIOUS CHAPTERS have dealt with the genesis of Southern Seminary, the milieu into which it was born, and the personalities and circumstances that shaped its destiny in its formative years. It is by no means a complete story, for no historian can ever describe or analyze historical realities in full. At best he must be selective, sifting out those factors that patently suggest themselves as most important and formative in the unfolding of any institution. Such a process of selectivity naturally involves a subjective element in the interpreter's analysis. To offset any excessive subjective bias a chapter dealing with the curriculum, the students, and the library, the instrumentalities among others of theological education, is appropriate at this point.

James P. Boyce's idea of theological education implied admission to the Seminary of both college-trained and noncollege-trained men. To make this possible, the elective principle of education, cherished by Broadus at the University of Virginia, was introduced at the beginning of Southern Seminary.

Men like Boyce, Broadus, Manly, and Williams, though highly educated men of culture, had close enough rapport with the temper of their age and the genius of their denomination to realize the need of a varied type of ministry. This explains that although the content of the theological curriculum established at Southern Seminary was similar to that of other seminaries, the method followed a different approach.[1]

---

[1] H. Richard Niebuhr, et al., *The Advancement of Theological Education* (New York: Harper & Brothers, 1957), pp. 2–5, throws light on the nine-

John A. Broadus has thus outlined the curriculum which Southern Seminary followed from its inception:

I. Biblical Introduction. In this school would be taught the Canon of Scripture and Inspiration, with Biblical Geography and Antiquities, etc.

II. Interpretation of the Old Testament. Here would be two classes,—(1) the Interpretation of the Old Testament in English; (2) Hebrew and Chaldee, and Hebrew Exegesis. Other Oriental languages, as Arabic, Syriac, etc., might also be taught.

III. Interpretation of the New Testament. (1) Interpretation of the New Testament in English. (2) New Testament Greek, and Greek Exegesis.

IV. Systematic Theology. (1) A general course, in which the instruction should not presuppose any acquaintance with the learned languages. (2) A special and more erudite course, in which there might be read theological works in the Latin, etc.

V. Polemic Theology and Apologetics.

VI. Homiletics, or Preparation and Delivery of Sermons.

VII. Church History.

VIII. Church Government and Pastoral Duties.[2]

A rather formidable curriculum to be divided among only four professors, with one of them, Dr. Boyce, serving as chairman of the faculty as well as treasurer and financial agent of the seminary!

It was provided that "in each of these schools a separate Diploma shall be given to those students who exhibit, upon due examination, a satisfactory acquaintance with the studies of that school. In those schools which comprise two schools, a general and a special course, the Diploma shall require a competent knowledge of both; while to those whose attainments extend only to a general or English course, there shall be awarded a Certificate of Proficiency." [3]

In modern parlance, the core course in this curriculum was the

---

teenth-century factors that influenced the pattern of theological education in America. While the European and Puritan tradition was in evidence, revivalist trends are also decisively important.

[2] Broadus, *op. cit.*, p. 157.

[3] *Ibid.*

English course, that is, the study of the Scriptures in the English language, and not, as heretofore in most American seminaries, the study of the Hebrew and Greek Bible. This English course was required of all students, regardless of previous preparation. However, those students who chose to study only in the Hebrew and Greek exegetical and language classes were permitted to omit the English course, but by so doing they forfeited their right to a diploma. In all schools of the Seminary, except Old and New Testament and systematic theology, only one class was provided for all types and grades of students.

It may be affirmed that in this emphasis on the English course Southern Seminary pioneered for American theological education. Dr. William R. Harper of Yale wrote to John A. Broadus and expressed his appreciation of his interest in pushing the study of the English Bible in the colleges and theological seminaries. "I have often thought of the pioneer work which you in your Seminary have done in this direction. I have never been able to explain to myself why other seminaries have not followed in your train." [4]

It needs no deep insight to discern that the curriculum which Southern Seminary adopted, based as it was on the elective system of studies, had both advantages and disadvantages. Dr. Broadus and his colleagues were aware of the criticism this procedure might engender. The really startling novelty of this type of theological education was the mingling of students of different educational preparation. But the founders of Southern considered this method best for their purposes. The difficulties of this approach they freely acknowledged, but reasoned Dr. Broadus:

The less erudite men soon find that work will tell, and that they can often share very comfortably in a recitation with some college graduate. At the same time, they have occasion to observe the advantage possessed by fellow-students, or the professor, from an acquaintance with the learned languages; and every year there are some men, endowed with a natural talent for language, who quit after one session,

---

[4] Robertson, *op. cit.*, p. 362.

and go off to college for a thorough course, or who go to work, by private instruction or resolute unaided study, to master Greek, some of them with real success. Others who come as college graduates, soon find, and show, that they have really little talent for language, and when disposed to leave the Hebrew and Greek, and confine themselves to the English course, they are not dissuaded. Thus the elements move freely up and down. Men do that for which they have preparation, turn of mind, and time or patience; and get credit for exactly what they do. Every year some men come for a single session, and are led to complete an English or a full course. . . . Here, as in the New Testament form of Church Government, the benefits of freedom far outweigh its inconveniences. The free choice of studies, provided for by James P. Boyce and his associates, has shown itself thoroughly adequate to furnish theological education for students of very diverse grades as to preparation, all in the same institution and for the most part in the same classes.[5]

Professor Charles A. McGlon has observed that

the consequent admixture of students of unequal age and educational background in the literary and theological institutions and in the independent seminaries effected something of a continuous testing of the curriculum. Older men availed themselves of certain courses in theology, history, and homiletics because of the elective system. Sometimes having less ability than well-developed concepts of what they needed for increasing the effectiveness of the religious work which they had left in order to enter the seminaries, they became potent forces in keeping the younger students and the professors close to the line of practicability.[6]

The same writer has also pointed out that the elective system of Southern Seminary enabled a Jewish rabbi, some Catholic leaders, and a Western cowboy to attend the classes of John A. Broadus in the School of the Preparation and Delivery of Sermons.[7]

The elective system, as Dr. Broadus indicated, naturally meant that graduation was extremely difficult. Until recent years exami-

---

[5] Broadus, *op. cit.*, pp. 160–61.
[6] McGlon, *op. cit.*, pp. 62–63.
[7] *Ibid.*, p. 72.

nations were exceedingly long. During the first thirty years of the Seminary's history these examinations lasted from nine to ten hours. In 1899 it was decided that all intermediate examinations should last only five and a half hours.

In time, of course, modifications in the curriculum have been effected to keep step with educational progress. In 1875 the degree of English Graduate was introduced for students graduating in all schools of the Seminary except Hebrew and Greek.[8] However, Dr. Broadus, on November 8, 1881, referred to the increasing tendency among students to be satisfied with the English course and the degree of English Graduate to the neglect of Hebrew and Greek. The subject was laid over for consideration at the next faculty meeting, but seemingly nothing was done about it. In later years both Hebrew and Greek were required of all graduates.

A resolution passed by the faculty on April 6, 1882, eventually led to the inauguration of graduate studies at the Seminary. The resolution asked the Board of Trustees to organize a higher course of study, "by taking from the present course of study and adding such other topics as the Faculty may determine upon and that Professor Broadus be appointed to draw up a schedule of studies to be submitted to the Board of Trustees at its approaching meeting." [9]

On October 27, 1885, Professor James P. Boyce, chairman of the faculty, read a memorial of the faculty to be presented to the Board of Trustees for sanction and action on certain changes and additions in the Seminary curriculum:

That the faculty be authorized for the School of Church Government and Pastoral Duties to confer separate Diplomas in these two fields—both of these to be required as heretofore for the degree of Full Graduate or of English Graduate.

That the faculty be authorized to confer Diplomas in Assyriac, in the Aramaic languages, Chaldee or Syriac or either of them, in Patristic Greek, in Patristic Latin, History of Preaching, in Foreign

[8] Broadus, *op. cit.*, p. 162.
[9] *Faculty Minutes,* book 1, p. 116.

116

Charles S. Gardner
Professor, 1907–29

W. Hersey Davis
Professor, 1920–50

William J. McGlothlin
Professor, 1896–1919

W. O. Carver
Professor, 1898–1943

A. T. Robertson
Professor, 1890–1934

Faculty, 1944-45 (seated, l. to r.) J. B. Weatherspoon, Gaines S. Dobbins, J. McKee Adams, S. L. Stealey, J. Leo Green (standing) O. T. Binkley, Charles A. McGlon, H. W. Tribble, H. C. Goerner, E. A. McDowell, Jr., R. I. Johnson

Hymnology, in Text Criticism of the New Testament, and in such other subjects as the Faculty may deem best, but that none of these Diplomas shall be required in order to secure the degree of English Graduate, or that of Full Graduate or received as a substitute for any of the Diplomas now required.[10]

The petition was granted by the trustees.

The degree of Eclectic Graduate was instituted in 1890 for those who would graduate in the Junior classes of Hebrew and Greek, systematic theology (the general or English course), church history, homiletics, and in any four of the remaining nine schools or classes. This degree might be earned by a well-prepared student in two years, by others in three.

In 1892 the Board of Trustees established a new system of titles or degrees as a reward for various types of study. The degree of English Graduate was to carry the title Th.G., or Graduate in Theology; the degree of Eclectic Graduate that of Th.B., or Bachelor in Theology. The degree of Full Graduate was to carry the title of Th.M., or Master in Theology. This degree was to correspond "very much to the famous old degree of Master of Arts in the University of Virginia, and to the similar M.A. in several Southern colleges." The degree of Th.D., or Doctor in Theology, was to be conferred upon any worthy student who, after having received the Th.M. degree, would remain "as a close student in the Seminary for at least one whole session of eight months, and has been graduated in at least five of the special departments of the Seminary, and, who, furthermore, has prepared a satisfactory thesis, presenting the results of original research or original thought in some subject connected with theological studies." [11]

Again, we wonder at the daring and audacity of the six professors who between 1885 and 1892 established thirteen separate departments of highly specialized studies—all this in addition to the regular theological course. This large program of studies was

---

[10] *Ibid.*, p. 148.
[11] *Ibid.*, p. 164.

no doubt far too extensive for their number or the resources of the Seminary.

The first Doctor in Theology degrees were granted in May, 1894, to Grant S. Housh, Weston Bruner, T. D. Stafford, and D. G. Whittinghill.[12]

THE STUDENTS OF SOUTHERN SEMINARY

Southern Seminary attracted from the start a varied group of students. This, as we have seen, was largely due to its peculiar theological curriculum and objective. Among the first twenty-six students who entered the Seminary in 1859, a plain country pastor, W. L. Ballard of South Carolina, forty-five years old, sat side by side with Crawford H. Toy, the brilliant M. A. graduate from the University of Virginia.

Many among the first students to matriculate remained for only one session. Others, like J. A. Chambliss, of Alabama, remained two years, he being the first Full Graduate of the Southern Seminary. G. W. Hyde, of Missouri, became a Full Graduate after three sessions. Others among the first matriculants were W. L. Curry, Hilary E. Hatcher, J. William Jones, Robert H. Marsh, C. H. Ryland, T. B. Shepherd, and W. J. Shipman, all of them household names among Southern Baptists.

During the second session, 1860–61, with impending war threatening the nation, some thirty-seven students were in attendance. Among them ten came from Virginia, five from Alabama, nine from South Carolina, five each from North Carolina and Mississippi, one each from Georgia, Missouri, and Massachusetts. Of this number, twelve had attended the first session.

A. W. Middleton from Mississippi belonged to this second Seminary class. At least one fellow student took notice of his airs, for he wrote of him,

He was a brother with opinions. Not infrequently would Middleton raise a breeze in the lecture room when Dr. Boyce held forth from the professorial chair in Systematic Theology. He could not endure

---

[12] *Ibid.*, book 2, pp. 5–6.

the perpendicular 'Calvinism' inculcated therefrom. His father had
written a book in which the age-hoary differences had all been sat-
isfactorily solved, and the son had proved apt scholar to the father.
Dr. Boyce was a younger man then than later, and he was no stran-
ger to the fiery zeal for dogma which usually inheres in men whose
minds and hearts are thoroughly inbred with this school of theology.
He did not take very patiently the dissent which the good brother
from Mississippi sometimes ventured to express quite emphatically.
Long since have I forgotten the particular points "argufied," but I
remember well Middleton's bold and confident manner as he told
the class "what father had said." [13]

Some remarks in one of the earliest issues of the student-edited
Seminary Magazine throw some light on student reaction to the
teaching and examination methods of the Seminary. "How may
one best pass the examination in Systematics?" The answer is quite
simple. "Cram Dr. Boyce's Theology the day before the examination, and forget it the day after!" Sensing, however, that
this advice, though witty, was too superficial to be taken seriously, the editor continued:

The method of cramming tends to make one's theology objective.
It moves the truths about God out of the sphere of conviction into
that of "the commonly accepted opinions." It tends to make religious belief a party matter, rather than a personal conviction. "What
is your religion?"—"I am with the Orthodox." Why, he does not
know and cares very little. This one thing he does, forgetting the
reasons for his faith, he goes on with the crowd. Hence, when one
fellow brings forth a heretical notion, and backs it up by even a
moderate array of facts, those who have accepted their theology at
second hand, are likely to be led astray. Thus we lay ourselves open
to the state of affairs that now prevails among the Baptists of England.[14]

Yet, when Dr. Boyce was absent in Europe to recover his
health, one editorial movingly wrote, "An ocean rolls between

---

[13] C. E. W. Dobbs, "Our Second Session and the Trying Days of '61," *The
Seminary Magazine*, III (April, 1890), 124–25.

[14] *The Seminary Magazine*, I (March, 1888), 74.

his pain-racked body and us. But no lapse of time or leagues of miles can keep his love away from us; and while we weep, and pray, and hope, the great, tender heart of Boyce, unchanged, unchanging, unchangeable, is throbbing in our midst." [15]

A wide range of topics were discussed both editorially and in informative articles. Whether it concerned the newly established University of Chicago or the manifestoes of the Landmarkers, the shortage of ministers or the propensities of religious crackpots, excessive organizationalism or the state of German theological science, the discovery of the *Didache* or of the Moabite Stone, the state of foreign missions or Baptist superiority complexes—these and many other important subjects came under critical review in this student journal. A few examples, taken at random, must suffice to show that the students of the late nineteenth century were alert to the world about them.

One editorial bemoaned the lack of charity

in that class of christians which is uncompromising in its dogma and incurably deaf to the opinion of others. When you have said your say, keep still and let some one else speak. The gods do not confer all reason, all judgment, all consistency, all purity of motive, all credible source of information, all keenness of insight on one man or even on one denomination. There seems to be in every denomination a sort of self-constituted aristocracy whose splendid abilities are clothed with I-thank-thee-that-I-am-not-as-other-men's garments. They are good men, and able men, and deserve great honor for their ruggedness of character. They have done great things for us all, some of them. But just on account of such men have the great religious questions remained so long unsettled, and causes of bad blood. . . . "Landmarkism" is a good thing if the position of the land marks can be determined beyond a peradventure. But when that is a matter of tradition and probability, it is, at least, becoming to greatness to admit that it may be otherwise. The simplicity of any theory is not conclusive proof of its truthfulness.[16]

When thirty-five Princeton Seminary students pledged themselves to foreign missionary service, one editor of the *Seminary*

---

[15] *Ibid.*, I (October, 1888), 176.
[16] *Ibid.*, I (December, 1888), 260.

Magazine wrote, "It seems that the Calvinistic Presbyterians are in advance of Missionary Baptists."[17] This same editor also reported that a Baptist student had refused to read a non-Baptist journal, "as if, forsooth, wisdom and truth touch the earth only where Baptists have consecrated the ground."[18]

One issue of the magazine in 1890 presented this intriguing item:

A fact that might now and then be stated, with no feeling of pride to be sure, is that there is not a student in our Seminary who is not a staunch disciple of the old orthodoxy. There is no taint of skepticism here, no striving after theological novelties, no fine rationalism; but the men are loyal to the old truth, and bear a zeal to proclaim it that means earnest lives and efficient work.[19]

Did the writer make these assertions with tongue in cheek? On the same page we find this bit of historical reminiscence:

Baptists have some queer things connected with their history. They were established in this country by a man who was probably never immersed, and as far as we can prove, never had any special sympathy with immersion—Roger Williams. They were Calvinists rather than Arminians in their doctrine, mainly through the influence of a Methodist—George Whitefield—who turned the Arminian current that threatened to take us all.[20]

In a world ridden with awesome fears, the students of 1890 knew of fears then gripping the minds of men:

If figures didn't lie, there would have been an eternal "smashup" long ere this. We are told that the Catholics will capture us; if not, whiskey will ruin us; if not, the Anarchists will burn us; if not, the capitalists will steal us; if not, the politicians will pocket the earth and then sail away to conquer other worlds. The statistician offers us gratis a dozen first-class routes to the de'il. . . . Oh, these mor-

---

[17] *Ibid.*, p. 268.
[18] *Ibid.*
[19] *Ibid.*, III (April, 1890), 155.
[20] *Ibid.*, pp. 155-56.

bid praters about destiny—how Providence rules above their bickerings and leads humanity towards the light.[21]

Two years earlier the editor responsible for local and personal news had reported with a glow of satisfaction that a Baptist minister at Hopkinsville, Kentucky, had baptized 122 persons in seventy minutes. "This breaks all previous records. Our sprinkling brethren could hardly make faster time than that." [22]

The same issue of the *Seminary Magazine* which through E. B. Hatcher gave an account of "An Important Discovery— The Didache" also informed the readers that there were some sixty million people in the United States. These multitudes were then being served by some seventy-five thousand churches with about eleven million members. The churches were said to own an aggregate wealth of eleven billion dollars. This editor seemingly knew his way around, for proudly he hailed these facts: the richest man in the world, Rockefeller, was a Baptist! The greatest preacher anywhere, Spurgeon, was a Baptist! The most popular author, John Bunyan, was a Baptist! And to clinch it all, the greatest theologian that ever lived, the apostle Paul, was, of course, also a Baptist! *Sancta Simplicitas!* [23]

The subject of "Science and the Bible" was of paramount interest in the last quarter of the nineteenth century. T. W. Young wrote discerningly about this issue under the heading "The Bible as a Book of Science." His analysis is intriguing. "The Bible," he writes, "is no scientific treatise; it has no theories of science to advance, and makes no such pretensions. Yet no book contains as much accurate scientific statements in so small a compass as does the first chapter of Genesis." Again, Young avows that geology teaches that the earth existed much longer than most men had formerly held. "The purpose of the Bible is not to teach physical science. If so, we would naturally expect an elaborate treatise with well formulated theories true to science for all ages." The

---

[21] *Ibid.*, III (January, 1890), 33.
[22] *Ibid.*, I (December, 1888), 268.
[23] *Ibid.*, II (December, 1889), 256.

Bible's purpose, then, is "to reveal to man his creation and fall, his reconciliation and redemption through the blood of Christ, rewards and punishments for the obedience or infractions of moral and spiritual laws, and his final sanctification and glorification when all things are completed." [24]

The missionary interest of the Seminary family was constantly kindled and rekindled through the Society of Missionary Inquiry and the regularly observed Missionary Day. Visiting missionaries and missionary secretaries would bring reports from distant fields, giving accounts of both victory and failure in the Lord's worldwide kingdom. In 1888 the editors of the *Seminary Magazine* proudly recorded the fact that half of the missionaries of the Southern Baptist Foreign Mission Board were graduates of the Seminary. But more recruits were desperately needed. "Dr. Yates is exhausted, Dr. Graves has returned home for reasons of health, Joiner is in Texas, Devault is in Heaven, and will not return to this port."

Four years later, in 1892, the centennial of modern missions was being observed. A hundred years had passed since William Carey's departure for India in 1792. The *Seminary Magazine* took due notice of this significant milestone in Christian history. Southern Baptists, ready to answer God's call, were girding themselves to send out one hundred new missionaries to foreign fields.

Dr. James P. Boyce had been appointed chairman of the Centennial Committee at the Southern Baptist Convention in Richmond, Virginia, in 1888. When he died near the end of that year, Dr. J. L. M. Curry took his place. Meetings were held in Atlanta in May, 1892, and Dr. John A. Broadus and the mighty B. H. Carroll of Texas delivered inspiring addresses. Celebrations of this missionary event were also held in Louisville. The sixteen thousand churches within the Southern Baptist Convention territory were encouraged to deepen their missionary passion and increase their missionary gifts.

The *Seminary Magazine* appeared until 1904, when it was re-

---

[24] *Ibid.*, I (November, 1888), 196 ff.

placed by a faculty controlled journal, *The Review and Expositor*. But enough has been mentioned to show how students of another generation faced the issues of their day.

Only one question remains: Did the students of other days have a sense of humor? From their class pictures one might be inclined to think that these bewhiskered theologues were far too serious for their own good. Yet, they were conscious of the lighter sides of life. For example, the *Seminary Magazine* reports that in a class where matters of textual criticism were being discussed, a professor asked, "What is an uncial?" A student replied, "The uncial is the skin of the papyrus, a plant which grows in the tropical regions."

While Dr. John A. Broadus was lecturing at Yale University in 1889, he sent a telegram of good wishes to the students in the Greek examinations. They wired back, "*Morituri te salutamus.* Safe Return. Grecians."

In more recent times, so we are reliably informed, one student became so exasperated by the sarcasm of Dr. A. T. Robertson that he followed the professor to his study after class and, taking off his glasses, said, "Take off your coat, prof. I'm going to beat the daylights out of you." Old Doctor Bob calmly said, "All right, all right, but let us first kneel down and pray!" Pray they did, and the old professor's hide was mercifully spared.

It would be unnatural to look for mention of disciplinary cases in the student-managed *Seminary Magazine*. The faculty minutes, however, on more than one occasion record a sad tale on this score. Students were summarily dismissed for cheating in examination, losing all credits and certificates in the process. In 1872, for instance, a student was accused of holding "opinions incompatible with his license to preach; his conduct being prejudicial to the discipline of the Seminary, and that his relations to the other students are exceedingly unpleasant." The faculty resolved to request that the brother in question not return to the Seminary.

In 1874 a student was charged with licentiousness. "After repeated equivocations, deception, he had finally confessed." He was asked to leave the Seminary at once and to stop preaching.

Another student, after acting dishonestly in examinations, showed himself penitent and willing to accept any punishment the faculty might see fit to inflict. It was decreed that he lose his diplomas for this and the past session but that he be permitted to return in the fall, since "he has a basis of Christian principle." [25]

Early in 1891 three students, one of them co-editor of the *Seminary Magazine*, had to be expelled from the Seminary for drunkenness. Dr. John A. Broadus had the painful duty of announcing their expulsion before the assembled student body. [26]

A terrible uproar occurred in October, 1892, in New York Hall. It seems that some students covered the floors of the Hall with molasses. The President was requested to set forth to the students the mortification felt over such unseemly behavior. [27]

When in a moment of mental aberration one student committed suicide, the whole Seminary family was plunged into unspeakable sadness. Though they cast the mantle of love over the unfortunate brother, a scar no doubt remained in the hearts of his friends. But such are the disciplines of life and death, of joy and pain. Suffering, commonly shared, has a way of knitting the ever endangered Christian fellowship. Despite human frailty, the Seminary family on the whole was a happy family. And God, the searcher of hearts, used these disciplines of joy and pain, deep anguish and gladsome labors, to accomplish his purpose through the various media that Southern Seminary had dedicated to his increasing purpose.

THE LIBRARY OF SOUTHERN SEMINARY

Next to a competent faculty a library is perhaps the most important educational instrument in any theological school. The founders of Southern Seminary realized that fact from the very start of their venture of establishing a central theological seminary for Southern Baptists. We have seen that their intellectual discipline had been received in the best schools of their day. All

---

[25] *Faculty Minutes,* book 1, pp. 39–40.
[26] *Ibid.,* pp. 197–98.
[27] *Ibid.,* book 2, p. 186.

of these four pioneers of Southern were also men of broad culture. They never were nor intended to be mere professional theologians.

Boyce, Broadus, Manly, Williams, and those that followed them—Toy, Whitsitt, Riggan, Sampey, Robertson, and Carver— were full-orbed men. They were the inheritors of the tradition of the Southern gentleman. That combination of professional competence and cultural appreciation was to be reflected in time in the library they sought to build.

The nucleus of the library of Southern Seminary lay in the library of the theological department of Furman University. This library of some two thousand volumes was transferred to the Seminary before its opening in 1859. Its first home was in the front room of the old First Baptist Church, the original and rented building of the new Seminary at Greenville, South Carolina.[28]

It was good that this Furman theological library was from the first supplemented by the private libraries of the professors. A total of ten thousand volumes was thus placed at the disposal of both students and teachers. Dr. James P. Boyce's library of some five thousand volumes was the largest of these private libraries.

On May 7, 1859, or several months before the opening of the first session of Southern Seminary, the committee on arrangements made this observation:

The Library of the Theological Department of the Furman University has not yet been valued. The Committee have had it catalogued and placed in such a condition as will enable those appointed to arrive at a fair estimate. From the Catalogue however it appears by no means so valuable as had been supposed, although it has many rare and valuable books. It is particularly deficient in modern works, such as will at once be needed in the departments of instruction. They would therefore suggest that the Faculty be authorized to draw and expend for books such as they deem necessary, an amount not exceeding five hundred dollars.[29]

---

[28] Leo T. Crismon, "Growing a Seminary Library," *The Tie*, XVI (March, 1948), 5.

[29] *Proceedings of the Board of Trustees*, book 1, p. 80.

During the second session of the Seminary, the trustees of Columbian College, Washington, D. C., presented a valuable collection of nearly two hundred books to the library. This was the first of many valuable and welcome gifts. During the session of 1868–69 Professor W. E. Bailey of South Carolina donated his library of classical, religious, and miscellaneous works numbering thirteen hundred volumes. Dr. Basil Manly, Sr., the first president of the Board of Trustees, directed before his death in 1869 that his library be given to the Seminary.[30] Before Dr. Boyce passed away in 1888, he had the grace of donating his entire theological library to the Seminary.

After the death of Basil Manly, Jr., in 1892, his fine theological library of thirty-five hundred books came into the possession of Southern Seminary, which he had served so faithfully for twenty-five years. During the session of 1894–95 the greater part of the library of Dr. William W. Gardner of Kentucky was donated to the library. Theodore Harris of Louisville gave in 1899–1900 the sum of five hundred dollars to endow a collection for the purchase of scientific books. He gave an additional five hundred dollars for the immediate acquisition of such books.

Some eight hundred volumes from the library of Dr. William H. Whitsitt were presented by his widow after his death in 1911. During the academic session 1927–28 a fine collection of more than a thousand volumes came to the Seminary from the library of Dr. W. T. Crenshaw of Atlanta, Georgia. A year later the library of Dr. E. C. Dargan and more than a thousand volumes from the private collection of Dr. E. Y. Mullins, the Seminary's fourth president, were given to the library.

In 1936 the Seminary library received fifteen hundred volumes from the library of Dr. E. F. Lyon of Vernon, Texas; and in 1937 the family of Dr. Charles A. Stakley of Montgomery, Alabama, gave over a thousand volumes from his personal library. In February, 1943, Ann Tarleton Carley of Georgetown, Kentucky, contributed three thousand dollars for the purchase of

---

[30] Crismon, *op. cit.,* p. 5.

new books. "From this fund many sets of works in the Loeb Classical Library were purchased." [31]

Since then other collections have been received from various donors: from Mrs. John S. Spalding of Atlanta, Georgia, a granddaughter of Governor Joseph Emerson Brown; from Dr. C. M. Thompson and Dr. M. P. Hunt, both of Louisville, Kentucky; from Dr. John Stuart some 250 volumes; and a thousand volumes from the library of the late Dr. John R. Sampey.

In 1956 Dr. Allen W. Graves, dean of the School of Religious Education of Southern Seminary, gratefully received for the Seminary the library of Professor William Williams, one of the original four professors of the Seminary.

At the beginning, as has been said, the library of the Seminary had only two thousand volumes. By 1888 it contained about fifteen thousand volumes. In view of the hard struggle which engaged both trustees and professors of Southern to sustain the Seminary, the gathering of a library of more than fifteen thousand volumes after less than thirty years of operation was no small achievement. Newton Theological Institution, established in 1825, reported after twelve years of operation that its library contained more than three thousand volumes. By 1866–67, after nearly forty-two years of operation, Newton's library had grown to twelve thousand volumes.

From 1888 to 1918, in the second thirty-year period of Southern's existence, its library grew to twenty-six thousand volumes, or an increase of eleven thousand volumes since 1888. In the latter year some 164 students were in attendance, while in 1918 the student body stood at 324.

During the next thirty years, i.e., from 1918 to 1948, the library of Southern Seminary grew to fifty-four thousand volumes or double the number of books available for research purposes in 1918. The student body numbered around eight hundred men and women in 1948. During the session of 1948–49, 204 students received degrees, among them being forty graduate students re-

---

[31] *Ibid.*

ceiving doctoral degrees. To say the least, by this time the resources of the library had fallen far behind those of other theological seminaries in the country.

Between 1948 and 1958 the library of Southern increased to
about 150,000 volumes. Annually, according to the librarian's report, about fourteen thousand dollars has been expended for the
acquisition of new books, and six thousand more has been spent on
the purchase of more than five hundred journals, audio-visual
aids, microfilm materials, and the binding of books and journals.

In the beginning of the Seminary's history, library facilities
were rather primitive. The first complete catalog of the library
dates from the year 1879. It must have taken some time to catalog the books of the library, since in 1869 a student had been engaged to do this work, the expense not to exceed fifty dollars. The
work was to be done during the summer vacation.[32]

In 1878 the faculty approved a recommendation of Dr. Boyce
to purchase Professor Marmon's library for two hundred dollars.
A year later, student C. P. Fountain was offered a hundred dollars to make a new catalog for the Seminary library. A few
months later the faculty generously increased the student's sti-
pend to $150.00.

In 1887 the faculty "beg leave to offer their most hearty thanks
to Hon. J. L. M. Curry, M.D., Minister to Spain, for presenting
the library of the Seminary a number of rare and valuable works
procured by him in Spain." [33] It was at this time that motion was
made "to fit the upper room in the north end of the Dormitory
Building and to occupy it as a Library."

In 1890 Dr. James L. Sampey, father of Dr. John R. Sampey,
was appointed librarian for one year at a salary of twenty-five
dollars a month.[34] In May, 1891, the faculty decided to request
that the Board of Trustees appoint Dr. John R. Sampey librarian
at a salary of four hundred dollars a year, out of which amount

---

[32] *Faculty Minutes*, book 1, p. 6.
[33] *Ibid.*, p. 159.
[34] *Ibid.*, p. 186.

he must pay assistance as he may need.[35] To think that in addition to his many other duties as teacher of Old Testament interpretation and Hebrew, dear old Tiglath had to manage a library of twenty-thousand volumes at so nominal a rate of remuneration!

A few days after Dr. Sampey's appointment as librarian, President Broadus and Professor Basil Manly suggested that he be made assistant professor, his salary being increased to sixteen hundred dollars and the librarian's salary to continue at four hundred dollars per year. His title was to be "assistant professor of Old Testament and homiletics."

Some students, even in those ancient days, must have been negligent in returning books. Others, then as now, tended to carry books away without checking them at the desk. At any rate, a watchman was engaged at the munificent sum of $1.50 a month to guard the library building.

While the benefactors of Southern Baptist Seminary have never been able to donate the large gifts which a university like Harvard has received through the years, their generosity has nonetheless been magnanimous. Whether these gifts were large or small, they all have made a contribution to the growth of the present library. For instance, the widow of a deceased missionary started in 1886–87 a special effort to develop a missionary collection for the library. The Sunday School Board of the Southern Baptist Convention has provided for a number of years one hundred dollars' worth of books for this missionary collection. Broadman Press, the publishing house of Southern Baptists, has in recent years given to the library a copy of each book that it has published.

At the meeting of the Executive Committee of the Board of Trustees of the Seminary, held on December 12, 1895, Professor John R. Sampey "called attention to the fact that at the meeting of the Board of Trustees in Washington, D. C., he had been authorized to raise a Broadus Memorial Book Fund of $60,000.00. Of this amount $50,000.00 was to be invested as an endowment

---

[35] *Ibid.,* p. 194.

for the Library, and $10,000.00 was to be employed to purchase a
house for the family of Dr. Broadus." [36] The treasurer of Southern Seminary reports that at present the Broadus Memorial Book
Fund contains the sum of $14,441.33, yielding an annual income
of about $620.00 for the acquisition of new books.

At the crucial Board of Trustees meeting of May, 1899, Dr.
Sampey, the librarian, was asked to raise ten thousand dollars for
much-needed books for the library, "provided that the time and
method of the effort be determined in conference and coopera-
tion with the President of the Seminary." [37]

In 1891 the Memorial Library, the first permanent home of the
Southern Seminary library, was erected. This building was
largely made possible through the generosity of Mrs. J. Lawrence
Smith of Louisville. This magnificent gift was first announced at
the faculty meeting of December 25, 1888.

The letter in which Mrs. Smith pledged this gift is worth re-
cording. It reads as follows:

As one by one those I love take their departure from the enjoy-
ments of earth, I hope to the better bliss of the life beyond, I feel
impelled to dedicate to their memory the substance that might have
been theirs had their span of life exceeded mine. In looking over
the many needs of humanity I desire that the study of the Bible
with all its helps through the Baptist Theological Seminary may find
a shelter for its books in a permanent building and something for
yearly expenditure for new books. With deep impressions of this
line of usefulness, I wish to place fifty thousand dollars for this purpose (in lots of unimproved property to be sold for the purpose of
such a fund) in the hands of the Trustees of this institution. [38]

Professor Basil Manly was requested by his colleagues to write
Mrs. Smith, expressing the profound thanks of the Seminary for
her "magnificent liberality."

The Memorial Library was opened and dedicated on May 6,

---

[36] *Minutes of the Executive Committee,* December, 1888, to January 26, 1911,
pp. 52–53.
[37] *Minutes of the Board of Trustees,* book 2, pp. 261–62.
[38] *Faculty Minutes,* book 1, pp. 166–67.

1891, with President William R. Harper of the University of Chicago delivering two addresses. The second library building of the Seminary was occupied on the new campus known as The Beeches in the spring of 1926 during the administration of Dr. E. Y. Mullins.

The first catalog of the library of Southern Seminary, completed in 1879, shows that its more than seven thousand volumes had been carefully selected. Next to Jerome's works (seven volumes, published in 1648) stood the complete works of Homer in an edition of 1662. The works of John Locke in an edition of 1823 and the works of Turrenttini in eight volumes no doubt provided much intellectual stimulus to the Seminary's first students. Flavius Josephus was represented by twelve sets of his works. The commentaries of Meyer and Lange, von Ranke's *History of the Popes*, and the complete exegetical and grammatical works of Moses Stuart of Andover Seminary were also included.

Konrad von Tischendorf, the great textual critic, was represented by seven entries in 1859–60. Francis Wayland of Brown University, Boyce's teacher, was of course a must. Seven books by this author were listed in the early catalog of the Seminary library. Science was represented by Sir Charles Lyell, the geologist; Alexander von Humboldt, the naturalist; and Justus von Liebig, founder of agricultural chemistry. Works by John Keble, the Tractarian, and Frederick D. Maurice, the Anglican, were also part of the original library at Southern.

The stern Hengstenberg of Berlin University loomed large with fifteen volumes. There were also four volumes by Johann G. Herder, the versatile idealist and friend of Wolfgang von Goethe. Martin Luther's *Galatians* was the only work of the great reformer in the original collection of the Seminary. John Calvin's works were naturally better represented in view of the Calvinistic outlook of men like Boyce and Manly.

Dr. Boyce's personal library was also available to the students and professors of the Seminary from the beginning. Since 1889 it has been an integral part of the library of the Seminary. The scope of Dr. Boyce's library is amazing; a collection of such dimensions reveals a man of great purpose and passion. The most impressive items are the many Bibles and New Testaments in more than twenty-five languages. Boyce must have thought greatly and reverently of the Bible.

Some rare and valuable works in Boyce's library date as far back as 1489, or nearly to the beginning of the art of printing. Many of these works, of course, are in Latin. A few of these are Beza's *Novum Testamentum* (Antwerp, 1583), in vellum; the *Disputationes de Controversiis* (Ingoldstadt, 1588–93) of Robertus Bellarminus in three volumes; J. Buxtorf's *Lexicum Chaldaicum et Talmudicum et Rabbinicum* (Basilea, 1690); and the *Gnomon Novi Testamenti* by the scholarly and saintly Johannes Bengel of the eighteenth century.

The Presbyterian and Huguenot background of Dr. Boyce is reflected in many French works bearing on the heroic conflict of the followers of John Calvin in France. Catholic works are also part of this library; there is also a complete collection of the Church Fathers. The Latin works of Sallust, Vergil, and Cicero, as well as those of Horace, Julian the Emperor, and twelve volumes of Plato, in French, are included.

In biblical science Boyce owned the best that the mid-nineteenth century had produced: eight Latin New Testaments; sixteen Greek New Testaments, including Erasmus' folio of 1522, Elzivir's of 1624, Stephens' of 1576, Beza's of 1653, and *Codex Vaticanus* of 1859. Tischendorf, of course, would be represented in such a library, as were Griesbach, Hahn-Tillmann, De Wette, Eichhorn, and Champollion by his epoch-making *Système Hiéroglyphique des Anciens Egyptiens* (Paris, 1828).

Eighteen lexicons, several Bible encyclopedias, and the earliest Plitt-Herzog, now Schaff-Herzog, *Encyclopedia of Religious Knowledge*, in German, were also part of Boyce's possessions. The Delphin Classics series of 182 volumes (London, 1825) is in this collection, as is the *New American Encyclopedia* (1858–60).

William Ellery Channing is represented by six of his works. The Princeton theologians—Archibald Alexander, Joseph Addison Alexander, and Charles Hodge—were represented as far as their works had been published. Cotton Mather's *Magnalia Christi Americana* and Increase Mather's *Remarkable Providences* add to the Calvinist atmosphere in Boyce's library. Comparative religious science was emerging in 1859. Boyce had at least some awareness of the new science, for he had purchased *Christianity Contrasted with Hindu Philosophy: An Essay in Five Books* in Sanskrit and English. The new orthodoxy of 1850 was also registering its claims, for a number of Horace Bushnell's writings such as *The Vicarious Sacrifice, Christian Nurture*, and *Sermons for the New Life* were purchased as they appeared.

Books by people of every age are included: Plato, Aristotle, Thomas Aquinas, Francis Bacon, Pascal, Voltaire, John Locke, Thomas Hobbes, Lucretius, Victor Cousin, Henry L. Mansel, John Hurst, Auguste Comte, Herbert Spencer, and Charles Darwin. Finally, large works in French are included: René Chateaubriand's *Le Génie du Christianisme*, Pierre Bayle's *Dictionarie Historique et Critique*, and *Biographie Universelle, Ancienne et Moderne*.

But why did a man as serious as Dr. Boyce have books like these in his collection: *Memoirs of a Doll, Fashionable World Displayed, Married or Single?, How Not to Be Sick, Anecdotes for the Family Circle*, and a biography of P. T. Barnum? Even more intriguing is the listing of French works on the art of cooking, such as Carême's *L'art de la Cuisine française au 19ième Siecle*, in five volumes.

6

Crawford Howell Toy

IN MAY, 1869, Dr. James P. Boyce presented a memorial to the Board of Trustees of Southern Seminary, urging them to appoint an additional faculty member. The reason for this petition was obvious. Boyce indicated that the peculiar character of the curriculum at Southern imposed upon the teachers a far more difficult task than would otherwise be the case. Many of the other, non-Baptist schools were better staffed. Princeton then had five professors, as did Union in New York, while Andover had seven. He says, "With five professors, our Southern Baptist Seminary will be working on a much larger scale than any other Baptist Seminary, and be in a position to rival, in magnitude and in all respects, the great Pedobaptist institutions mentioned." [1]

In missionary operations, Boyce contended, Southern Baptists could not yet compare with what Northern Baptists were doing, but in theological education, if the request for another teacher were granted, "in a few years Southern will become the largest Theological school in America, while it will continue to have the advantage of being carefully and thoroughly adapted to the wants of our Baptist ministry." [2]

In this memorial to the trustees, the faculty expressed the hope that the forward strides of the Seminary might encourage brethren of wealth to support it more loyally. They were willing to forego promised increases in salary if through the appointment of a new professor the effectiveness of the school might be enhanced and the ministerial supply increased. The presentation of

---

[1] *Proceedings of the Board of Trustees*, book 1, pp. 95–97.
[2] *Ibid.*

this memorial resulted in the election of Dr. Crawford Howell Toy to the faculty of Southern Seminary in May, 1869.

Professor C. H. Toy, one of nine children, was born March 23, 1836, at Norfolk, Virginia. His father was the proprietor of a wholesale and retail drug firm. The elder Toy was a devout Baptist, a charter member of Freemason Street Baptist Church, Norfolk, and a gifted student of languages, including Hebrew.

According to Professor David Gordon Lyon of Harvard University, Toy was "of excellent stock, the inheritor of the best traditions in regard to learning." [3] He enjoyed rare opportunities educationally, was endowed with native ability, and had the will to make the most of these. When young Toy graduated from Norfolk Military Academy, he received the complete works of Shakespeare as a graduation present for excellence. In 1852 he entered the University of Virginia, taking a full course in liberal arts as well as in constitutional and international law, graduating in 1856 with the M.A. degree. He attended the first session of Southern Seminary, 1859–60.

After teaching English at a female institute in Virginia and mathematics at the University of Alabama, Toy became professor of Greek in Richmond College; for one year, 1865–66, he taught Greek at the University of Virginia. During the War Between the States he served as a private and later as a chaplain.

Toy, eager for wider horizons, spent two years in advanced work at Berlin University, studying theology under Dorner, Sanskrit under Weber, and Semitics under Roediger and Dieterici. Upon his return to America, Toy taught Greek for one year at Furman University and then was called in 1869 to become professor of Old Testament at Southern Seminary.

Professor Toy's inaugural address there was on the subject "The Claims of Biblical Interpretation on Baptists." Toy believed that upon Baptists devolves a special obligation with regard to the Scriptures because they put their complete dependence on the Bible. They accept all it teaches and nothing else.

---

[3] David Gordon Lyon, "Crawford H. Toy," *Harvard Theological Review,* XIII (January, 1920), 2. A very valuable biographical account.

If we could lean on the decisions of Councils, Convocations, or Assemblies, . . . royal or episcopal decrees, array of patristic, scholastic, and other lore, . . . it might not be so needful for us to cling close to the Word of God as our sole guide; but now we have no other resource. It is our pole-star. Without it we are on a boundless ocean, wrapped in darkness.[4]

In order rightly to interpret the Bible, Dr. Toy argued, Baptists need on the one hand "learning and thought" and on the other, "the inspiration and guidance of the Holy Spirit."

After discussing at length the history of interpretation, Professor Toy then emphasized that in exegeting Holy Writ each passage must be explained in terms of the meaning of the words, the context, the relations of this passage to the whole of divine revelation of truth, the Christian consciousness—and all this with the solemn invocation of the presence of the Holy Spirit. "A fundamental principle of our Hermeneutics must be that the Bible, its real assertions being known, is in every iota of its substance absolutely and infallibly true."[5]

For ten years Professor Toy taught at Southern and was considered by both students and colleagues the most learned man on the faculty. One of his students and later colleague at Harvard, Professor David Gordon Lyon, wrote that "in the classroom he seemed to know everything about the subject which he taught. He criticized the textbooks with freedom, and sought not to fill the minds of the students with facts, though he never minimized the value of a fact, but to stir up the mind and to exercise its own powers."

Some of Dr. Toy's teachings were both novel and disturbing. It became known even during his first session as a teacher in the Seminary that Dr. Toy had accepted Charles Darwin's theory of evolution. He had also become convinced of the plausibility of the Kuenen-Wellhausen theory of Pentateuchal criticism. Dr. Broadus has commented on this painful matter as follows:

---

[4] Broadus, *op. cit.*, p. 211.
[5] *Ibid.*

If the Darwinian theory of the origin of man has been accepted, then it becomes easy to conclude that the first chapter of Genesis is by no means true history. From this starting-point, and pressed by a desire to reconstruct the history on evolutionary principles, one might easily persuade himself that in numerous cases of apparent conflict between Old Testament statements and the accredited results of various sciences the conflict is real, and the Old Testament account is incorrect. This persuasion would seem to the critic to justify his removing various books and portions of books into other periods of the history of Israel, so as to make that history a regular evolution from simpler to more complex. For example, it is held that the laws of Moses cannot have arisen in that early and simpler stage of Israelitish history to which Moses belonged, but only in a much later and more highly developed period,—all of which might look reasonable enough if we leave the supernatural out of view. Then the passion grows stronger for so re-locating and reconstructing as to make everything in the history of Israel a natural evolution; and the tendency of this, if logically and fearlessly carried through, must be to exclude the supernatural from that history altogether. These views would of course be supported by certain well-known theories to the effect that the first six books of the Old Testament were put together out of several different documents, as indicated by certain leading terms, and other characteristic marks of style and tone.[6]

Dr. Toy was asked to desist from teaching these theories. He sincerely promised to do so, but in the end he found it impossible to keep his promise. "He was entreated to let those theoretical questions alone, and teach the students what they needed."[7] It was argued that "the great majority of the students were quite unprepared for fitting examination of any such theoretical inquiries, and needed to be instructed in the Old Testament as it stands."[8]

Dr. Broadus also was sure that

it was hard for Dr. Toy to realize that such teaching was quite out of the question in this institution. He was satisfied that his views would promote truth and piety. He thought strange of the predic-

[6] *Ibid.*, pp. 260–61.
[7] *Ibid.*, p. 262.
[8] *Ibid.*

tion made in conversation that within twenty years he would utterly discard all belief in the supernatural as an element of Scripture,—a prediction founded upon knowledge of his logical consistency and boldness, and already in a much shorter time fulfilled, to judge from his latest books.[9]

Dr. Lyon has testified that Dr. Toy "never demanded that his views on any subject should be accepted without question. With transparent fairness he gave the arguments pro and con on any disputed question that came up, and stated his own preference or convictions, but preferred that the student should in the presence of all the facts form his own judgment." [10]

Dr. C. H. Toy finally resigned from the Seminary faculty. The Board of Trustees at its Atlanta meeting in May, 1879, accepted his resignation. Two members of that board, it ought to be stated, Doctors Gwin and Chambliss, "submitted their protest against the policy and action of the Board in connection with the resignation of Dr. Toy, and asked that the same be spread on the Minutes." [11]

Dr. Toy's decision was regretfully accepted. Although students and friends urged him to appeal to the Convention, he politely declined. He was basically a man of peace, not of strife and contention. Dr. Broadus has recorded the personal grief of Dr. Boyce over Professor Toy's leaving the Seminary. As Broadus and Boyce accompanied their departing colleague to the railroad station in Louisville, Dr. Boyce, standing with his friend in the waiting room, threw his left arm around Toy's neck and, lifting his right arm, said, "in a passion of grief, 'Oh, Toy, I would freely give that arm to be cut off if you could be where you were five years ago, and stay here.' " [12]

After a year of private study in New York, Dr. Toy was appointed by President Eliot of Harvard University as Hancock Professor of Hebrew and other Oriental languages.

---

[9] *Ibid.*, pp. 262–63.
[10] Lyon, *op. cit.*, p. 7.
[11] *Proceedings of the Board of Trustees*, book 1, p. 19.
[12] Broadus, *op. cit.*, pp. 263–64.

While Toy was living in New York City, he wrote a charming letter to John A. Broadus. He addressed him as "Dear Bro. Broadus," and encouraged him to continue his work on his *Commentary on the Gospel of Matthew*. "There is still great need of a good book, which shall devoutly apply modern methods to the exegesis of the evangelical history."

Dr. Toy also spoke of his research studies at the Astor Library, whose Semitic resources he found respectable, though he found its Assyrian and Babylonian material less than complete. He also took notice of the fact that at Johns Hopkins University only eighteen out of sixty-four students (including fellows) were "pursuing languages, and of twenty fellows only three, of which twelve are in Greek. That does not look well for the humanities. But I have faith in men's sense of the useful, in the long run; I do not doubt that, allowing for temporary movements in one direction and another, the world will give us as much attention to Greek and Latin as they deserve." [13]

Dr. Toy's accomplishments at Harvard University were many. He inaugurated the Semitic department, in 1881 established the Harvard Semitic Club, a year later organized the Harvard Semitic Seminar, and a little later also the Harvard Club for the Study of the History of Religions. The latter organization honored Dr. Toy with a *Festschrift* in celebration of his seventy-fifth birthday. This festive tome bore the title *Studies in the History of Religions* and was edited by David G. Lyon and George Foote Moore. Among the contributors to this volume were leading scholars from both European and American Universities such as Jastrow, Torrey, Gottheil, Wolfsohn, Karl Budde, and others. [14]

C. H. Toy made a considerable contribution as a writer. With John A. Broadus, as we have noted before, he translated 1 and 2 Samuel in Lange's commentary. While still at Louisville he wrote a number of articles on Hebrew and Yoruba philology.

---

[13] Letter of C. H. Toy to J. A. Broadus, October 31, 1879 (Seminary Library).
[14] Lyon, *op. cit.*

During his Harvard tenure of office, Dr. Toy published a good many important works.[15] In addition to these he also contributed articles for about twenty journals, both technical and literary. An article on Pope Leo XIII (1878–1903), the Roman pontiff who opened the Vatican library to all scholars at the behest of von Pastor, appeared in the *Christian Register*.[16] Dr. Toy was likewise on many editorial boards such as that for the *Jewish Encyclopedia*, being in charge as co-editor of Hebrew philology and Hellenistic literature and writing articles for all of its twelve volumes.

An article by C. H. Toy entitled *Panbabylonianism* shows him to have been a judicious critic of the views of men like Stucken, Winkler, and Alfred Jeremias. He accused them of extreme generalizations, charging them with failure to distinguish between the origin of ideas and the forms in which these ideas clothe themselves. His conclusion on this theory is that "astralism is positively hostile to an understanding of the Bible." [17]

After Dr. Toy's death, one writer interpreted him as follows:

Dr. Toy was essentially an investigator and pioneer. His studies in Biblical Science and in Religion, and his frankness of utterance mark the beginning of a new epoch in American scholarship. Yet he seemed altogether unconscious of his own greatness. With all his learning and honors he was at heart as simple and guileless as a child. He belongs in the class of the sages of olden times. He followed after wisdom, and received the fulfilment of her promise, "Length of days, and years of life, and peace." [18]

Are we unduly proud if we of Southern Seminary lay claim to C. H. Toy as part of us, although he felt constrained to tread a path that led him far away from his original moorings? And must

---

[15] Among them *Quotations in the New Testament* (1890), *The Book of the Prophet Ezekiel* (1899), *A Critical and Exegetical Commentary on the Book of Proverbs* (1899), and *Introduction to the History of Religions* (1913).
[16] January 18, 1900.
[17] C. H. Toy, "Panbabylonianism," *The Harvard Theological Review*, III (January 10, 1910), 47–84.
[18] *The Harvard University Gazette*, May, 1919. Cf. Lyon, *op. cit.*

we conclude as have some that his becoming a Unitarian confirmed the rightness of the judgment of his brethren in 1879 when they accepted his resignation from his professorship at Southern Seminary?

It is a matter of record that Dr. Toy reaffirmed the basic faith of Southern Baptists upon leaving Southern. The Harvard Divinity School history declares that when Dr. Toy joined the Harvard faculty he considered himself an orthodox Baptist. Yet after the lapse of only eight years he became a Unitarian.

Today the critical views which Dr. Toy espoused in the seventies are receiving a hearing in the classes of Southern Seminary without, however, being made into shibboleths. Moreover, much of Wellhauseanism has been subjected to sharp critical review by many Old Testament scholars of recent decades. Suffice it to say, however, that the founding fathers of Southern Seminary were wise in resisting speculative critical tendencies which, when followed to their logical conclusions, have led in many quarters to the utter repudiation of evangelical Christianity.

Professor W. O. Carver has ventured to suggest that the critical trends in Dr. Toy's thinking might not today be "regarded as sufficiently revolutionary to call for drastic action." He also considered it

one of the tragedies of the situation that in the resolution accepting his resignation it is set out as if it were the determining factor that his remaining in the Seminary would hinder the raising of money for the endowment. Whether by patience and fraternal conference Dr. Toy might have been led into a deeper and more comprehensive understanding of the principles of progress must remain an open question. If this could have been done he might have become the leader of a new era of insight and interpretation of the Old Testament and of a better understanding of the Hebrew religion and the principles of religion in general.[19]

In view of Dr. Toy's later development and final nonaffiliation with any church, Dr. Carver felt that the Board of Trustees of Southern Seminary was justified in accepting his resignation.

---

[19] W. O. Carver, "Unpublished Notes," p. 26.

7

William Heth Whitsitt, Church Historian

IT WAS THE JUDGMENT of the revered Dr. W. O. Carver that "no man in the history of the Southern Baptist Theological Seminary ever received so little recognition for so great service as William H. Whitsitt, its sixth professor and its third president." [1]

W. H. Whitsitt was born November 25, 1841, near Nashville, Tennessee. He was like Boyce of Scotch-Irish ancestry. His forebears had come in 1741 from Ireland into Virginia via Pennsylvania. They were, most of them, Presbyterians. James Whitsitt, the grandfather of William H., found Christ in a Virginia revival and became a Baptist in 1789. A year later the family moved to Davidson County in Tennessee, where James Whitsitt labored as a zealous gospel preacher in the beautiful Cumberland Valley. He was a man of unusual native ability and strong reasoning powers and a great friend of missions. James's son, Reuben Ewing Whitsitt, was the father of the subject of this chapter. He died when William Heth Whitsitt was but eleven years old.

Young Whitsitt attended Mill Creek Academy, then Mt. Juliet Academy, and finally Union University, all of them located in his native state. He entered Union University in 1857, graduating with honors in 1861 and receiving the M.A. degree. Soon after finishing college, Whitsitt enlisted in the Confederate army as a private. Later he became a fighting chaplain. Like C. H. Toy, his colleague-to-be, Whitsitt was captured by the Union army and later exchanged.

---

[1] W. O. Carver, "William Heth Whitsitt: The Seminary's Martyr," *Review and Expositor*, LI (October, 1954), 449.

In 1866 Whitsitt entered the University of Virginia, taking a "stiff ticket" in Latin, Greek, mathematics, and moral philosophy. A year later he matriculated at Southern Seminary. He graduated in 1869 with diplomas in biblical introduction, Hebrew, Old Testament interpretation in English, New Testament interpretation in English, Greek, systematic theology in English, church history, church government, and pastoral duties.[2]

Upon the advice of Dr. Broadus, Whitsitt spent two years studying at the universities of Berlin and Leipzig. He studied with men like Luthardt, Curtius, Lipsius, and Tischendorf. Here he was instructed "in the patient, scientific methods of investigation, which characterize the best type of German scholarship." [3] His work under John A. Broadus had prepared Whitsitt for the exacting discipline that German centers of learning offered during the last century.

Upon his return from Europe, Whitsitt served for but a few months as pastor of the Baptist church at Albany, Georgia, when in May, 1872, he was called as assistant professor of ecclesiastical history and biblical introduction of Southern Seminary. In 1879, upon Manly's return from Georgetown College to Southern, Whitsitt took over polemic theology in addition to his regular duties in church history, dropping biblical introduction. When in 1895 he became president of Southern, Whitsitt surrendered this subject, polemic theology being given to Assistant Professor Herbert H. Harris.

W. H. Whitsitt was an able and resourceful scholar. At first he did not easily impart his learning. Gradually, however, by precept and example he gained the attention of his students. He made them dig for facts. When he spoke, he usually had something to say. Possessed of ample mother wit, Whitsitt kept his students on their toes.

Whitsitt supplemented his teaching with his writings. His in-

---

[2] John R. Sampey, *Southern Baptist Theological Seminary* (Baltimore: Wharton, Barron & Co., 1890), p. 208.

[3] E. B. Pollard, "The Life and Work of William Heth Whitsitt," *Review and Expositor,* IX (April, 1912), 163.

tention from the very beginning of his career had been to write a scientific history of the Baptists. This interest was stimulated by various factors: the looseness of the Baptist fellowship, its excessive individualism, the ecclesiastical atomism of the "local church" idea so entrenched among Southern Baptists of that day, and the lack of Baptist histories written from an impartial point of view. Whitsitt, however, never came to write that history. At best he wrote only the prolegomena of that history, and even that got him into serious trouble.

Whitsitt's inaugural address of 1872 dealt with the "position of the Baptists in the History of American Culture." It was published in pamphlet form and appeared in a second edition in 1874. These were the concluding words of that address:

The people with whom your lot is cast, my brethren, have emancipated the intellect, and have opened the Bible to all. You will be called to move among men of active, independent minds. Your principal claim to their respect, and, as a consequence, your best prospects for usefulness, will depend upon your intellectual and moral endowments and culture. They recognize the validity of no sacramental theories: you will therefore be surrounded by no halo of priestly sanctity. Hence it is imperatively necessary that you should employ diligence in arming yourself thoroughly for the duties before you. Remember, too, that the pulpits of a people professing these levelling, humanitarian principles, these earnest Gospel truths, are no fit theatre for over-cultivated, weak–thoughted, intellectual exquisites, doling out diluted and harmless treatises on philosophy or aesthetics. Men of robust spirit are in demand, who, like our blessed Master, keep in sympathy with the common people, and are gladly heard by them; who in connection with apostolic ruggedness and vigor cultivate also apostolic gentleness and simplicity.[4]

Most of the writings of W. H. Whitsitt were set in local or denominational patterns. Among them were short monographs on *The Rise of Infant Baptism*, *The History of Communion Among Baptists*, and *The Origin of the Disciples of Christ*, written as a contribution to the centennial of the birth of Alexan-

---

[4] Broadus, *op. cit.*, p. 226.

der Campbell, whose activities had caused such a disturbance among Southern Baptist churches. Dr. Pollard of Crozer found a number of faults in the latter work.

Whitsitt also wrote a book on "Sidney Rigdon, the Real Founder of Mormonism." Mrs. Whitsitt and Dr. Broadus urged him to publish this large book by all means. Broadus even suggested that Whitsitt use the twenty-three hundred dollars he had for a down payment on a home to put this work into print. "If the Seminary," argued Whitsitt, "would pay me at the same rate as it pays my colleague the book would be easily published." [5] This study of Mormonism remained unpublished. Today it may be found in the Library of Congress in Washington, D. C.

At this juncture it may be of interest to review briefly the manner and content of some of Professor Whitsitt's teaching. His lectures delivered in the seventies in the field of biblical introduction will engage our attention first.

Following German precedents, Dr. Whitsitt lectured at first on theological encyclopedia and methodology. In this he was concerned to show the students the organic whole of the science of theology; the relation, for instance, between exegesis and history and of both to systematic theology; and of all these to practical theology.

The aim of this endeavor, Whitsitt held, was the prevention of the fragmentation of theological study, the desultory and unscientific heaping up of materials without philosophical organization of these materials into a unified whole. "Theological Encyclopaedia is so to speak the architect of our theological acquirements."

It will prevent the exegete from looking with more or less contempt on the labours of the ecclesiastical historian and the dogmatician from turning too much away from the exegete. . . . It would also prevent a vast deal of vulgar bickering among our professors were they to realize the interdependence of all they do.[6]

---

[5] Carver, "William Heth Whitsitt: The Seminary's Martyr," *op. cit.*, p. 459.

[6] William H. Whitsitt, unpublished lectures on biblical introduction (class of 1873–74) (Southern Seminary Library), p. 28.

Whitsitt was also deeply interested in maintaining the rapport between theology and other disciplines and to kindle the conversation between the sacred and the secular.

Whitsitt defined theology as a positive science. This means that its materials are not elaborated from reason but posited by the revealed Word of God. His definition has a Barthian flavor, for he said:

Theology, at least Christian theology, is not something which might be determined on *a priori* grounds, but it is dependent upon fixed and settled revelation of divine truth and the divine will. It is a matter concerning which we can judge only *a posteriori*. No man by consulting the movings of his own mind and heart and the revelations of natural religion could arrive at the truths of Christian theology. Revelation is above reason. Even after the plan of redemption and other central facts of theology are stated and explained, unaided reason recognizes in them the great "mystery of godliness." [7]

Theology, according to Dr. Whitsitt, is also an applied science. "There would be no science of medicine if there were no sick. So theology is an applied science, i.e., it makes use of history, philosophy, poetry, elocution, psychology and everything imaginable for the sake of explaining and enforcing the Scriptures (the reproving, warning and edifying of the body of Christ). Now the only nexus which binds all these together is the desire of being useful to the Church of Christ." [8]

Theology, Whitsitt continued, is not only a science but also an art. First the theologian must seek to comprehend, then try to apply what has been understood and believed. What has been gained through hard study of theology needs to be clothed in understandable words and thoughts. Theology, man's reflection on the nature and reach of God's redemption, must be projected in the form of preaching. This witness, like all theologizing, must be done in the expectation that God will again speak and attest his own witness.

[7] *Ibid.*, p. 29.
[8] *Ibid.*, p. 30.

Whitsitt had also a constructive word to say on the relationship between theology and philosophy. The latter ought to be a constant attendant to the former. But special care ought to be taken lest the two be mingled together. Each must remain within the bounds of its own province. Philosophy, as Whitsitt conceived it, involves more than the use of logic or criticism of theological tendencies.

But philosophy in the sense here employed is the recognizing of events by their causes, the tracing of effects to their sources . . . Philosophy's function in theology is to organize the vast material there into a higher unity and bring it under better control.[9]

Whitsitt did not encourage theological students to follow any particular philosophical system. He tried rather to induce them to philosophize on their own, i.e., to trace the connection of theological ideas and principles with each other, thereby gaining a broader view. He had little patience with those who railed against philosophy or theology. There is no theory without practice, nor practice without an implied theory. Ignorant folk are the more likely to fall for foolish theories and the riding of hobbies.

As Dr. Whitsitt explored theology further he came to divide it into exegetical, historical, systematic, and practical theology. Baptists, Whitsitt believed, together with the Presbyterians, must of necessity give priority to exegetical theology, for Holy Scripture is the source and touchstone of all their doctrines. He pointed out, for instance, that in the South the two principal chairs in the Seminary were in biblical introduction, while in the North, at Newton and Crozer, systematic theology occupied the center of interest.

It was Whitsitt's feeling that where systematic theology occupies the center of the theological endeavor, men may be tempted to engage in a priori thinking, thus developing a Christian theology on merely speculative grounds. Such thinkers,

---

[9] *Ibid.*, p. 37.

Faculty, 1949-50 (first row, l. to r.) Dale Moody, O. T. Binkley, J. B. Weatherspoon, Ellis A. Fuller, W. O. Carver, E. A. McDowell, Jr. (second row) Wayne E. Oates, Phillip E. Rodgerson, William A. Mueller, V. L. Stanfield, Findley B. Edge, William H. Morton, V. Lavell Seats (third row) Gaines S. Dobbins, H. E. Turlington, Heber F. Peacock, Jr., Theron D. Price, Clyde T. Francisco, H. R. Peterson, H. C. Goerner, Charles A. McGlon

Old Norton Hall

however, forget that theology is a positive science and that it ignores the "givenness" of its materials at its peril.

Next to exegetical theology Dr. Whitsitt placed historical theology, which concerns itself with the earliest monuments of Christian history. A work on church history, Whitsitt affirmed, that should ignore the life and labors of our Lord would be a theological monstrosity. In church history are confronted the history of the constitution, the outward fortunes, and the teachings of the churches of Christ. The study of dogma is a valuable auxiliary to systematic theology, yet the latter's findings are not to be based on dogmatic theology.

With regard to exegetical theology, sometimes also called biblical theology, Whitsitt found its task in the interpretation of the Scriptures of the Old and New testaments. He held that for Baptists the distinction between biblical and ecclesiastical theology was invalid. The reason for this was obvious, for "their ecclesiastical theology is also Biblical theology. In other words, Baptists propose to follow no practice and adopt no teaching in the Church which is not founded upon the Scriptures." The auxiliaries of exegetical theology, according to Whitsitt, are the Bible, the study of the canon, philology or the knowledge of the biblical languages, biblical antiquities, geography, and Near Eastern history.

Whitsitt also dealt in detail with the relationship of biblical criticism to the task of exegesis and exegetical theology. They are mutually interrelated. He sounded this warning:

But those who know nothing or next to nothing about the ancient languages and who have little skill and practice in the independent interpretation of the Greek and the Hebrew Scriptures, ought to have very little to say about Biblical Criticism or its results. It is beginning at the wrong end to be talking about specious passages. That is the business of the old and experienced scholar. A man must first learn the true sense of the text of any author and enter fully into its spirit before he is prepared to decide whether it is corrupt or no. Nothing has impaired the science of Biblical Criticism so much or rendered common people so suspicious of theological schools, as the unfortunate habit of young men who know nothing about exegesis to be talking in season and out concerning spurious passages. Dr. Broadus has banished this study to the Senior class in our Seminary, and that with eminent propriety.[10]

In order to be a good exegete or interpreter of God's Word, one ought to study hermeneutics, the art of interpretation. It is both an art and a science. In general, this discipline is governed by the same principles that obtain in other areas of interpretative endeavor. But historical imagination and deep reverence for God's Word are needed for one to become a sound exegete.

Whitsitt was of the opinion that an extreme emphasis on grammar and dictionary does not for any long period command respect. On the contrary, a preoccupation with these matters often tends to produce the opposite extreme, namely undisciplined allegorizing.

With respect to practical theology, that is, the application of theological insight to exegesis, to historical and systematic theology, and all of these to the practical life of God's people, great wisdom is required. The edification of God's people is a delicate art. "Don't lug your scientific claptrap into the pulpit where it does not belong," was Dr. Whitsitt's plea with his students.

Like his colleague Dr. Broadus, Whitsitt encouraged his students to cultivate a love for poetry, music, painting, and sculpture and to lay them under tribute to their ultimate concern, the proclamation of the gospel of God's grace. However, he warned his students not to indulge in preaching "spread-eagle rhapsodies." He was conscious of the possibility that some of his students might misunderstand him and while indulging in the most unreasonable balderdash, yet claim their professor's authority for their antics. To forestall such an eventuality, Dr. Whitsitt entreated them to remember "that I am opposed to all kinds of extravagances."

When Dr. W. O. Carver entered Southern Seminary in 1891, he was at once impressed with the qualities of Dr. W. H. Whit-

---

[10] *Ibid.*, pp. 47–48.

sitt as a creative theological teacher. However, Carver felt that since Whitsitt was essentially a university lecturer rather than a classroom instructor questioning students on material they had supposedly prepared, his teaching methods were none too well adapted to the average student. But although Whitsitt was not in step with the teaching methods then being used at Southern Seminary, Carver found him exceedingly fascinating. Let Carver, therefore, be heard with regard to his impression of this able man:

Whitsitt spoke deliberately and quietly, with none of the tricks for stimulating attention, to say nothing of enthusiasm, in his students. His vocabulary frequently had words used with quaint meanings and in a sense sometimes different from current connotation of words. His dictation was too slow to compel the constant attention of listeners. For myself he was fascinating, even though I was well able to understand why he was regarded as somewhat dry. In almost every lecture there was something which I felt was amply worth sitting through an entire hour to get even though it sometimes would be a single sentence. He frequently used epigrammatic expressions but without the air which impressed you with the terseness and pointedness of the truth he was presenting. For one example: I could never forget, "I would rather have ten words written on the spot than a cartload of reminiscenses." Or, "Brethren, the Lord is always going to look after the plain people. The Episcopalians were eminently respectable; and the Lord raised up the Methodists and the Baptists to look after the common people. And now, Brethren, the Methodists and the Baptists are getting to be eminently respectable; look out for the Salvation Army." That saying has helped me through sixty years of observation, study and interpretation of trends in our Christian conditions.[11]

PRESIDENT OF SOUTHERN SEMINARY, 1895–99

When, in May of 1895, after the death of John A. Broadus, William Heth Whitsitt was unanimously elected the third president of Southern Baptist Theological Seminary, the faculty numbered eight teachers. The latter in the order of their election were: Whitsitt (1872), John R. Sampey (1887), F. H.

---

[11] Carver, "Unpublished Notes," p. 17.

Kerfoot (since 1887 co-professor in systematics, and full professor in that field after Boyce's death in 1888), A. T. Robertson (1888), E. C. Dargan (1892), W. J. McGlothlin (1894), W. O. Carver and H. H. Harris (1895). The student body of the Seminary stood at 267 at the end of the academic session of 1894–95.

The equipment of the school had been greatly enhanced since 1880, with Governor Joseph Emerson Brown's gift of fifty thousand dollars toward the Seminary's endowment. This was increased to three hundred thousand three years later, and by 1891 it had reached four hundred thousand.

New York Hall had been completed by 1888, furnishing rooms for two hundred students. Thanks to the gift of Mrs. John Lawrence Smith of fifty thousand dollars, the Memorial Library was completed by May of 1891. Three years later Norton Hall, a new classroom and administration building, was made possible through the largess of the Norton family of Louisville. It was erected at a cost of sixty thousand dollars and stood on the south side of Broadway between Fourth and Fifth streets.[12]

The controversy in which President Whitsitt became involved after his first year of administration has somewhat overshadowed the accomplishments made under his leadership. But these accomplishments are the more remarkable in view of the disturbing conditions under which Dr. Whitsitt was forced to labor.

During Whitsitt's first year as president of Southern the student body rose from 267 to 316 students. During the session of 1896–97, when the controversy was in full force, the student body went down to 290, but in the following year it had rallied, standing at 301. Whitsitt's last year, with excitement running at high tide in the Southern Convention territory, that is, the session of 1898–99, saw 262 students registered.

Other achievements were the erection of the Levering Gymnasium at a cost of ten thousand dollars. The building was a

---

[12] Robertson, *op. cit.*, pp. 398, 414.

gift of Joshua Levering, the chairman of the Board of Trustees, and was first occupied in 1897. Mr. G. W. Norton, a member of the board, had donated five thousand dollars toward the John A. Broadus Memorial Book Fund, of which mention was made in a previous chapter.[13] John D. Rockefeller again came to the rescue when during this time he gave twenty-five hundred dollars to cover the deficit in current expenses.[14] The salaries of A. T. Robertson and Edwin C. Dargan were at this time raised to twenty-five hundred dollars a year. Moreover, the Board of Trustees authorized the treasurer of the Seminary, Dr. F. H. Kerfoot, to acquire a house in Louisville for the family of the late President John A. Broadus at a cost of about twelve thousand dollars.

Still another boon came to the Seminary when the Basil Manly library of thirty-six hundred volumes was given to the Seminary, bringing the Seminary Memorial Library up to twenty thousand volumes.

Another notable event was in the realm of curriculum. In November of 1896 a new division of graduate work into major and minor subjects was effected. The purpose behind this change was the desire of the faculty to arrange major and minor studies according to the difficulty of the subjects involved and to prevent an easier course of doctoral candidates.[15]

In March, 1897, Dr. Robertson suggested in a faculty meeting that the class in missions should henceforth have the same standing as any other class in the Seminary.[16] This action laid the foundation for the later expansion of the department of comparative religion and missions under the competent leadership of Professor William Owen Carver.

Other advances were made. The first course of lectures on the Gay Foundation, established through the gift of William David Gay of Montgomery, Alabama, in honor of his father, Julius

---

[13] John R. Sampey, *Memoirs of John R. Sampey* (Nashville: Broadman Press, 1947), pp. 74–75.
[14] *Minutes of the Board of Trustees*, book 2, p. 215.
[15] *Faculty Minutes*, book 2, p. 49.
[16] *Ibid.*, p. 56.

Brown Gay, was given in March of 1895 by Henry Herbert Harris. These lectures were published in that same year.[17]

During this same month the faculty mourned the early death of their gifted colleague, Dr. H. H. Harris. He served but two years on the teaching staff of Southern. The faculty minutes record a beautiful eulogy to his memory.

Professor John R. Sampey also became secretary of the faculty in 1895, when W. H. Whitsitt became president of Southern. The latter, after Professor C. H. Toy's leaving, had served in that capacity from 1879 to 1895.

Professor F. H. Kerfoot, who had entertained some ideas of becoming the successor of John A. Broadus, relinquished his duties as financial agent of the Seminary but remained its treasurer for several years more. Dr. Carver has intimated that Kerfoot was not entirely mistaken in his expectations. When the choosing of a new leader came in 1899, Dr. Kerfoot was again in the picture. He was even nominated for the presidential office but was not elected.

It was during Whitsitt's administration that the faculty lost one of its most faithful secretaries, Mr. A. D. Almond, who had served the school for fifteen years. He died in the spring of 1897.

Various disciplinary cases had to be handled during this time. One of these involved two students who appeared before the faculty to explain their conduct with regard to theater attendance. Both promised to mend their evil ways, and the president was asked to give them a most earnest admonition on their waywardness.[18]

Everything else considered, the achievements under W. H. Whitsitt's all too brief administration were quite remarkable. Had he been able to weather the storm, his being at the helm of Southern Seminary might have added many other worthy accomplishments to his record. But despite the loyalty of his con-

---

[17] Leo T. Crismon, "Southern Baptist Theological Seminary," *Encyclopedia of Southern Baptists* (Nashville: Broadman Press, 1958), II, 1270.

[18] *Faculty Minutes*, book 2, pp. 80–81.

freres and most of the alumni, "Uncle Billy," as he came to be affectionately called by the students, was to undergo a painful ordeal before his administration came to an end.

THE WHITSITT CONTROVERSY

The immediate cause of what has been called the Whitsitt controversy was an article on Baptists which Dr. Whitsitt wrote and which was published in *Johnson's Universal Cyclopedia* in 1893. In this article Whitsitt wrote that Roger Williams was probably baptized by sprinkling rather than by immersion and that immersion of believers among English Baptists was "invented" by Edward Barber in 1641. The basis for these statements was the three months' research that Dr. Whitsitt had carried on in England in 1880. Upon his return to the United States he published, anonymously and editorially, his findings in the *Independent*, a pedobaptist journal published in New York City. He also reported on his findings to the faculty and students of the Seminary in the opening address of the session of 1880–81.

It was Dr. Whitsitt's statement about the origin of believers' baptism by immersion that caused many of Whitsitt's Baptist brethren in the Southland to rise up in a fury of protest. To earnest, orthodox Southern Baptists of 1896 it was an unshakable conviction that their life and thought, the very principles of their being and existence, were rooted in the teachings of the New Testament. Most Baptists had been taught that the early Christian movement in apostolic days had all the earmarks of a modern Baptist church. Therefore, to assert as had Whitsitt in his articles of 1880 and 1893 that immersion was first "invented" by British Baptists in 1641 seemed to many to be a blasphemous heresy, utterly contrary to old and cherished beliefs.

To be sure, not all Baptists, either North or South, were disturbed by Whitsitt's findings, but many were. Baptist writing of history, it must be admitted, up to that time had tended at least to encourage the belief in the absolute distinctiveness of the Baptist witness. Zealous Baptist preachers had encouraged that belief; many Baptists believed that they could trace, with a good conscience, their ancestry and their practices straight to the churches of the New Testament. Since most Baptist histories were, in addition, extremely polemical, they encouraged a view of Christian history that tended to ignore other equally valid and equally important developments in the history of the Christian church.

Moreover, Baptists were still a frontier denomination in the nineties, at least in the deep South, fighting hard for survival both economically and denominationally. And Northern Baptist societies were at this very time making strong overtures toward a united Baptist witness in North America, another factor that brought anxiety to many Southern Baptist hearts.

Still another observation is in place here. The strange response that Dr. Whitsitt's articles on British Baptist origins found among his brethren must have appeared as a threat to the security both of the Landmarkers and many of the half-illiterate preachers of the South. Their fervent and simple preaching gloried in these Baptist distincitives which Whitsitt's theory seemed to endanger. Instinctively these people reacted against Whitsitt's ideas as undermining not only the basic Baptist position but their own prestige and influence. Although the leader of the Landmarkers had recently died, the movement itself had received a new impetus in the "gospel missionism" idea.

A more remote cause of the controversy was this Landmark movement, which swept through the Southern Baptist Convention churches shortly after they had separated from their Northern brethren. The movement reached its height in the early fifties of the nineteenth century and is still a force to be reckoned with in Southern Baptist life.[19]

The Landmark movement, as Professor W. W. Barnes has keenly observed, may be interpreted as part of the passionate search for authority that marked much of nineteenth century ecclesiasticism.

---

[19] John E. Steely, "The Landmark Movement in the Southern Baptist Convention," in Duke K. McCall, compiler and editor, *What Is the Church?* (Nashville: Broadman Press, 1958), pp. 134 ff.

In the midst of complex religious and political situations, there was in Europe and America a passion for antiquity in the search for authority. The papalists found it in the Bishop of Rome—to them, the successor of Peter—and recognized him as infallible. The high-churchmen of the Church of England found it in the church, the body of Christ, speaking through all the bishops. Among Baptists, there were three reactions to the search for authority. The Camp-bellites emphasized, first, historicity (Thomas Campbell); then, apostolicity (Alexander Campbell). The latter "restored the ancient gospel." J. R. Graves "reset the old landmark" and stressed both apostolicity and historicity. The Hardshell (antimission) Baptists simply named themselves "Primitive" Baptists and pursued the even tenor of their way.[20]

This Landmarkian emphasis on apostolicity and historicity was connected with a certain theory of succession.

In the course of their history Baptists had developed various theories of succession. Some groups had argued in favor of church succession, another group for apostolic succession. Still others were ardent defenders of baptismal succession. Finally, there were the advocates of spiritual succession, the theory which emphasizes the necessity of being true followers of Jesus Christ as Lord and Saviour. This is a succession of genuine Christian experience.[21]

Dr. J. R. Graves (1820–93), a native of Vermont, was converted at fifteen years of age, joined the North Spring Baptist Church in his native state, and settled in Nashville, Tennessee, around 1845. According to Professor E. B. Pollard, Graves was a man of considerable native ability, some learning, and unusual polemic skill. He was personally shy and somewhat withdrawn, but when set on fire by an idea or a sermon, he had great kindling power. Dr. Graves succeeded Dr. R. B. C. Howell as editor of the *Tennessee Baptist* in 1846. In that capacity he wielded tremendous influence. Again and again he engaged in sharp controversies with the Methodists and Campbellites and anyone who seemed to imperil Baptist orthodoxy as he conceived it.

[20] Barnes, *op. cit.*, p. 99.
[21] *Ibid.*, pp. 100–101.

Graves, like Whitsitt, had become profoundly disturbed about the question of the true nature of the church. In the pursuit of this inquiry he gave the current Baptist theories of succession, none of which had ever gained full acceptance by any or all Baptist groups, a peculiar twist by identifying the church of Jesus Christ with the kingdom of Christ. All true churches of Christ, Graves believed, constitute the visible kingdom which Christ came to establish. From this he inferred that if Christ's kingdom has stood unchanged through the centuries since its establishment, there must always have existed true and uncorrupted churches, since his kingdom cannot exist without true churches.

Dr. W. W. Barnes has quite accurately characterized Dr. Graves's identification of church and kingdom and his theory of church succession as being closely akin to that of the Roman Catholic Church. It is significant, moreover, that while contemporary Landmarkers shy away from speaking of the Baptist *church* and rather speak of Baptist *churches*, Dr. Graves used that term quite often.[22]

From his understanding of the nature of the church and church succession, J. R. Graves drew a number of correlative principles:

1. The primacy of the local church. The New Testament knows only local churches composed of regenerated and baptized believers. The sole hope of believers in such local Baptist churches lies in Jesus Christ as the only mediator of justification.

2. This being so, true Baptist or Old Landmark churches, if they would be faithful to Baptist beliefs, cannot recognize those societies not organized according to the pattern of the "First Baptist Church" in Jerusalem.

3. Non-Baptist churches have no right to call themselves true gospel churches. Therefore, Baptists may not recognize their ministers as true gospel ministers, and it is not permissible to

___
[22] *Ibid.*, p. 102.

allow the ministers of non-Baptist churches to preach in Baptist churches.

4. To invite, however, non-Baptist ministers to Baptist pulpits is virtual recognition of them as true ministers, which they are not.

5. On the basis of Old Landmark Baptist principles it is not proper for New Testament Baptist churches to invite non-Baptists to the Lord's Supper. Nor is it scriptural for one local Baptist church to allow members of another local Baptist church to participate in the Lord's Supper celebration. The latter is strictly a local church ordinance. Church discipline becomes an impossibility when people are freely admitted to the Supper of a local Baptist church, unless they are members of that body.

The name "Landmark" derives from a book written by Dr. J. M. Pendleton, a Baptist pastor in Bowling Green, Kentucky, entitled *An Old Landmark Re-Set*. Dr. Graves published this work in 1854. Its meaning is obvious: the phrase "an Old Landmark" was to be suggestive of the ancient moorings or principles of Baptist beliefs with regard to church order.

It was this viewpoint, so vigorously advocated by J. R. Graves, J. M. Pendleton, and A. C. Dayton, that agitated Southern Baptists in the fifties of the last century. Landmarkism, for a time, threatened to destroy the Southern Baptist Convention. "By 1880 Graves could boast that a majority of denominational papers had endorsed Landmarkism." [23] When the Whitsitt controversy erupted in 1896, the Landmarkers rose to the fray. Others joined them and, as in the fifties, personalities and personal ambition also became entangled in the controversy. One may even say that the Whitsitt controversy was but a continuation of the attack which was launched against Professor William Williams in the seventies.

Thus, when W. H. Whitsitt's theory of Baptist origins first became known to the larger Southern Baptist constituency, a strong reaction soon set in, both in the denominational press and

---

[23] W. Morgan Patterson, "Landmarkism," *Encyclopedia of Southern Baptists*, II, 757.

in the various Baptist state conventions and associations. At once people began taking sides. Those who from the first had been opposed to Seminary education or had absorbed Landmark sentiments of opposing all denominational organizations were naturally predisposed to find fault with Professor Whitsitt's ideas.

Articles appeared with almost monotonous regularity in the *Western Recorder*, Baptist weekly of Kentucky. This paper was edited by Dr. T. T. Eaton, pastor of the Walnut Street Baptist Church as well as a trustee of the Seminary. Other Baptist journals joined in the debate, and the files of the *Religious Herald* of Virginia, the *Christian Index* of Georgia, the *Biblical Recorder* of North Carolina, the *Tennessee Baptist*, and the *Baptist Standard* of Texas furnish a rich source of the pro and con of the controversy. The editors of these papers, in whose pages this matter was chiefly fought out, were not trained church historians. They cared little for the niceties of theological or historical erudition and were unwilling to listen to anything, however learned and scientific, that might undermine the solid faith of Southern Baptists.

The *Western Recorder*, it seems, carried most of the articles. Baptist writers, North and South, and even from Europe, made their contributions to the discussion of the issues. Julius Grimmel, editor of *Der Sendbote*, corresponded with T. T. Eaton. John Christian; Dr. King, pastor of the First Baptist Church of Providence, Rhode Island; and Dr. B. H. Carroll of Texas were Eaton's allies. C. S. Gardner of South Carolina, C. B. Willingham of Georgia, E. M. Poteat of Philadelphia, and Professors Robertson and Sampey of the Seminary were among Whitsitt's staunchest defenders and most loyal supporters. Professor A. H. Newman, then of Toronto's McMaster University, wrote with discrimination and good judgment.

Numerous articles were published in the various journals during the spring and summer of 1896, following the publication of Whitsitt's articles in *Johnson's Universal Cyclopedia*. In August and September a number of associations resolved that the Seminary trustees take action at once against Dr. Whitsitt.

Unless the latter should of his own free will resign, support was to be withdrawn from the Seminary. These associations also intimated that failure to act on the part of the trustees would result in losing thousands of friends of theological education. Continuing dissatisfaction, they argued, "is most likely provoking the opening of a number of theological schools among Baptists of the South." [24]

At this stage of the controversy Dr. Eaton, editor of the *Western Recorder* and avowed foe of Dr. Whitsitt, was willing to give the trustees of the Seminary the benefit of the doubt, although they had until then done nothing to remedy the situation. "We are satisfied that their doing nothing has been because it was not clear to them what was the best thing to do, rather than because of any indifference either to the character of the teaching of the institution, or the will of the denomination." [25]

When Dr. Whitsitt's book, written in defense of his earlier statements, appeared, Dr. Eaton discussed it in detail in six or more issues of the *Western Recorder*.[26] The scholarship displayed in this book, *A Question in Baptist History*, deterred Eaton and his cohorts not a whit. The opposition remained quite vocal and pressed its campaign with unmost vigor and determination. Charges of dishonesty, cowardice in reporting his findings, and infidelity against the Baptist faith continued to be heard against Dr. Whitsitt.

But Whitsitt's friends were not idle. Some of them defended him to the fullest. In the fall of 1896 the Long Run Association (Louisville) held its annual meeting. Here Dr. John R. Sampey, Dr. Whitsitt's colleague in the Seminary, secured the floor against a bedlam of voices and talked in a passionate manner for over an hour on the issue. Boldly he defended Dr. Whitsitt's integrity, scholarly competence, and Baptist orthodoxy. Eloquently Sampey spoke in favor of freedom of research. Letters poured in

---

[24] *Western Recorder*, August 13, 1896, p. 5.
[25] *Ibid.*, August 30, 1896, p. 8.
[26] September 24, October 1, 8, 15, 22, 1896.

from near and far commending Dr. Sampey's courageous defense of his colleague. Friends of Whitsitt rejoiced while the enemies gnashed their teeth.

Individual members of the faculty of Southern Seminary, among them particularly Robertson, Sampey, and Carver, unflinchingly stood by their friend and colleague. But the faculty had never acted as a body in defense of their embattled president and fellow teacher. Finally they did act. The faculty minutes dated September 29, 1896, record that on that day the members of the faculty met at Norton Hall at four o'clock in the afternoon. Professor E. C. Dargan led the opening prayer. President W. H. Whitsitt withdrew immediately after he had opened the meeting.

The following statement, drawn up by Drs. Kerfoot, Dargan, and Harris, was presented to the faculty, and after full discussion it was unanimously adopted. "As a token of the hearty unanimity prevailing, each professor appends his signature." The document reads as follows:

To Southern Baptists, Dear Brethren,
In view of the recent agitation affecting the Southern Baptist Theological Seminary, we, the undersigned members of the Faculty, reassembled to take up the work of another session, deem it proper to make to you the following frank statements:
First of all, we assure you that you cannot have more solicitude for the orthodoxy of our beloved Seminary than have we ourselves. It is our great concern at all times that the teaching of each member of the Faculty shall be in strictest accord with the Word of God, and with all the accepted tenets of our denomination. We recognize to the fullest extent our responsibility to the constituency of the Southern Baptist Convention, and the perfect right of the brethren to concern themselves in all proper ways as to the teaching of each and every professor.
In reference to the great anxiety recently manifested, and the variety of opinion publicly expressed, as to some of the teachings of our President, Dr. Wm. H. Whitsitt, we desire to say:
1. That Dr. Whitsitt, in some of his utterances, has certainly been greatly misunderstood, and has been supposed by some to teach what he did not mean and does not hold. His recently published book, en-

titled *A Question in Baptist History*, states his position more fully than he had stated it before, and we think it ought to be accepted as a frank and satisfactory explanation of just what he meant in any previously published articles of his on the same subject.

2. After a careful reading of the book, we think it perfectly clear that he never meant in any sense to recognize as real Baptists any persons who did not practice immersion; and he never meant to teach that the immersion of believers began at the time which he claims as the date of its reintroduction into England. The sole question which he seems to have had in view was concerning *the date at which genuine Baptists first appear in English History*.

3. As to this historical question touching the first appearance of Baptists in England, it would be unseemly for us as a body to express any opinion. Our line of special study have not lain in this direction, and, like the great majority of our brethren, we can only weigh the evidence as presented and decide each for himself. But we may with propriety say, after careful reading of his book, that Dr. Whitsitt has unquestionably made out a strong case, certainly strong enough to justify him in publishing the results of his researches. Nor can we fail to recognize his scholarly ability, his breadth of view, and calmness of discussion, as well as the force of the evidence he has brought forward.

4. As to the complaints which have been made about the way in which Dr. Whitsitt gave to the world the results of his investigations, we deem it due him to say that no one who knows him as we do could ever suspect him of any disloyalty to the denomination or unfaithfulness to the people with whom he is identified.

5. As to the charge that Dr. Whitsitt is unsound on certain scriptural doctrines, we refer the brethren to the Fundamental Articles of our Seminary, to which he subscribed on becoming a professor, and all of which he has recently declared he "still lovingly and joyfully holds." We refer them also to his position and emphatic denial of the teachings and the views attributed to him. These denials we accept as honest and truthful, and we believe him to be a sound scriptural Baptist.

In view of all these things we beg to remind our brethren that we have a great charge upon our hands, entrusted to us by you. Dr. Whitsitt is the President of the Seminary. In his election there was singular unanimity. The first year of his administration was a remarkable success. The prospects are exceedingly bright. But the work of your Faculty, both President and professors, has been made more difficult and burdensome by this unfortunate agitation.

Your Seminary, with its property and endowment of over eight hundred thousand dollars, with all its heritage of labors and sacrifices and blessed memories, with its prestige for theological soundness and large attendance—all this, along with the growing interest of Southern Baptists in ministerial education, cannot but suffer from acrimonious discussion. It is much easier to pull down than to build up.

We, therefore, appeal to you to stand by us, as we stand by our honored President, and to continue to give the institution your fervent prayers, your liberal support, your undiminished confidence. Then, with the blessings of God, we may confidently hope to realize in some measure the expectations of our fathers, and accomplish something for the more faithful preaching of a pure gospel.

> F. H. Kerfoot
> John R. Sampey
> A. T. Robertson
> E. C. Dargan
> W. J. McGlothlin
> H. H. Harris [27]
> W. O. Carver [28]

It was deemed best to publish these statements in the denominational press, should Dr. Whitsitt approve. Professors Dargan, Harris, and Sampey were appointed a committee to improve the literary finish of the paper, with power to act.

> John R. Sampey, Secretary. [29]

The controversy went on with unabated vehemence. Dr. Sampey's impassioned speech at the Long Run Association had pleased his friends but had inflamed the opponents of Dr. Whitsitt even more. Charges and countercharges flew thick and fast in the denominational press. The moderates of either side were shouted down. And the opposition acknowledged no defeat.

The records of the Board of Trustees of Southern Baptist Seminary as also of the Executive Committee of the school disclose that no action was taken in the Whitsitt affair either in 1896 or during the first months of 1897.

---

[27] Space was left for the signature of Prof. Harris, but not obtained through oversight. He signed, however, the original paper.

[28] Dr. W. O. Carver must have been absent on this day, but later he signed, "Approved, April 28, 1897."

[29] *Faculty Minutes,* book 2, pp. 43–48.

Buildings of the School of Church Music

Cooke Hall

Barnard Hall

Air View of the Seminary Campus in Louisville

But at the May, 1897, meeting of the Board of Trustees, Dr. B. H. Carroll of Texas offered a resolution with regard to Dr. Whitsitt's teachings on Baptist history. Former Governor W. J. Northen, of Georgia, offered a substitute motion which was discussed by Brethren B. H. Carroll, T. T. Eaton, J. H. Hudson, H. McDonald, J. H. Kilpatrick, J. W. Warder, W. R. L. Smith, and W. E. Hatcher. Northen's substitute was passed in lieu of the resolution of Brother Carroll. It read as follows:

The Trustees of the Southern Baptist Theological Seminary, assembled in their annual meeting in Wilmington, N.C., May 6th, 1897, desire to submit to the Baptists of the South the following statement in regard to the institution whose interests have been committed to their care and management:

1. That we account this a fitting occasion to reaffirm our cordial and thorough adhesion to the Fundamental Articles adopted at the time when the Seminary was established and to assure those in whose behalf we hold in trust and administer the affairs of this institution that it is our steadfast purpose to require in the future as in the past that the fundamental laws and scriptural doctrines embodied in these Articles shall be faithfully upheld by those who occupy chairs as teachers.

2. That we cannot undertake to sit in judgment upon questions of Baptist History which do not imperil any of these principles concerning which all Baptists are agreed, but concerning which serious, conscientious, and scholarly students are not agreed. We can, however, leave to continued research and free discussion the satisfactory solution of these questions.

3. That, believing the Seminary to hold an important relation to the prosperity and usefulness of Southern Baptists, we consider it our duty, while demanding of those in charge of its departments of instruction, the utmost patience in research and the greatest discretion in utterance, to foster, rather than repress the spirit of earnest and reverent investigation.

4. That, having fully assured that the tender affection which we cherish for this institution founded by our fathers and bequeathed by them to us, is shared by the Baptists of the South, one can safely trust them, as we ask them to trust us, to guard its honor, promote its usefulness and pray for its prosperity." [30]

---

[30] *Minutes of the Board of Trustees*, book 2, pp. 221–22.

A committee consisting of W. E. Hatcher, B. H. Carroll, and H. McDonald was appointed to invite Dr. Whitsitt to appear before the board and make such statements as he might wish. On the next day, May 7, 1897, Dr. Whitsitt appeared before the members of the board, as requested, at nine o'clock. He made the following statement:

DEAR BRETHREN:

I beg leave to return sincerest and heartiest thanks for the noble and generous treatment that you have bestowed upon me. I have only words of affection for every member of the Board. After consulting with the committee I have the following to say:

1. That in regard to the articles written as editorials for the *Independent*, I have long felt that it was a mistake and the generous action of the Board of Trustees renders it easy for me to make this statement. What I wrote was from a Pedobaptist standpoint with a view to stimulating historic research with no thought to disparage Baptist doctrine or practices.

2. That the article in *Johnson's Encyclopedia* has probably passed beyond my control, but it will be very pleasing to me if I can honorably procure the elimination from it of whatever is offensive to any of my brethren.

3. Regarding the charge that I expressed a conviction that a kinswoman of mine ought to follow her husband into a Pedobaptist church, that it was never my intention to indicate a belief that the family outranked the Church of God. I believe that obedience to God's commands is above every other human duty, and that people in every relation of life ought to obey God rather than men.

4. That on the historical questions involved in the discussion I find myself out of agreement with some honored historians; but what I have written is the outcome of patient and honest research and I can do no otherwise than to reaffirm my convictions and maintain my position. But if in the future it shall ever be made to appear that I have erred in my conclusions I would promptly and cheerfully say so. I am a searcher after truth and will gladly hail every helper in my work.

5. That I cannot more strongly assure the brethren that I am a Baptist than by what I have recently declared with regard to the Abstract of Principles set forth in the Fundamental Laws of the Seminary. I am heartily in accord with my Baptist brethren in every distinctive principle that they hold. My heart and life are bound up

with the Baptists and I have no higher thought on earth than to spend my days in their fellowship and service, in the name of the Lord Jesus Christ.

Respectfully submitted

Wm. H. Whitsitt.[31]

Brother B. H. Carroll moved that Dr. Whitsitt's paper be appended to the resolutions adopted by the board. This motion was amended to the effect that Carroll and Hatcher write a sentence connecting the two papers and present them to the Convention of the Southern Baptists then in session in Wilmington, North Carolina, and to the general public.

After Dr. Whitsitt had ended his statement, the hymn "How Firm a Foundation" was sung, and the members of the board pressed forward to grasp the hand of the president. Finally, Dr. Whitsitt and Brother McDonald from Atlanta led in prayer.

This indeed looked like real victory.

It ought to be stated that the Northen resolution leading to the declaration of confidence of the Board of Trustees in Dr. Whitsitt had been proposed to counteract and in a way answer a deluge of letters that Chairman Joshua Levering had read to the board—letters addressed to the board by certain associations in Kentucky with regard to Dr. Whitsitt's views of Baptist origins.

When the board's statement and that of Dr. Whitsitt were presented to the messengers of the Southern Baptist Convention the next day, President Whitsitt received an ovation from the people gathered at this annual session. A sense of victory surged through a letter written by Dr. A. T. Robertson to his colleague, Dr. John R. Sampey, while the latter traveled in the Holy Land. Dr. Robertson wrote:

The Lord be praised. It is a great victory and brings a serious situation, especially in Kentucky. The Trustees refuse to have a heresy trial, passed resolutions indicating freedom of research, before Whitsitt made a single statement. This was Thursday night. Next

---

[31] *Ibid.*, pp. 223–24.

morning Whitsitt appeared and made his statement similar to his of last summer save the further one that he is willing to eliminate opinion especially from the Encyclopedia articles if that could be done, but he distinctly and strongly affirmed his historical position and would make no change anywhere on that. You know by now, I suppose of the ovation he received in the Convention. We have victory and shall have peace by degrees. Eaton is talking much privately and publicly, but we are keeping silent and shall continue to do so. Silence, peace, and hard work is our motto.

It has been a hard and stubborn fight, but everything held together and nobody wavered and God's Spirit did the rest. This is a great day for Southern Baptists and marks a long stride forward.

The students are elated. Dargan is happy with the Students' Fund out of debt ($2,000.00 at Wilmington); Rockefeller gave $2,000.00 to pay for the deficit in current debt. Boards are out of debt too— You and I are going to suffer for a while for our forward stand, but we can stand that for the good that has come.[32]

Dr. Robertson also reported that there were 290 students at the end of the session of 1896–97! Moreover, most of the state papers had come out against any conviction of Dr. Whitsitt, and no serious trouble was to be anticipated.

But the end was not yet in sight. Dr. Whitsitt, upon his return to the Seminary from the Convention, spoke in a most conciliatory tone to the students. "It behooves us to be humble men. Let none of us conceive that we own the Baptists of the South, and have under our control the decisions of the Southern Baptist Convention. On the contrary, we should walk humbly with our God and our brethren." [33]

Dr. Whitsitt warned against anything that might savor of exaltation. He urged patience in the presence of contradiction and reproach. "Did not our blessed Lord who endured contradiction from sinners give us the best example? Let us, therefore, learn one and all to be quiet. The world and the brethren alike are weary of our controversies. Should we continue in

---

[32] Letter of A. T. Robertson to Dr. John R. Sampey (May 21, 1897).
[33] Whitsitt's speech to the students of Southern Baptist Seminary, *Western Recorder*, May 27, 1897, p. 5.

them, shortly they will weary of us." Whitsitt also asked those present to be considerate of the trustees. "They have trusted us so fully and so generously. Hence, it behooves us to imitate their virtues."

Lastly Whitsitt counseled,

Let us all be considerate of our beloved brethren, sincere and devoted men. Though we differ with them and they from us, we have faith in them. Let us cultivate that faith more and more. Let us esteem and honor them. Let us love them honestly and heartily. They are strong and worthy men. I believe that none of them will reject the olive branch that we offer. On the contrary, they will be glad of any sincere and kindly advance that we may make. Let nothing be said or done to give them pain. They are not striving to lord it over us; neither do we desire to lord it over them. They are honored brethren; in God's name let us love them as Christian brethren." [34]

Whitsitt firmly believed that the victory in Wilmington had been due to the prayers of thousands of churches, homes, and individuals throughout the Convention. But the passions of men were still excited.

I request that everyone will earnestly pray for the peace of Jesus. We are weary of strife and bitterness. We sincerely desire the respect and sympathy of all our brethren. Peace will promote the glory of God and the comfort of souls. Peace will cheer our aching hearts. O Lord, send peace, sweet peace, holy peace, for thy name's sake. . . . Peace will introduce a season of great work. Holy Ghost religion and hard work are the best things in the world for Baptists.[35]

But before things got better they had to become still worse.

Dr. John R. Sampey in his extemporaneous address at Long Run Association had cried out that "to muzzle now this discussion is nothing short of tyranny." Of course, when victory seemed to be in sight, it was only natural that Dr. Whitsitt's friends and supporters longed for the end of the debate. The

---

[34] *Ibid.*
[35] *Ibid.*

opponents, however, thought differently. They complained about the tyranny of shutting off discussion.

It was particularly Dr. B. H. Carroll, pastor of the First Baptist Church in Waco, Texas, and trustee of the Seminary, who reopened the discussion. In many ways Dr. Carroll was a most remarkable man. His parents had moved from Mississippi, where he had been born, to Burleson County, Texas, in 1858. An avid reader, Carroll, according to his own confession, was for a time an unbeliever. At the age of thirteen he could give pat answers to questions bearing on salvation without believing a word of what he said. Yet he was baptized. Later, however, during the Civil War he was thoroughly converted to Jesus Christ at a Methodist camp meeting. In time Carroll graduated from Baylor University, became widely known as a debater and orator, and in 1871 was called as pastor of the First Baptist Church in Waco. He remained in this pastorate until 1899.

As professor of Bible at Baylor, Carroll wielded a large influence. He helped establish Southwestern Theological Seminary, today the largest theological school in the world. He was also active in the promotion of Sunday school work and was in the thick of the contest that led to the founding of the present Sunday School Board in Nashville. Then, too, Carroll was an enthusiastic advocate of home and foreign missions.

In his heart beat a great love for the common, the average man. He was a man of marvelous gifts and sterling character and was in every respect a worthy opponent of Dr. Whitsitt.

In June of 1897 Dr. Carroll wrote an article, "Back to the Realm of Discussion," that stirred up the controversy afresh. In this article the great Texan made much of the fact that the Whitsitt matter had been widely discussed in the United States, Canada, Great Britain, and even in Continental Europe. To Dr. Carroll the reason for this worldwide interest in the Whitsitt affair was quite obvious:

Thoughtful and well-balanced minds never attribute such widespread interest to any local jealousy or antagonism. The wide-spread leaders of human thought do not rush into the arena of conflict at the call of petty, local jealousy. Angus, King, Lorimer, Thomas, Vedder, Newman, Hiscox, and the like beyond our boundaries would never have responded to such a bugle.[36]

But, argued Carroll, not only great Baptist leaders but the common people have also been aroused. Associations and conventions in Kentucky, Mississippi, Arkansas, and Texas, where "J. R. Graves' soul goes marching on," have registered their protest in the Whitsitt affair. "Unlettered, backward people, you say. May be so. But there are nearly half a million of them in touch with a million more who have not spoken." [37] Baptists may ignore such a voice, but often they do it at their peril.

Dr. Carroll had reopened the discussion.

When the Southern Baptist Convention held its next session at Norfolk, Virginia, in May, 1898, it was Carroll who presented to the messengers a resolution that looked toward the severance of Southern Baptist Seminary from the Convention. He honestly believed that his action was in the interest of the Convention in order to safeguard its purpose and unity as basically a missionary and evangelistic agency of God's Kingdom. The substance of Carroll's resolution, which was duly seconded and passed, to be presented for a vote at the next Convention in accordance with its constitution, was as follows:

Resolved, That this Convention, without expressing any opinion whatever on the merits of the controversy concerning Seminary matters, about which good brethren among us honestly differ, but in the interest of harmony, particularly with a view to preserve and confirm unity in mission work, does now exercise its evident right to divest itself of responsibility in the Seminary management, by dissolving the slight and remote bond of connection between this body and the Seminary; that is, that this body declines to nominate trustees for the Seminary or to entertain motions or receive reports relative thereto, leaving the Institution to stand on its own merits and be managed by its own trustees.[38]

[36] *Western Recorder,* June 3, 1897, p. 4.
[37] *Ibid.*
[38] *Proceedings of the Southern Baptist Convention,* May, 1898, p. 23.

On motion of J. B. Hawthorne, of Tennessee, it was ordered that a committee of one from each state report at the next session of the Southern Convention on the advisability of changing relations of the Convention to Southern Seminary as provided by the charter of the Seminary.

Whitsitt and his supporters felt another blow at almost the same time. A large number of protest letters were read before the Board of Trustees, which met a day earlier than the Convention. Nearly twenty-five letters came from Baptist associations in Kentucky alone. Ten letters had arrived from Arkansas, seven from Tennessee, one each from Louisiana, Missouri, and Mississippi. Four letters of indictment of Whitsitt's teachings had been sent by state conventions within the bounds of the Southern Baptist Convention.[39] All this, together with several years of intense strain, broke Dr. Whitsitt and led him to resign his office.

Dr. A. T. Robertson had been sure of victory until now. But in July, 1898, he wrote to Dr. John R. Sampey this pathetic word: "I have written Whitsitt giving him ten reasons why he ought to announce his resignation just before the Missouri Convention to take effect at the close of next session. . . . Help Norton to see the importance of action now. . . . If Norton agrees to the idea, Whitsitt will do it." [40] In a postscript to this letter Robertson added that he had written Dr. William E. Hatcher of Richmond, Virginia, fourteen pages with eighteen reasons why Whitsitt "ought to resign Wednesday. I expect him to telegraph Whitsitt."

One of the early supporters of Whitsitt, Dr. I. J. Van Ness, editor of the *Christian Index*, also strongly favored Whitsitt's resignation. There was a reason for Van Ness's pressure. He felt that not only the Landmarkers but also a widening circle of other honest Southern Baptists were losing confidence in Whitsitt's leadership. He thought that Whitsitt's resignation would be the best thing that could happen.

So, despite the endorsement by the faculty and the Board of

[39] *Minutes of the Board of Trustees*, book 2, pp. 232–33.
[40] Letter of A. T. Robertson to Dr. Sampey, July 10, 1898.

Trustees of the Seminary, Dr. Whitsitt, no doubt influenced by the counsel of well-meaning friends, resigned on July 13, 1898, as president and professor of church history. The resignation was to take effect at the end of the academic session of 1898–99.

Some of Whitsitt's most ardent supporters felt that he had left them hanging in the air. If the president of Southern Seminary no longer thought it worthwhile to continue the fight, why should his friends continue it? Without a leader, the cause seemed doomed.

The end came in May, 1899, when the Board of Trustees of the Seminary met in Louisville, where the Southern Baptist Convention was also holding its annual sessions. Although the Visiting Committee presented a glowing report about the past academic year, particularly stressing, with remarkable unanimity, "the high moral tone existing through the entire body" of Seminary life, it did not surprise anyone when the chairman of the board, Joshua Levering, read the following telegram:

> To Hon. Joshua Levering, President of the Board of Trustees of The Southern Baptist Theological Seminary, Baltimore, Md.:
> I hereby resign my office as President of The Southern Baptist Theological Seminary and professor of Church History to take effect at the close of the session of 1898–1899.
> Louisville, Ky., July 13, 1898.
> Wm. H. Whitsitt.[41]

In addition to this telegram from Dr. Whitsitt, Mr. Levering also presented about sixty communications from individual persons and Baptist bodies in the South which were either in favor of or against the acceptance of Dr. Whitsitt's resignation by the board. By consent these communications were laid on the table.

There had been one last attempt on the part of Dr. E. M. Poteat and Dr. John R. Sampey to start a circular letter among the trustees to nullify Dr. Whitsitt's resignation. This movement began about a month before the board met at Louisville. Poteat and Sampey tried to enlist C. S. Gardner of South Carolina,

---

[41] *Minutes of the Board of Trustees,* book 2, p. 248.

but although he confessed to having been a stout friend of Whitsitt's through the years, he did not feel that such a circular letter at this late juncture would do any good. He wrote:

I feel toward Whitsitt as I always have. I love him as much as ever. I think the fight against him has been, on the part of the leaders, unjust, ungentlemanly, un-Christian, and immoral. I think the Seminary will be a great sufferer from his removal. My opinion of the whole matter has undergone no change, unless it has become stronger.[42]

Dr. Gardner felt that things had advanced to such a stage that it was not certain whether those who stood by Whitsitt prior to his resignation would do so now. Some of the trustees, moreover, were weighing the possibility of accepting Dr. Whitsitt's resignation as president of the Seminary but retaining him as professor of church history.

Throughout the nine months after Whitsitt's resignation had been sent to Mr. Levering, A. T. Robertson had feared that the opponents of Whitsitt would not cease until all those who had been active in Whitsitt's support would also be forced to resign. However, several trustees, among them Dr. Gardner and Dr. I. J. Van Ness, assured Robertson again and again that there would be no danger of disciplining or dismissing Whitsitt's supporters.

The board accepted Whitsitt's resignation on the evening of May 11, 1899, after Carroll, Hatcher, Kilpatrick, and Warden had spoken to the motion to accept it. The vote was taken at eleven o'clock in the evening. First, the trustees voted on Whitsitt's resignation from the presidency of Southern Seminary. The record simply states that the resignation was accepted.

Next came his resignation as professor of church history. On a division the resignation was accepted by a vote of twenty-two to twenty. That was a narrow margin indeed and revealed that many trustees still felt that Whitsitt might have fruitfully carried on as a teacher of the institution.

The next step that the trustees of the Seminary had to take

---

[42] Letter of C. S. Gardner to John R. Sampey, April 3, 1899.

was the election of a new president. At first it was thought wisest to defer the election of a new leader for the ensuing year. Dr. John R. Sampey was proposed as interim chairman of the faculty for the following year. But that suggestion was not accepted by the board.

A pathetic letter addressed to the trustees by Dr. F. H. Kerfoot complicated matters. Although Kerfoot disavowed any aspirations to the presidency, he must have had his eyes on the position even when Broadus died in 1895. Kerfoot intimated that he had perhaps suffered as much, if not more, than Dr. Whitsitt during the recent controversy. He had tried, he wrote, to be faithful to the President and to his beloved Seminary while at the same time trying "to hold a large part of our constituency to the Seminary which I felt would be hopelessly estranged if I allowed myself to become a partisan fighter." [43]

Though he had been wounded in the house of his friends and been subject to grave misunderstanding by many, Kerfoot felt highly gratified that so "many of the friends of the Seminary have been desirous of seeing me elected President of the institution, but I learn that there are many who insist that my election cannot bring peace to the denomination. I am unwilling to allow the Board of Trustees to be embarrassed by this question. I'm unwilling to give the denomination any occasion to do anything that may embarrass or in any wise hinder the prosperity of the Seminary for which I began to work 28 years ago." [44]

The trustees accepted this letter with thanks.

Immediately after the reading of Dr. Kerfoot's letter, Brother H. McDonald moved the election of Brother J. P. Greene of Missouri as president of the Seminary. Remarks on the motion were made by Carroll, Hatcher, Tichenor, Ryland, and Hudson. Brother Hudson offered an amendment to the effect that Dr. Greene be also elected to fill the vacant chair of ecclesiastical history and polemic theology. Discussion by several of the brethren, followed, and then came the vote. Dr. Greene, presi-

---

[43] *Minutes of the Board of Trustees,* book 2, p. 254.
[44] *Ibid.*

dent of William Jewell College, Liberty, Missouri, was unanimously elected president of Southern Baptist Theological Seminary.

It is a matter of record that Dr. Greene finally declined the presidency of Southern Seminary. Under the date of June 2, 1899, Dr. Greene wrote to the chairman of the Board of Trustees that he regretfully declined the proffered election.

The trustees met in Atlanta on June 29, 1899, at a called meeting for the express purpose of electing a president. Dr. Kerfoot's name was again presented. Dr. Carroll of Texas and other brethren also made suggestions. But finally former Governor Northen of Georgia prevailed with his resolution to proceed with the election of a president of the Seminary.

It was a dramatic moment when Dr. W. E. Hatcher rose to nominate Dr. E. Y. Mullins as the fourth president of Southern Baptist Theological Seminary. Landrum, Tribble, Marvin, Ryland, Eager, Smith, Thomas, Eaton, Thornhill, Freeman, Warder, Edmonds, White, Levering, and Connally spoke to the motion made by Dr. Hatcher. Dr. Kerfoot's name was withdrawn by Brother Connally at McDonald's request. Then the vote was taken on Dr. Hatcher's motion to elect Dr. Mullins. The vote was unanimous, and Dr. E. Y. Mullins was elected president of Southern Baptist Theological Seminary.

At the time of his election Dr. Mullins was pastor of the First Baptist Church at Newton Centre, Massachusetts. This church is located at the foot of the hill on which Newton Theological Institution, now Andover-Newton Theological School, has carried on its fruitful labors for more than a century.

Former Governor Northen was sent to Newton Centre in order to convey in person to Dr. Mullins the invitation of the board to become the fourth president of Southern Baptist Seminary. He appeared at the parsonage of Dr. and Mrs. Mullins on a hot Fourth of July, 1899, apologizing for his unkempt appearance.

The next morning, when breakfast was over, the Governor delivered his formal message. A discussion of every phase of

Southern Baptist life and the Seminary situation followed. To Mrs. Mullins this discussion seemed never to end, since the messenger of the Board of Trustees was eager to carry back with him an unequivocal acceptance by Dr. Mullins. But the president-elect promised only that he would go immediately to Louisville to confer with the faculty, and only after knowing their mind would he give his answer.

Dr. Mullins soon made his way to Louisville and conferred with the Seminary faculty. For a few brief days he also stayed with Dr. Sampey at the latter's country parsonage in the bluegrass region of Kentucky. Brief notes to his wife kept her posted on his movements.

When Dr. Mullins finally arrived back home, his wife, who had been waiting for him on the veranda, was petrified. "Then he came swaying up the walk like a drunken man. She flew to him: 'What is the matter? Are you sick?' tumbled out in consternation as she helped him along. He only nodded his head to the last; did not attempt to speak." [45]

Dr. Mullins had returned from his momentous journey to Louisville a very sick man. The doctor was quickly summoned. He got from him "what details he was able to get from a man almost in delirium from excessive fever." [46] Weeks of anxiety followed, and for days Mrs. Mullins did not learn of the result of her husband's trip to Louisville, nor did she at the moment care to know. Gradually the patient improved, and only when Dr. Mullins was out of danger and the nurse had left did they talk of the problem. "Then he said with tears: 'The task is mine —ours.' And they wept together." [47]

Mrs. Mullins was a bit apprehensive as to whether her husband would enjoy teaching at the Seminary. Just before leaving Newton Centre she had occasion to talk to Dr. William Newton Clarke, professor at Colgate Theological Seminary, about her

---

[45] Isla May Mullins, *Edgar Young Mullins* (Nashville: Sunday School Board of the Southern Baptist Convention, 1929), p. 113.
[46] *Ibid.*
[47] *Ibid.*

fears. He smiled at her and said, "I have tried both, and there is nothing in the world so stimulating as a group of young men studying for the ministry sitting before you and drinking in eagerly everything you say; while you, on your part, know that you are speaking to unseen thousands who will look to these men to give them the Bread of Life." He continued, "I want you to do something for me. After your husband has taught three weeks in the Southern Baptist Theological Seminary, I want you to write me a letter and tell me how he likes teaching." Mrs. Mullins later wrote to Dr. Clarke and confirmed his prediction.

A new leaf had been turned in the lives of Dr. and Mrs. Mullins. Years of hard but fruitful labors lay ahead for them. When they arrived in Louisville, Dr. Robertson, his wife, Ella Broadus Robertson, and the beloved Mrs. John A. Broadus were on hand to extend to them the Seminary's welcome.

With the coming of Dr. Mullins to the presidency of Southern Baptist Seminary a new chapter in its history began. In more than one way it was a grand history that commenced.

8

E. Y. Mullins, President

THE LANDMARKERS and other opponents of Dr. W. H. Whitsitt had seemingly won the struggle. But the Board of
Trustees of the Seminary had once again reaffirmed their full
confidence in Dr. Whitsitt's loyalty to basic Baptist beliefs and
their advocacy of reasonable freedom of research. In fact, the
opponents of Whitsitt were dumfounded by his resignation, and
there was a movement on foot to nullify it so that he might be
deposed with due decorum. But that movement failed. Hence, as
Professor W. W. Barnes of Southwestern Seminary has well
said, "Landmarkism won the battle, but lost the war. The Southern Baptist Theological Seminary 'lost its president, but did not
lose its soul.'"[1]

As one reflects on the circumstances preceding the election of
Dr. E. Y. Mullins in July, 1899, one cannot help wondering
about the strange ways of God and man. Some ten years prior
to his return to Louisville, Dr. Mullins had received a call to a
church in San Antonio, Texas. He had accepted the call, and
only the illness of Mrs. Mullins prevented their leaving the pastorate in Harrodsburg, Kentucky. Instead their path led to
Baltimore, then to Richmond, Virginia, and from there in 1896
to Newton Centre's First Baptist Church. Had Mullins been in
Texas at the time of the Whitsitt controversy, it is very likely
that he would never have become president of Southern Seminary.

Thus, although Mullins had been on the side of Whitsitt and
had even written some articles for a Southern Baptist journal,

[1] Barnes, *op. cit.*, p. 138.

he was not identified with either side of the controversy in the minds of those who elected him in 1899.

Dr. E. Y. Mullins was well prepared for the difficult task that awaited him in Louisville. Born January 5, 1860, in Franklin County, Mississippi, of godly parents, he grew up near Corsicana, Texas. His father was a farmer-teacher-preacher, as had been his father before him. Mullins' grandfather on his mother's side had been an influential member of the Mississippi legislature.

English, Irish, and French strains were blended in his ancestral heritage. With eleven children to rear, his parents had their hands full. Being the first boy, young Mullins had to help earn money so that the older girls of the family might go to college. He worked at odd jobs, being a printer's devil, newsboy, type-setter, printer, messenger boy, and telegrapher. "At fifteen he was in full charge of a telegraph office with a man's pay." [2]

Mullins received his college education at the Agricultural and Mechanical College of Texas. Here an excellent liberal arts course was combined with military training, all of which stood him in good stead in later life. Converted under Major Penn of Dallas, Mullins was baptized by his father on November 7, 1880. The young convert had first planned to become a lawyer. In fact, he even studied law for a short time, only to exchange it for the ministry when he sensed that God was calling him into his service.

Between 1881 and 1885 E. Y. Mullins was a student at Southern Baptist Theological Seminary. He was twenty-one when he matriculated and proved to be a methodical, persistent, and eager student. His talent for leadership was soon recognized by his fellow students, for they chose him as manager of Waverly Hall. In that capacity Mullins proved to be a most capable caterer, the food he served being both cheap and extremely palatable. He held this position till he left the Seminary in 1885.

During his third year as a Seminary student, Mullins met Miss Isla May Hawley at a student reception at Walnut Street

---

[2] Mullins, *op. cit.*, p. 11.

Baptist Church. The tall six-footer easily won the heart of the young and beautiful lady who was to become his life's companion.

When E. Y. Mullins graduated in the class of 1885, he really wanted to go as a missionary to Brazil. But Dr. John A. Broadus, who had occasionally talked with the young graduate about his future, predicted that "wherever you are, I think your work will be educational." Before that prediction was to be fulfilled Mullins had to acquire considerable experience. He successfully served the First Baptist Church at Harrodsburg, Kentucky (1885–88), and Lee Street Baptist Church in Baltimore, Maryland (1885–95), and after a brief interval as associate secretary of the Southern Baptist Foreign Mission Board in Richmond, Virginia, he became pastor of the First Baptist Church of Newton Centre, Massachusetts (1896–99).

In all these ministries Dr. Mullins quickly and easily won the hearts of the people, preaching quickening sermons, visiting people in their homes, and being a good pastor to those in trouble. The call to the presidency of Southern Seminary came as a complete surprise. Though he loved his work at Newton Centre, there was no hesitancy in his accepting this position of trust in Louisville.

Mullins was near forty years of age; he had gathered valuable experience as pastor, mission secretary, and leader of men. He was God's man for this hour in the Seminary's most crucial period of its history. For when Dr. E. Y. Mullins became president of Southern Seminary, forty years of its history lay behind. It now needed to face toward a brighter future with enlarged horizons and deepened purposes.

The faculty was wholeheartedly behind its new leader. It was a comparatively young faculty, with F. H. Kerfoot fifty-two, E. C. Dargan forty-seven, John R. Sampey thirty-six, A. T. Robertson thirty-five, William J. McGlothlin thirty-two, and W. O. Carver thirty-one years of age. All of them were capable and devoted men of the finest cultural background, intellectual training, and wide experience. It was a superb team. Its strength,

181

won through the recent conflict, augured well for a happy and creative future. And it was a group of promising young scholars with which Dr. Mullins came to be associated.

On the whole, Southern Baptists had favored the election of E. Y. Mullins. Friends and alumni gathered about him to lend him their hearty and prayerful support. Yet it required great skill, much tact, and much patience to rally the Baptist constituency and to steer the Seminary into quiet waters. But in time the high goals that Dr. Mullins and his co-workers set to attain were achieved, and the school moved from strength to strength, from honor to honor.

The first time that Dr. Mullins was present at the faculty meeting was on July 19, 1899. All but Dr. Robertson were present. Dr. F. H. Kerfoot gave notice that he had been elected corresponding secretary of the Home Mission Board of the Southern Baptist Convention. Since he had the offer under consideration, the faculty postponed the rearrangement of teaching assignments.

The next day, July 20, it was agreed that in case of Dr. Kerfoot's continuing with the Seminary, Dr. Mullins was to teach church history, while Dr. Carver was asked to teach polemic theology. As it turned out, Dr. Kerfoot did leave the Seminary, and Dr. Mullins was made responsible for systematic theology as his primary teaching assignment. Professor McGlothlin took church history. Dr. Carver continued with missions, junior Greek, and polemic theology. It was thought that in the latter subject he would be a "safer" teacher than in church history, where he might be tempted to teach Whitsitt's ideas. Soon, however, Carver proposed that he be permitted to drop polemic theology and in its place inaugurate a full department of comparative religion and missions. Permission was willingly granted.

One of the first proposals that Dr. Mullins made to his colleagues was that thirty thousand dollars be raised during the next session so as to secure sufficient funds to meet current expenses. Of this amount five thousand dollars was to be used for the purchase of needed books for the library, while the remainder was to be applied to current expenses. The faculty heartily concurred with President Mullins' proposals, and soon things began to hum.

A number of advances may be noted during the first decade of Dr. Mullins' administration. After the strife of the Whitsitt controversy the faculty felt that a strengthening of the curriculum of the school would be one of the best means of commending the Seminary to the Baptist constituency and to present and future students. Thus, in October of 1899 the faculty decided that the standard for graduation in all special classes would be 80 per cent for the present session and 85 thereafter.[3]

Requirements in the graduate school were from this time on steadily increased. In May, 1900, the faculty resolved to modify the requirements for candidates applying for the Doctor of Theology degree as follows:

If one who has taken the degree of Master in Theology afterwards spends at least one full session of eight months in the Seminary, devoting himself to graduate study, and receives Diplomas in not less than five special classes (four of which shall be taken after graduation as Master in Theology, the selection of all classes to be approved by the Faculty not later than October 10th of each session), and presents a satisfactory thesis showing original research or original thought on some matter connected with theological studies, he shall have a Diploma with the title of Th.D., Doctor in Theology. The standard for all work toward the doctorate is eighty-five per cent.[4]

The admission of young ladies to the classes of the Seminary after 1900 was highly welcomed by some and vigorously opposed by other well-meaning people. Rev. E. Z. Simmons, missionary to China, had approached Dr. Mullins and the faculty in 1900 with a view to establishing a training school for women missionaries and Christian workers in Louisville. Two years later, in May, 1902, the Board of Trustees authorized the opening of the Seminary's classes to women preparing for Christian work.

---

[3] *Faculty Minutes,* book 2, p. 98.
[4] *Ibid.,* pp. 104–105.

However, while these women were allowed to take examinations, they were not matriculated as students. For the session of 1903–1904 Dr. Mullins reported that forty-eight women were attending lectures regularly. Of these, ten were expecting to be missionaries while the remainder were preparing for other Christian work. The majority of the whole number in that year were wives of Seminary students.[5] In that same report Dr. Mullins also informed Southern Baptists that through the gift of a Christian woman in Louisville the Seminary had been able to establish a special training class in practical mission methods for women and that Dr. W. O. Carver had been asked by the faculty to teach that class.[6]

Dr. Carver subsequently exercised a considerable and decisive leadership in the venture that led in 1907 to the establishment of Woman's Missionary Union Training School, now called the Carver School of Missions and Social Work in honor of Dr. Carver. In the year of its founding the Board of Trustees of Southern Seminary surrendered to Woman's Missionary Union the entire management and control of the new school. But it also offered all the advantages of study in the Seminary's classes to the students of the new training school.[7]

Still another significant forward step in the life of the Seminary was the inauguration of a quarterly theological journal, first called *The Baptist Review and Expositor*. This journal began publication in 1904 and has appeared since then without interruption. It has been from the beginning a faculty venture, although the Seminary administration has generously helped it along with financial subsidies through the intervening years.

This journal, now called simply *The Review and Expositor*, has attracted contributors and subscribers among the alumni of the Seminary and in other parts of the world.

The first issue of this theological journal appeared in April,

---

[5] Carrie U. Littlejohn, *History of Carver School of Missions and Social Work* (Nashville: Broadman Press, 1958), p. 19.
[6] *Ibid.*, p. 20.
[7] *Ibid.*, p. 42.

1904. Its contents indicated the intention of the editors to minister constructively and creatively to as wide a constituency as possible. The pages of the first issue of the *Review and Expositor* contained, among others, articles on "The Purpose and Meaning of an Educated Ministry" by Dr. Milton G. Evans, of Crozer Seminary; "Symbolism in the New Testament" by W. T. Whitley, of England; "An Analysis of the Sermon on the Mount" by Professor J. H. Farmer, of Toronto; "The Code of Hammurabi and the Laws of Moses" by John R. Sampey; and "Is Jesus Christ the Author of Christian Experience?" by the editor-in-chief, Dr. E. Y. Mullins.[8]

The editors of the new journal expressed their realization of the need of constructive theological thinking. While much of modern doubt, they argued, is of the earnest kind which arises in the minds reared under Christian influences, there is also a cynical sort of doubt that corrodes the soul of man. Everywhere sincere people are troubled by the advance of modern science and perplexed by the questions that modern philosophers are raising. They need guidance and help. And the help they need is not that of the mere dogmatist whose stock in trade is bald assertion, but rather the appreciative and sympathetic help of a sober and careful effort to meet their difficulties in an adequate way on the high plane of reasoned exposition and discussion.

The editors, however, also clearly stated that the merely critical and analytical process of theological scholarship had been overdone in certain quarters. While not at all denying the value of legitimate criticism, the *constructive* element in theological reflection, they avowed, deserved greater emphasis.

Furthermore, the editors declared in the first issue of the *Review and Expositor*, they would steer between a cheap and easy neutrality on the one hand and narrow traditionalism and sectarianism on the other hand. Truth from all sources would be welcomed. "It will be neither possible nor desirable to main-

---

[8] *Review and Expositor*, I (April, 1904), p. 1.

tain a rigid doctrinal uniformity . . . for considerable diversity of opinion will appear." [9] That policy implied, among other things, that Baptist and non-Baptist contributors would be welcomed to the pages of the new journal.

During the more than fifty years of its existence the *Review and Expositor* has stimulated conversation among Christian theologians, preachers, philosophers, scientists, and humble believers. Scholars of repute like James Orr, D. C. Macintosh, A. M. Fairbairn, James Stalker, George Cross, I. S. Gubelmann, John Horsch, A. H. Newman, H. Wheeler Robinson, P. T. Forsyth, S. Angus, Augustus H. Strong, J. A. Faulkner, W. T. Whitley, Ralph K. Knudsen, R. B. Hoyle, Gunnar Westin, Herman H. Horne, W. W. Barnes, Austen K. de Blois, W. Y. Fullerton, John A. Mackay, Theodore Gerald Soares, Benjamin Bacon, John Wick Bowman, Halford Luccock, Kenneth S. Latourette, Johannes Schneider, and George A. Buttrick have contributed to this ever-needed theological conversation.

A seminary is a school where theory and practice must ever go hand in hand. The founders of Southern were very conscious of this combination. John A. Broadus, the homiletician and careful New Testament scholar, and Basil Manly, Jr., the professor of Bible and Old Testament, were unceasingly active on behalf of improving the teaching ministries of Southern Baptists.

Both Broadus and Manly actively promoted Sunday school work within the bounds of the Convention. They helped create its first literature and also were deeply interested in better church music. These two men were responsible for the organization of the first Sunday School Board of Southern Baptists. Basil Manly, Jr., the real founder of that Board, was also its first president, while John A. Broadus became part-time secretary with an annual salary of three hundred dollars.[10]

It was therefore quite natural that the new Sunday School Board, established in 1891, desired to provide lectures on Sunday

[9] *Ibid.*, p. 3.
[10] Homer L. Grice, "Sunday School Board of the Southern Baptist Convention, 1863–1873," *Encyclopedia of Southern Baptists*, II, 1340–41.

school work in the Seminary. In February, 1902, Dr. W. E. Hatcher inaugurated this lectureship. The messages he brought were so popular and suggestive that the students clamored for their publication.

Later, in May, 1906, the Board of Trustees of the Seminary recommended the establishment of a new chair of Sunday school pedagogy, the professor in charge of this chair to be supported jointly by the Seminary administration and the Sunday School Board in Nashville, Tennessee. The Sunday School Board took the initiative in this matter, proposing

to raise the endowment through gifts from Sunday schools through-out the South, donating $1,000.00 to the endowment for every $2,000.00 contributed by the Sunday schools, up to $20,000.00. The proposal for the endowment came in connection with the celebration of the jubilee year of the Seminary, when the board made an initial gift of $5,000. By April, 1922, amounts contributed from the Sunday schools supplemented by gifts from the Sunday School Board totaled $73,766.01.[11]

Dr. B. H. Dement was proposed as the first incumbent of this chair that was later renamed the Basil Manly Chair of Religious Education and Church Administration. Other occupants of this important chair in the life of the Seminary and the denomination have been Landrum Pinson Leavell, who served from 1915 to 1920; Gaines Stanley Dobbins, who served from 1920 to 1956; and the present incumbent, Professor Findley Bartow Edge, who has served since 1947.

The development in modern Baptist life of the Baptist World Alliance is of the utmost importance. That less than six years after the end of the Whitsitt controversy men like Dr. A. T. Robertson, the budding Greek scholar, should envisage the idea of the Baptist World Alliance is highly gratifying.

To be sure, as far back as 1678 a General Baptist in England, Thomas Grantham, had conceived the idea of "all congregations of Christians of the world that are baptized according to the

---

[11] *Ibid.*, pp. 818–19.

appointment of Christ would make one consistory at least sometimes to consider matters of difference among them." [12] Then in 1790 John Rippon of London, England, had suggested that a world organization of Baptists meet, probably in London, "with a desire of promoting a universal interchange of kind offices among them," but nothing came of it.

Around 1895 Dr. W. W. Landrum talked to Dr. R. H. Pitt, editor of the *Religious Herald*, of Virginia, about a pan-Baptist conference. Although Dr. Pitt wrote a brief article about this suggestion, the idea remained still-born. Seemingly the time was not yet ripe for its realization.

It was in the early years of this century, that Dr. A. T. Robertson, professor at Southern Baptist Seminary as well as a contributing editor of the *Baptist Argus* of Louisville, Kentucky, suggested to Dr. J. N. Prestridge, its founder and editor-in-chief, that he issue each year a "Baptist World Outlook" number. This was done with considerable success and wide acclaim. Finally, early in 1904 Dr. Robertson conceived the idea of a world gathering of Baptists in London, England. He put his idea into the form of an editorial in the *Baptist Argus* after conferring with Dr. E. Y. Mullins and Dr. Prestridge and securing their full approval.

Marked copies of this editorial by Dr. Robertson were then sent to Baptist leaders all over the world. Dr. Prestridge continued to advance the idea of a Baptist World Congress, and soon Baptists everywhere responded with enthusiasm to the idea.

The eminent Dr. J. H. Shakespeare, of London, editor of the *Baptist Times and Freeman*, threw himself with unstinting energy into this endeavor. The issue of all these efforts was the first Baptist World Congress, which met in London, England, in July, 1905, and the establishment of the Baptist World Alliance.

Dr. E. Y. Mullins, Dr. W. O. Carver, Dr. C. S. Gardner, and Dr. A. T. Robertson were present on this memorable occasion. Dr. Robertson was quite fittingly made a member of the first

---

[12] Louie D. Newton, "Baptist World Alliance," *Encyclopedia of Southern Baptists*, I, 127–28.

executive committee of the Baptist World Alliance. He served on that committee from 1905 to 1923. In that year Dr. E. Y. Mullins, president of Southern Seminary, was elected president of the Baptist World Alliance at the third congress of Baptists at Stockholm, Sweden. He served with distinction from 1923 to 1928.[13]

Since the founding of the Baptist World Alliance, Southern Baptists have been most ardent supporters of this worldwide fellowship. Through the years the faculty and administration of Southern Seminary have shown a strong interest in its affairs and development. Four Southern Baptists have been elected president of the Baptist World Alliance: E. Y. Mullins (1923–28), George W. Truett (1934–39), C. Oscar Johnson (1947–50), and Theodore F. Adams (1955–60). Two of these leaders, E. Y. Mullins and C. Oscar Johnson, were graduates of Southern Baptist Theological Seminary, as was also Dr. Walter Oliver Lewis, who from 1939 to 1948 was the second general Secretary of the BWA.

At the suggestion of Dr. J. L. Burrows, an alumnus of Southern, the faculty of the Seminary decided in the fall of 1906 to inaugurate Founders' Day. The birthday of James P. Boyce, the first chairman of the faculty, was designated for that purpose.

Dr. Burrows was elected to deliver an address on the first Founders' Day on Dr. James Petigru Boyce, while Dr. William H. Whitsitt, since 1901 professor of philosophy at the University of Richmond, was chosen to speak on John A. Broadus. The first observance took place on January 11, 1907.[14]

This day of remembrance has been observed ever since. Founders' Day at Southern Seminary has been among the finest days in the experience of the Seminary family. Such days keep fresh

[13] F. Townley Lord, *Baptist World Fellowship* (Nashville: Broadman Press, 1955), pp. 1–5. Cf. A. T. Robertson, "The Real Origin of the BWA," *Review and Expositor*, XXV (October, 1928), 469–72; L. D. Newton, *op. cit.*; Robert G. Torbet, *A History of the Baptists* (Philadelphia: Judson Press, 1950), pp. 188–215.

[14] *Faculty Minutes*, book 3, p. 153.

the memory of the virile and often agonizing struggles of the past and are a constant source of reflection and new vision for the future. "What thou hast inherited from thy fathers, conquer it in order to possess it!" This word from the poet laureate Friedrich von Schiller, whose complete works Dr. Boyce had in his private library, ought to be inscribed upon the heart of every alumnus and friend of the Seminary.

From the day that Dr. Mullins began his work at Southern in 1899, the idea of an adequate endowment for the Seminary had been constantly on his mind. With the rapid increase of churches in the Southern Baptist Convention, the anticipated growth of the student body, and the need of capturing the imagination of the friends of the Seminary by some bold and forward-looking venture, the movement toward an adequate endowment was highly desirable. Therefore, at the request of Dr. Mullins and his colleagues, the Twentieth Century Endowment Campaign was recommended by the executive committee to the Board of Trustees early in 1902.[15] To expedite matters Dr. E. Y. Mullins induced the messengers of the Southern Baptist Convention of 1903 to appoint a committee which was to study the needs of the Seminary.

As so often in the school's history, the Norton family of Louisville came forward with a gift of fifty thousand dollars to get the campaign under way. Mr. Mellen Bray, an influential layman of Dr. Mullins' former church at Newton Centre, Massachusetts, sent a check for five thousand for the increase of the endowment.

By May, 1907, President Mullins was able to report a large gift of sixty thousand dollars from Theodore Harris, a Louisville banker and loyal trustee and member of the executive committee of the Seminary. The faculty requested that the Board of Trustees designate this gift for the endowment of the chair of Old Testament Interpretation. Needless to say these large gifts brought to the members of the Seminary family great joy for God's gracious leadings.

---

[15] *Minutes of the Executive Committee,* book 1, p. 101.

The goal of the Twentieth Century Endowment Campaign had been to raise the sum of $500,000. Before the Jubilee Campaign had ended, the Seminary's endowment had been increased to $600,000. By 1919 it had been increased to a total of $1,336,-000, and by 1928, the end of Dr. E. Y. Mullins' term of office, it had reached a total of $1,803,000.

One of the results of this endowment campaign were increases in faculty salaries. By 1911 the executive committee recommended that the salaries of professors be increased from $3,000 to $3,500 per year, such increase, however, to be made gradually. The salary of the president was to be raised to $5,000, but even in his case such increase was to be effected only gradually as the funds of the Seminary might justify.

However, both President Mullins and the trustees realized that the faculty of only six teachers was utterly inadequate for as large a student body as Southern Seminary enrolled around 1900. In that year Dr. George Boardman Eager (1847–1929) was elected professor of biblical introduction and associate professor of practical theology. He served in that capacity until 1920, when he retired.

Dr. Eager was a man of broad and generous culture and distinguished, even elegant, bearing who had an unusual gift of friendship. He had held pastorates in Lexington, Virginia; Mobile, Alabama; and Montgomery, Alabama.

Dr. W. O. Carver believed Dr. Eager to have been "the most distinguished member of a distinguished family of denominational workers and leaders." Mrs. Carver used to say to her husband that the Seminary could well afford to pay Dr. Eager's salary, if only to give the students a chance to see a Christian gentleman in the flesh.

Mrs. Eager was her husband's equal as a lady of distinctive tastes and a woman of breeding. Before her marriage she had been an Episcopalian. Along with Mrs. Maud Reynolds McLure, Mrs. S. E. Woody, Eliza Broadus, and Fannie E. S. Heck, Mrs. George B. Eager "more than any other person was responsible for the adoption of the Home and the authorization of the W.M.U. Training School," [16] now the Carver School of Missions and Social Work.

As a teacher Dr. Eager was none too successful. Nor was he ever very popular with students, though they liked his easy examinations.

The other members of the faculty—Sampey, Robertson, Dargan, Carver, McGlothlin, and Mullins—made up for what was lacking in the less able members of the teaching staff. Dr. E. Y. Mullins reveled in teaching theology. His students were delighted by the range of his thinking, the clarity of his expression, and the form in which he clothed his ideas. He was an able interpreter of the drama of redemption. Christian experience was the focal point of his theological reflection, although in that he was perhaps unduly influenced by Schleiermacher and William James.

Mullins, despite the distractions of administration, was ever busy with his pen. As editor-in-chief of the *Review and Expositor*, a writer for other journals, and a welcome lecturer on college and seminary campuses, he made a singular contribution to sound thinking and Christian statesmanship.

At the first session of the Baptist World Congress in London in 1905 Dr. Mullins gave an address on "The Theological Trend." Dr. J. H. Rushbrooke said of it: "He arose to speak, a man practically unknown east of the Atlantic, and sat down with a world reputation." This address appeared in the fall issue of the new Seminary journal.

During the same year Dr. Mullins published a provocative and informing text in Christian apologetics under the title *Why Is Christianity True?* In its 450 pages the author grappled with current issues and the problematic of the Christian faith. He explored the bearing of the faith on the newer disciplines of psychology, sociology, biology, and the questions arising out of the interaction of Christian beliefs with contemporary philosophical tendencies.

---

[16] George A. Carver, "Carver School of Missions and Social Work," *Encyclopedia of Southern Baptists*, I, 237.

Dr. Edwin Charles Dargan (1852–1930) had come to the faculty in 1892 when John A. Broadus was president. He was in every way one of the choice teachers of the Seminary and was an instant success. His background, his widely recognized ability as a preacher, and his denominational standing commended him both to the trustees and his colleagues. Dargan came at a considerable sacrifice in salary, since he had been pastor of the influential Citadel Square Baptist Church in Charleston, South Carolina. His initial title was that of associate professor of homiletics and Latin theology. But within two years of his coming to Southern his second field was changed to biblical theology.

In 1905 Dr. Dargan published his *Ecclesiology*, the best work in this field by a Baptist author up to that time. The first, though smaller, edition of this work had appeared in 1897. The revised edition of 1905 was considerably enlarged, running to nearly seven hundred pages. His next work, *Society, Kingdom, and Church*, appeared in 1907. These works show historical perspective, keen judgment, and a fine style.

Dr. Dargan left the Seminary in 1907 for a pastorate in Macon, Georgia, much to his own regret, for he loved teaching. A family problem lay behind this decision. But he continued writing, and between 1907 and 1912 he brought out a *magnum opus*, his two-volume *A History of Preaching*. Its enduring quality is attested by the fact that it is still being used widely as a text.

A smaller work, *The Bible Our Inheritance*, appeared in Spanish translation in 1936 as *La Biblia Nuestra Herencia*. Still another work, *The Art of Preaching in the Light of History*, delivered as the Holland Lectures at Southwestern Baptist Theological Seminary in Texas in 1921, first appeared in a series of articles in the *Review and Expositor*.

Dargan's surrender of his professorship was a real loss to the Seminary. After a lapse of years in the pastorate in Georgia, Dr. Dargan became editor of publications of the Southern Baptist Sunday School Board in Nashville. There he carried on with distinction for many years until his death in 1930. His extensive library was given to the Sunday School Board, forming the nucleus of the library of the Southern Baptist Historical Society. It is now called the Dargan-Carver Library, containing forty-five thousand books and a large collection of archival material.

Dr. William Joseph McGlothlin (1867–1933), of Tennessee, came to Southern as a student in 1891. He was a graduate of Bethel, where he had established a splendid record. He secured the B.A. and M.A. degrees from that college in 1889 and 1891, and received the Th.M. degree from Southern Seminary in 1894 and the Ph.D. degree from Berlin University under Adolf von Harnack in 1901.

After teaching in public schools in Tennessee, at Bethel College, and at the Baptist Institute at Bardstown, Kentucky, McGlothlin became professor of church history at Southern Seminary. McGlothlin was tall and well proportioned; his red hair matched his complexion. He was a friend of Dr. Carver, with whom he had roomed at the Seminary during his middler year. They remained friends for life.

At first McGlothlin taught Greek and Hebrew and soon won the respect of his colleagues and students. He was a superb teacher as well as a hard taskmaster in teaching the rudiments of the biblical languages. In 1896, when Whitsitt became president, McGlothlin was elected assistant professor of Old Testament interpretation. A year later, however, he was asked to teach biblical introduction while retaining a partial interest in Old Testament interpretation.

The departure from the Seminary of Dr. Whitsitt in 1899 changed the picture once again, for now there was a vacancy in the field of church history. The faculty had decided to prevail upon Dr. Mullins to teach church history, and as we have seen, it seemed that he would. But Mullins' first love was theology; therefore, he himself asked the faculty that they allow him to teach in that field. It was then necessary to find a man for church history, and McGlothlin seemed to be the man for the place. He was consequently appointed professor of ecclesiastical history and associate professor of Old Testament interpretation. After

1915 Dr. McGlothlin's work was limited to church history, and he taught that subject with considerable effectiveness until he left the Seminary in 1919 to become president of Furman University.

With Whitsitt and Harnack as his great mental tutors in church history, Dr. McGlothlin's work in that field might have been more significant than it was. Dr. W. O. Carver felt that McGlothlin's bent for denominational leadership might have had something to do with the fact that his literary output remained comparatively small. Dr. Norman W. Cox in a Founders' Day address has summed the matter up as follows:

Dr. McGlothlin, superb and great teacher that he was, was not the author of great works as were Doctors Broadus, Dargan, Robertson, Mullins and others who have served or who now serve on this faculty. This was not because he lacked the gift of literary expression. His diction and style were clear, terse and pungent. He possessed abundant resources of material from which great books could have been written. I believe his failure to create books was due to three things. He was absorbed in his work as a student and teacher. He lacked the compelling inner urge that is the fruit of more imagination than he possessed. Unfortunately he left the Seminary just at the time of life, fifty-two, when he was ready to do his best writing. His entrance upon administrative work, as the President of Furman University, was a new venture in his experience. This doubtless dissipated his writing impulses.[17]

This measured judgment of Dr. Cox was shared by others who knew McGlothlin intimately. However, he did write a number of books which are still worth reading. They were *History of Glen Creek Baptist Church* (1900); *Die Bernischen Wiedertäufer* (1902); *A Guide to the Study of Church History* (1908); *Kentucky Baptists, the Seminary, and Alien Immersion* (1908); *Baptist Confessions of Faith* (1910); *A Vital Ministry* (1913); *Infant Baptism in History* (1915); *The Course of Christian History* (1917); and *Baptist Beginnings in Education, A His-*

---

[17] Norman W. Cox, "W. J. McGlothlin, Scholar and Teacher," *Review and Expositor*, XXXIX (April, 1942), 158.

tory of Furman University (1926). Of these works McGlothlin's *Baptist Confessions of Faith* has been most widely used and quoted by church historians.

Dr. McGlothlin was president of the Southern Baptist Convention from 1930 to 1932. He died in May, 1933, after an automobile accident.

Dr. W. O. Carver, a bosom friend of McGlothlin, became a member of the faculty of Southern Seminary in 1896. Together with Sampey and Robertson, he belongs to the famous triumvirate of the second generation of teachers in the Seminary who served a total of 150 years on the faculty. Each of these three worthies made signal contributions to the life of the Seminary as teacher, writer, and denominational leader.

Dr. Carver's life spanned the years between 1868 and 1954—nearly the whole period of the Seminary's one hundred years' history. In the preceding pages we have often had occasion to refer to his pervasive influence and his mature judgment on the Seminary's history. Like Broadus and Robertson, Dr. Carver brought the school with which he was so long connected world renown. A host of missionaries on the more than thirty mission fields of Southern Baptists remember their professor of missions and comparative religion with gratitude and delight.

In a posthumously published work, *Out of His Treasure*, William Owen Carver described his entry into the world in these words:

I was born in the home of my Carver grandparents, April 10, 1868, three years and one day after Lee's surrender at Appomatox. Thus I entered upon life in a crisis in the life of America. Throughout my life I have seen much and learned a little about crises, transitions, and eras; learned that life is always under tension; that progress is achieved by adjustment among tensions, and understanding gained by resolving paradoxes. In the course of my years I have seen, and shared in, more than one epochal transition in the life of our country.[18]

---

[18] William Owen Carver, *Out of His Treasure* (Nashville: Broadman Press, 1956), p. 1.

Carver grew up in humble circumstances. A log cabin was the home where his parents began their married life. It was a small farm which they tilled, enduring the hardships of Reconstruction days. Despite many handicaps Carver secured a good education, attending country schools with superior teachers and later being privately tutored in Latin, algebra, and physics. After one year at Doyle College he entered Richmond College in Richmond, Virginia.

Here in the "dominion state" W. O. Carver came into a different atmosphere from that which had prevailed in the section of Tennessee from which he came. Dr. J. R. Graves, according to Carver, "ecclesiastically a narrow dogmatist and the supreme authority for most Baptists in a half dozen States," provided him with the first doctrinal book he ever read. It was Graves's *Intercommunion of Churches Unscriptural.* The *Tennessee Baptist,* of which the doughty Landmarker was the spirited editor, was the only religious weekly in the Carver home. Carver's laconic comment on this circumstance was, "Thus I was brought up 'after the most straitest sect of our religion,' with Graves the high priest of my orthodoxy." [19]

Most of Carver's teachers at Richmond were able men, both scholars and active churchmen. One of them, E. B. Smith, was a veritable genius in mathematics, and Carver was greatly impressed by him. From this school Carver received in due time the A.B. and M.A. degrees, the latter degree being conferred in 1891. W. O. Carver received his Th.D. degree from Southern in 1896. His dissertation, handwritten, dealt with "Gentile Opposition to the Jews in the First Century." He had entered the Seminary in 1891.

The minutes of the trustees' meeting at Chattanooga, Tennessee, on May 7, 1896, record these words:

We recommend the employment of Mr. W. O. Carver as an Assistant Instructor in the Seminary at a salary of $600.00. Mr. Carver is an ordained Minister, a native of Tennessee, a Master of Arts of

---

[19] *Ibid.,* p. 25.

Richmond College, a doctor of theology of the Seminary and has had experience as a teacher.[20]

Thus began an auspicious career that was to end only in 1954 when the Lord called home his servant.

Two years after Carver's initial appointment he became assistant professor of New Testament interpretation and homiletics with an increase in salary of two hundred dollars a year. When Dr. Mullins became president, Carver was asked to concentrate on missions, but he continued teaching polemic theology, which after 1900 was changed to apologetics. In the catalogue of 1900 Dr. Carver is listed as professor of comparative religion and missions and associate professor in New Testament interpretation. This designation continued until 1923, when he was simply listed as professor of comparative religion and missions.

One interesting item at this point of the story is that Southern Seminary nearly lost Dr. Carver during the first decade of this century. Behind this lay Dr. Dargan's leaving in 1907 and partly the desire of Dr. E. Y. Mullins to draw Dr. W. T. Whitley, a British Baptist historian, to the Seminary faculty.

Dr. Whitley had in 1906 delivered the Gay Lectures under the title "The Story of Missions on Five Continents." His survey of the movement of the Christian gospel through the centuries had been quite impressive. Several of the members of the faculty seriously considered the wisdom of inviting Dr. Whitley to come to Southern. Hence, when Dr. Dargan left the chair of homiletics, Dr. Mullins and Dr. Robertson wondered whether Dr. Carver might be willing to change from missions to homiletics. They actually proposed this to their colleague, but it made no appeal to him whatever, nor did he evince the slightest inclination for such a weighty step. When Dr. Mullins seemed disposed to press the matter, Dr. Carver plainly told him that if he and the faculty seriously desired to call Dr. Whitley to occupy the chair of missions, he would resign and leave.

Dr. Carver gave two reasons for his adamant refusal. First,

---

[20] *Minutes of the Board of Trustees*, book 2, p. 211.

homiletics did not seem to offer to him a large enough challenge for fresh research and original thinking; second, he felt that the professor of homiletics ought to exemplify his teaching in his practice, that he ought to be a good preacher before he engaged in teaching others how to preach effectively. Since he did not believe he was qualified on this last point, Carver felt justified in saying no to Dr. Mullins' proposal.

In the end both Dr. Mullins and Dr. Robertson desisted from their plan and assured Dr. Carver that they had had no intention of displacing him unless he were fully committed to teaching the art of preaching.

Carver published four books between 1903 and 1910. The first book bore the title *History of New Salem Church* (1903); the second was *Baptist Opportunity* (1908); *Missions in the Plan of the Ages* (1909) was the third; and *Missions and Modern Thought* appeared in 1910.

Of these four works the third, *Missions in the Plan of the Ages*, has come out in many editions, the last being that of 1951, an indication of its abiding worth and influence. The same is true with regard to his *The Course of Christian Missions*, first published in 1932.

During the first decade of the century Dr. Carver was in the poorest of health, requiring a leave in 1900 and 1907. It is amazing that he accomplished so much in so short a time. Dr. Carver had intended pursuing advanced studies at the University of Berlin during his sabbatical of 1907–08. But illness shattered his plans. Yet he visited Gustav Warneck, pioneer of missions at Halle University, and met other distinguished men of affairs. And during this trying period, hindered by bodily weakness, he wrote his *Missions in the Plan of the Ages*. It was published by Fleming H. Revell Company. Dr. Carver always considered this book his "first real book and the first of eight dealing with missions."

Missions and Modern Thought, published by Macmillan in 1910, was also a fruit of Dr. Carver's stay in Europe. This work was not as successful as *Missions in the Plan of the Ages*, yet when it first appeared the critics received it with considerable interest and even enthusiasm. Carver had written this book for a prize competition of *The Christian*, a British journal, which Carver avidly read while living in London in 1908.

Missions and Modern Thought, appearing as it did during the year 1910, when the first modern World Missions Conference met in Edinburgh, Scotland, confronted the crucial issues of the missionary enterprise. Carver sharply discerned the trends of the times and the spirit of the age.

The first chapter, "Outlook on the Situation," was a clarion call to clear thinking. Carver was quite aware of the "acids of modernity" that were then eating into the very substance of contemporary life. He saw both the good and the bad, the seeds of promise and the seeds of corruption at work in the world around 1910.

The nineteenth century, Carver maintained, was in many ways an iconoclastic century. It destroyed the scientific theories inherited from the sixteenth and seventeenth centuries. It meanwhile constructed its own theories, "until it came to be a maxim of science that no book more than ten years old is worth shelf-room." [21]

Carver believed that he could discern a tremendous spirit of self-sufficiency in certain scientific circles, while in the realm of philosophy a spirit of dissolution seemed to be at work. He diagnosed the situation in these words:

Philosophy [at the time of Hegel] found itself in the grasp of a new spirit, took the wings of imaginative logic, and reached wonderful heights of speculation concerning the Absolute. But just when it seemed to be perched upon the summit of perfection it dropped to ruin, and the last half of the century knew only forms of eclecticism. With the turn of the new century we find philosophic thought under the lead of a new conception, calling itself "Pragmatism," and "Humanism," which is, after all, the negation of philosophy in the true sense, and only an effort to make man content with a theory compre-

---

[21] W. O. Carver, *Missions and Modern Thought* (New York: The Macmillan Company, 1910), p. 9.

hending human life and the present order, and to stop with that. To be sure, this is leading the way to a philosophy which will base itself on the spiritual experiences of the soul, but we are still without a philosophy.[22]

Yet Dr. Carver in 1910, amid the most conflicting tendencies of the age and the lowly state of theological thinking, discerned the movement of the Holy Spirit in a broken and unbelieving world. He was able to discern, for instance, a new ethical sensitivity, a yearning for practical religion, and a deepened sense of the bonds that united or might unite all men into a wholesome social community.

Confession of sin, devotion to righteousness, yearning for the realization of the Kingdom are some of the marks of this revival in Japan and India, as well as of the notable work of grace in Manchuria and in China. Only let these fundamental effects of the Spirit continue and multitudes of new disciples will be won to Christ.[23]

Carver also noted that in theological seminaries, as well as in universities and colleges, lecture courses and even professorships in missions were being established, all of which seemed to suggest a new interest in the things of the spirit and world missions. The Student Volunteer Movement received Dr. Carver's hearty endorsement, and he often attended its sessions and world gatherings.

Dr. Carver welcomed the fact that the day of polemic theology was past. And while many Christians still believed, and rightly so, "that the content and nature of the church's mission . . . was to carry a certain body of doctrines and forms into so much of the world as Christianity might claim," he argued for a wider and deeper conception of missions. That meant to Carver the realization that Christianity must be conceived "as a redemptive factor in the total life of humanity, with the goal of a redeemed race. That conception belongs to the developing con-

---

[22] *Ibid.*
[23] *Ibid.*, p. 24.

ceptions of race, society, history and religion. Christianity is now conceived as living rather than established, as growing rather than fixed, and, by consequence, capable of almost indefinite adaptation to environment." [24]

For forty-eight years Dr. William Owen Carver labored as a teacher of missions and comparative religion at Southern Baptist Theological Seminary. Until the early twenties he also was associate professor of New Testament. Even after his retirement in 1943 he was called back into service in 1947 as acting head of the department of theology. Until his death in 1954 he continued as professor emeritus, ever accessible to troubled students, whom he helped with the problems which they brought to him.

During his long career Dr. Carver engaged in many controversies, discomfiting his foes and challenging his friends. He was ever eager to be reconciled to his adversaries but held staunchly to the truth as he saw it. As counselor of the Foreign Mission Board, as visitor to the mission fields in 1922–23, as a promoter of the Woman's Missionary Union Training School now bearing his name, Dr. Carver rendered inestimable service through the years. The faculty eagerly sought his advice, missionaries abroad praised his sagacity and understanding, and the best students in the Seminary always knew his worth.

When he published his *The Glory of God in the Christian Calling*, a study of Paul's letter to the Ephesians, the literary editor of *The Christian Century*, Professor W. E. Garrison, acknowledged that Carver's exegesis was stimulating to the extreme and that his scholarship had not abated with advancing years.

"Among the teachers at the Seminary that left a lasting impression on me," wrote Professor Dale Moody, "none did more than Dr. Carver. His interest in the theology of all Christian groups opened a wider world of thought and vision for me that remains the most important factor in my life. In many ways he represented the whole history of the Seminary—loyalty to the

---

[24] *Ibid.*, pp. 11–12.

Baptist cause and concern for the whole world. The longer his memory lingers the greater his soul appears." [25]

When in the spring of 1953 Dr. Carver lectured at Central Baptist Theological Seminary in Kansas City, Kansas, its president, Dr. William W. Adams, wrote, "Never have I known anything that went beyond the visit to our campus of Dr. and Mrs. Carver. He lifted the entire intellectual and spiritual level of our seminary family. Faculty and students alike agree to that. Never shall we forget his closing message, given on his eighty-fifth birthday." [26]

The June, 1954, issue of *The Tie* recorded this news: "Dr. William Owen Carver, professor emeritus of comparative religion and missions, died May 24, 1954, at the Kentucky Baptist Hospital, Louisville." Thus a rich life, full of the fruits of the Spirit of God, came to a victorious end and a new beginning in God's eternal presence.

Dr. Archibald Thomas Robertson, Carver's older colleague, has already been mentioned in this and previous chapters. Among all the teachers of Southern Seminary, past and present, Dr. Robertson attained to perhaps the highest stature as a writer and scholar. His forty-five books, numerous articles in journals and encyclopedias, and his *opus magnum*, *A Grammar of the Greek New Testament in the Light of Historical Research*, published in 1914, bespeak his diligence, scholarly erudition, and enormous capacity for hard work.

The big *Grammar*, a volume of 1,367 pages in the first edition and of 1,500 in the fifth, received the acclaim of scholars all over the world. Professor Adolf Deissmann of Berlin University praised Dr. Robertson's *Grammar* in words of highest esteem. An expert in Greek papyri, Professor Edwin Mayser, also of Germany, hailed Robertson as a master. Professor F. W. Grossheide of Amsterdam's Free University compared Robertson with Melanchthon, the friend of Luther. American colleagues in the field of New Testament like Professor Edgar J. Goodspeed of

---

[25] Letter of September 18, 1958.
[26] *The Tie*, XXI (September, 1953), 2.

the University of Chicago and Professor Benjamin W. Bacon of Yale University were unanimous in praising the philological erudition embodied in the *Grammar*. Dr. Henry Cadbury, later of Harvard University, wrote:

It is not difficult for the reader who has made his way through this formidable volume to appreciate something of the author's own sense of rejoicing at the completion of what is practically a life work. Here are assembled . . . and classified the whole linguistic phenomena of the New Testament. This is not only the most modern of such grammars; it is much the completest.[27]

A recent Founders' Day speaker, Dr. Harold Graves of California, facetiously referred to the remark of a Catholic scholar in Rome who is reported to have said that he wondered how the apostle Paul could ever have written his epistles without Dr. Robertson's big *Grammar*.

But only those close to Dr. Robertson realized the vast labors which the writing and publication of this *Grammar* entailed. At times Dr. Robertson nearly despaired of ever getting it published. He borrowed against his life insurance policies and from other sources and still was unable to meet the demands of the publishers. One day he said to Dr. Carver that this venture would utterly ruin him. "I wish the whole thing were in the bottom of the Atlantic Ocean."

At this crucial juncture Dr. Mullins, realizing the great importance to the Seminary of Dr. Robertson's work, came to the rescue. A publishing fund was authorized by the trustees to the amount of ten thousand dollars, later supplemented by an additional four thousand, which made possible the eventual publication of Robertson's *Grammar*. Though he had to assign all royalties from his great work for the reimbursing of this fund, Dr. Robertson derived deep satisfaction from the wide acceptance of the effort on which he had spent twenty-six years of his life.

---

[27] Henry J. Cadbury, *The Harvard Thological Review*, IX (January, 1916), 138–40.

But Dr. Robertson was more than a scholar of repute. In his classroom, at pastors' conferences, at the Northfield gatherings, and on special lectureships he engaged in the task of faithfully interpreting and illuminating the New Testament, which he knew so well and loved so much.

As a teacher in the classroom Dr. Robertson used, as a rule, the recitation method. This tended to keep his students wide awake, but to many of his best students it often seemed a waste of time, especially in view of the large classes of more than two hundred students. Robertson was at his best in his seminars. Here students from many lands came to know him intimately and learned to appreciate the wide range of his learning, the keenness of his intellect, and the depth of his Christian convictions.

Dr. Robertson was a progressive convervative. During the Whitsitt controversy he stood valiantly for freedom of research within the gospel of Jesus Christ that he believed with all his heart and mind. When, in the early twenties, ardent fundamentalists within the Southern Baptist Convention sought to impose an anti-evolutionist creed upon the Seminary faculty, both Robertson and Carver adamantly refused to yield to this unseemly pressure.

In his exegesis Dr. Robertson was simple, direct, and often forceful. When a real textual difficulty confronted him, he refused to evade the issue. Though Southern Baptists firmly believe in "eternal security," Robertson squarely faced up to what Hebrews 6:4–6 has to say on the matter. He wrote, "It is a terrific picture and cannot be toned down. The one ray of light comes in verses 8 to 12. The present active infinitive *anakanizo* . . . with *adunaton* bluntly denies the possibility of renewal for apostates from Christ."

Was Jesus truly human? Dr. Robertson had no doubt about it whatever. "He began life in the flesh as a child; he was a real child. Would he laugh? Would he cry? Would he jump? Some pious people say he never laughed. Did he ever play? Did he afterwards like children's games as one that enjoyed them for himself?"

Students who were overly eager to abandon their studies in order to be able to preach heard this warning from Doctor Bob: "Though possessed of so much knowledge (at 12) Jesus did not enter on his life work at once. No posing as a boy preacher. He goes back to the shop, making plows and living with the birds, waiting his time." [28]

Generations of Southern Seminary students recall with delight Dr. Robertson's whimsical references to Rabbi Smelfungus and how Jesus evidently taught without a permit from that representative of a stodgy piety. The strangest stories are still being heard of how Dr. Robertson exhibited special skill in taking the starch out of prissy or forward students.

But the great New Testament scholar seemed happiest when he stood before a congregation pointing men and women to the Lord Jesus Christ as their only Master and Saviour.

Dr. Robertson has bequeathed to Southern Baptist Seminary a noble and rich heritage: an example of utter faithfulness through nearly fifty years of teaching, writing, and lecturing. How he accomplished so much is still the wonder of many of his former students and of his successors in the field of New Testament at Southern Seminary.

Another scholar of competence under Dr. Mullins' administration was Dr. Charles Spurgeon Gardner, who in 1907 succeeded Dr. Dargan in the chair of homiletics and Christian sociology. Prior to his coming to the Seminary as a teacher, Dr. Gardner had served with distinction in several Baptist churches of the South. An outstanding preacher for twenty-three years, Gardner was also a man who knew his way among books. He "taught ecclesiology with a difference," as Dr. Jesse B. Weatherspoon has put it, introducing his students to the larger implications of Christian churchmanship.

When Dr. Gardner began teaching at Southern in 1907, America was astir with the spirit of social reform. In that year Walter Rauschenbusch published his epoch-making book *Christianity*

---

[28] A. T. Robertson, unpublished lectures in New Testament interpretation (1928), p. 39.

and the Social Crisis. Dr. Gardner, a progressive evangelical, was fully aware of the great changes going on in the society of his day. Consequently he strongly emphasized the relevance of sociological insight, psychological acumen, and ethical motivation to life-centered preaching.

Dominant in Gardner's thinking was the kingdom of God as the supreme and comprehensive ideal of a Christian social order. Only under the sovereign reign of God's love and grace may man's total nature find fulfilment and redemption.

Dr. Herbert Gezork, now president of Andover-Newton Theological School and one of the last graduate students to receive his doctorate under Professor Gardner, has spoken of Gardner's superior scholarship, the serenity of his mind, and his ability to probe deeply into the problems of Christian thought and action.

Dr. Weatherspoon, who became Dr. Gardner's successor in 1929, has credited his predecessor with having pioneered in at least three distinct areas at Southern Seminary: sociology of Christianity, religious education, and psychology of religion.[29]

In a Founders' Day address of 1945, Dr. Gardner, then eighty-five years of age, delivered a forceful message on "The Seminary as a Factor in the Kingdom of God." He called for open-minded conservatism in a time of rapid change, practical efficiency in churchmanship, a lofty view of the Bible, and the advocacy of a universal gospel centered in God's supreme revelation in Jesus Christ.

Space forbids to speak in greater detail about other faculty members, a number of whom came to teach at Southern after 1920. Among them were Professors Hersey W. Davis, Frank M. Powell, Kyle M. Yates, J. McKee Adams, Inman Johnson, and Harold W. Tribble. All of them have made their contribution to the life of the Seminary, some of them rising to eminent stature as writers or administrators. Dr. Yates is the author of several popular books and is now distinguished professor of Bible at

---

[29] J. B. Weatherspoon, "Charles Spurgeon Gardner," *Review and Expositor,* LII (April, 1955), 190.

Baylor University. Dr. Tribble was president of Andover-Newton Theological School from 1947 to 1950 and has been, since 1950, president of Wake Forest College at Winston-Salem, North Carolina.

Dr. Tribble, in a Founders' Day address in 1952, summarized the achievements of Dr. Edgar Y. Mullins, his mentor, in this fashion:

I think a good insight into the administrative ability of a school president may be found also in the ability and productivity of the faculty that he maintains. I shall give only one set of figures on this score. From 1859 to 1898 the faculty of the Seminary wrote 22 books; from 1899 to 1928 they wrote 89 books; from 1929 to 1951 they produced 57 books.[30]

Soon after the fiftieth Jubilee of the Seminary in 1909, a climactic event in the history of the school, the trustees realized that the noise and bustle of the downtown campus interfered with the proper function of the Seminary. It was therefore decided in 1910 to look toward the eventual removal of the school to a more suitable location. But it was not until 1921 that property of fifty-three acres was acquired in the Crescent Hill section of Louisville. Ground-breaking for the new Norton Hall, the present administration building, occurred on November 29, 1923. Meanwhile, the cornerstone of the Western Baptist Theological Seminary, then in the possession of the First Baptist Church of Covington, Kentucky, had been secured, and on November 5, 1924, George W. Norton laid it on the beautiful new campus. In the spring of 1925 Mullins Hall, the new men's dormitory, was started, and on March 26 and 27, 1926, the Seminary moved from Broadway to "The Beeches" at 2825 Lexington Road, six miles from the old location.

The campus of Southern Baptist Seminary is both spacious and beautiful. Its buildings are in Georgian colonial style, and they are modern and well equipped. Adjoining the Seminary

---

[30] Harold W. Tribble, "Edgar Young Mullins," *Review and Expositor*, XLIX (April, 1952), 132.

campus is the Carver School of Missions and Social Work. The Seminary is within easy reach of downtown Louisville and near the Crescent Hill and St. Matthews business districts.

While Southern Baptists had contributed only about $50,-000 for the erection of the four buildings at Fifth and Broadway, they rallied to the support of the Seminary, contributing about $800,000 for the building of the new campus, the cost of which ran considerably over the $2,000,000 mark before all the projected buildings had been completed.

The old library on the southwest corner of Broadway and Fifth Street was sold for $150,000, an increase of over $130,000 above its original purchase price. The other property was leased for ninety-nine years at an annual income of about $37,500. When the new campus was occupied, a debt of around $1,000,000 remained still to be paid. It was to prove quite a burden when the great depression of 1929 ushered in an era of gloom in American economic history, but resourceful leaders like Dr. John R. Sampey, the successor of Dr. Mullins after 1928, and Dr. Gaines S. Dobbins, the treasurer of the Seminary, liquidated that fearful debt before the depression had ended.

During the time that the new campus was being projected and built, Dr. E. Y. Mullins had also been elected president of the Baptist World Alliance at its sessions in Stockholm in 1923. The duties which this office and the building campaign imposed upon the president of the Seminary were an almost unbearable strain. In March, 1925, he underwent a major operation. He needed a vacation badly, but the necessities of the campaign made that impossible. Shortly after the occupancy of the new campus, Dr. Mullins had to undertake still another journey to Europe in the interest of the Baptist World Alliance and the stricken churches of the Continent. It was his seventh trip to Europe since he had assumed the presidency of Southern Seminary. His whole tour, while terribly exhausting, was one continuous triumphal journey. Everywhere Baptists received him gladly. While in Lodz, Poland, he became seriously ill, but received wonderful care in the Peabody-Montgomery Memorial

Hospital and was able to complete his journey. But he returned to America weakened in body and weary of spirit. When the Southern Baptist Convention met in Louisville in the spring of 1927, Dr. Mullins lay ill, unable to present the new campus, the gift of his brethren, to the Convention.

The academic year of 1927–28 moved along with Dr. Mullins still at the helm of the Seminary. Eagerly he looked forward to the sessions of the Baptist World Alliance in June of 1928, at which time he would preside and deliver the presidential address. But illness again overtook him, and his address had to be delivered by Dr. George W. Truett of Dallas, with Dr. Mullins remaining in Louisville. The address was a superb defense of the Baptist position on religious liberty.

During the summer of 1928 and into the fall of that year Dr. Mullins lingered on, his family and friends quietly hoping against hope that he might yet recover. He greatly enjoyed seeing the Levering Gymnasium erected on the new campus, but he had to reduce his activities to the minimum. His last piece of business was to deed to the Seminary a lot within two squares of the school on which the president's home was someday to be built.

On November 23, 1928, at high noon, Dr. Mullins died, completing his earthly pilgrimage in the city of Louisville, which shortly before his death had declared him its first citizen. His monument in chaste Vermont granite of Grecian Doric design in Cave Hill Cemetery records the eventful career of Edgar Young Mullins, the fourth president of the Southern Baptist Theological Seminary (1899–1928), president of the Southern Baptist Convention (1921–24), president of the Baptist World Alliance (1923–28), preacher, teacher, scholar, administrator, Christian statesman, world citizen, and servant of God.

With Dr. Mullins' going an epoch in the Seminary's history came to an end, an epoch full of signal achievements and victories. Ere a year had passed, the great stock market crash of October, 1929, had plunged the people of the United States into one of its greatest economic disasters. But in God's providence the Seminary also survived this period of trouble.

9

Sampey, Fuller, and McCall

JOHN R. SAMPEY was in many ways a most remarkable man. Of Methodist, Anglican, and Huguenot background, Dr. Sampey in time became involved in a world-encircling ministry of preaching, writing, and teaching.

Sampey was born September 27, 1863, at Fort Deposit, Lowndes County, Alabama, and died, at a ripe old age and laden with honors, on August 18, 1946, at Louisville, Kentucky. Converted at fourteen and licensed to preach at sixteen, he delivered his first sermon at Mt. Lebanon Church, near Ramer, Alabama, on August 1, 1880. His subject was "Eternity"; his text was Psalm 90:2; and he kept on preaching the eternal gospel of the Son of God on four continents till the Lord called him home. On his sixtieth anniversary as a minister Sampey rejoiced to preach on the same text and theme at Broadway Baptist Church in Louisville. To the end he felt that men were ever in desperate need of the saving grace of God revealed in Jesus Christ our Lord.

Sampey graduated from Howard College with the A.B. degree in 1882, being the valedictorian of his class. In the fall of that year he entered Southern Seminary, taking the full course and graduating in 1885. From that time until his election as president of Southern Seminary in May, 1929, Sampey taught Old Testament and Hebrew and continued to carry a full load of teaching while administering the affairs of the Seminary.

It is difficult to do justice to a life so rich and full of grand achievements as that of John R. Sampey.

First of all, Sampey was ever an inspiring teacher. More than seven thousand students sat in his classes. As he unfolded the vast sweep of God's purpose in the life of Israel, as he dramatically described the princely prophet Isaiah or the hardpressed Jeremiah, as he unfolded the prophetic witness of the Old Testament to the coming Messiah, students often sat spellbound and enraptured by his fervor and eloquence.

As pastor of country churches in Kentucky for more than thirty years Dr. Sampey kept close to the people and their needs. In his *Memoirs* he made a special point of the fact that most of the members of the faculty of Southern knew how to preach, and he argued that a theological teacher had to have pastoral experience if he would minister effectively to young preachers and future pastors.

Sampey was also an evangelist at large. He was widely in demand as visiting evangelist in churches and on college campuses. Three times he visited Southern Baptist mission fields in South America, preaching to large numbers in Brazil and elsewhere, and he had the joy of seeing more than a thousand people accept Jesus Christ as Lord and Saviour during these evangelistic meetings. Again in 1936 he visited Japan and China and preached with power and fervor to the people of those lands.

From 1895 to 1942 Dr. Sampey was a member of the International Sunday School Lesson Committee. For forty-six years his influence was deeply felt in this interdenominational body preparing the lessons for most of the evangelical churches in North America. Sampey's scholarly abilities, trained under men like William Rainey Harper, came into fruitful play as he served as chairman of the Old Testament section of the American Standard Bible Revision Committee from 1930 to 1938.

Within the Southern Baptist Convention Dr. Sampey was a power to be reckoned with. All held him in high esteem. Often he preached the Convention sermon, and three times he was elected president of that body, from 1935 to 1938.

From 1900 onward Dr. Sampey participated also in great international Christian gatherings, such as the International Sunday School Conventions, the Baptist World Alliance sessions of 1934 and 1939, and the great ecumenical gatherings on life and work and faith and order at Oxford, England, and Edinburgh, Scotland, in 1937. In 1936 he participated in the China Baptist Centennial at Shanghai.

Dr. John R. Sampey was nearly sixty-six years old when he assumed the presidency of Southern Seminary in May, 1929, after having been acting president since the death of Dr. E. Y. Mullins in November, 1928. Would he measure up to the strain of the office of president of a great school like Southern Seminary?

The nearly fourteen years that Dr. Sampey served as president of the Seminary were punctuated by cataclysmic events that were a mixture of pathos, disaster, and tragedy. The year that Dr. Sampey assumed the presidency of Southern Seminary was also the beginning of the great depression of the thirties. In 1931 the Japanese invaded Manchuria; two years later, in January of 1933, Adolf Hitler seized power in Nazi Germany. Then, in September of 1939 World War II began with all its tragic consequences.

The Seminary itself was burdened down with a terrific debt of nearly one million dollars. Some have spoken of Dr. Sampey's administration as a holding operation. It was that, to be sure, but it also was marked with resolute determination to cope with existing hardships.

Administratively, Dr. Sampey honestly tried to follow the pattern of his predecessors—Boyce, Broadus, Whitsitt and Mullins—that is, to continue what he liked to call a "democratic administration of Seminary affairs." According to Dr. Carver, "he earnestly increased the standing and responsibilities of the faculty and limited independent responsibilities and functions of the president." But Dr. Sampey also soon discovered that the huge debt; the precarious condition of the Southern Baptist Convention, most of whose boards were then in debt; and the decrease of the student body made faculty participation in the solution of urgent problems less and less practicable and possible. Toward the end of his term of office questions arose concerning his lack of authority for dealing with certain rather serious and delicate matters. In time, however, these problems found their proper solution.

One of the wisest acts undertaken in this period was the appointment of Dr. Gaines S. Dobbins as treasurer of the Seminary in 1933. Dr. Dobbins held this office until 1942 without additional salary. The combined efforts of President Sampey and Dr. Dobbins won the day with regard to the liquidation of the huge debt. A refinancing program through the Mutual Benefit Life Insurance Company of New York, reducing the interest rate of the loan, saved the Seminary from possible default on its heavy debt.

The stringency of the times made it necessary in 1932 to reduce faculty salaries by 20 per cent shortly after the faculty had volunteered of its own account to reduce their salaries by one tenth. For several years Dr. Sampey had desperately tried to protect his colleagues against these salary cuts, but in vain.

In the academic sphere Dr. Sampey was also able to make reasonable progress. Dr. Jesse B. Weatherspoon joined the faculty in 1929 as the successor of Dr. C. S. Gardner as one of the most valuable additions to the teaching staff during the past thirty years. Dr. Harold W. Tribble had become full professor after Dr. Mullins' death, and the latter's mantle fell upon him as teacher of systematic and biblical theology. The death of Dr. A. T. Robertson in September, 1934, made Professor W. Hersey Davis head of the New Testament department, and a year later Dr. Edward A. McDowell was added to the faculty to teach in the same field. Two years later Dr. McDowell became assistant professor in New Testament interpretation, while Dr. H. C. Goerner, after a three-year instructorship, was made assistant professor in comparative religion and missions in 1938. Also in 1938 Mr. Inman Johnson, for many years a teacher of speech and music, was elevated to a professorship, and Dr. Hugh R. Peterson became registrar, student counselor, and later secretary of the faculty. In 1941 Dr. Leo Green came into the Old Testament department where he proved an effective teacher until he left the Seminary in 1948 to take a pastorate. Dr. Leo T. Crismon was elected assistant librarian in 1938 also, and through the years he has rendered a great service to an ever larger student body and faculty.

The completion of the J. Frank Harrison endowment of the Chair of New Testament Interpretation in 1933 and, largely through the persistent efforts of Dr. Dobbins, of the John R. Sampey Chair of Old Testament Interpretation of a hundred thousand dollars, added to the academic as well as financial strength of the Seminary.

In 1928 the Seminary had instituted the Doctor of Philosophy degree in lieu of the Doctor of Theology degree in the belief that Southern Baptist colleges and universities would thereby receive a steady supply of competent teachers in the field of religion. Ten years later the faculty unanimously re-established the Th.D. degree program, especially in view of the requirements of the American Association of Theological Schools.

In 1938 laymen preparing for the vocation of religious education were permitted for the first time to enrol in the classes of the Seminary. This was a wise decision, as subsequent developments have shown. From 1940 onward Negro students were privately taught by members of the faculty; and before another decade had gone by, members of the Negro race were admitted to all the facilities of the school.

The student body stood at 435 when Dr. Sampey became president. It dropped to 417 by the end of 1930. Four hundred eighteen were registered the next year, with 27 students from foreign countries. The enrolment fell to 391 by the end of the academic year of 1931–32 and reached a low ebb in 1933–34, when only 343 students matriculated. But during the next session the situation improved as 353 registered. The session of 1935–36 saw 389 students matriculated; the next year there were 407 students; and during the session of 1941–42 the number rose to 520 students.

Despite depression and impending war, Dr. Sampey and his devoted colleagues kept the Seminary on its course. There were setbacks, but on the whole there was steady progress and much reason for encouragement. In spite of financial difficulties, students put forth their best efforts to gain their diplomas. Some of the splendid young men that now serve on the faculty of Southern underwent a rather serious intellectual discipline under men like Robertson, Carver, McDowell, Adams, Weatherspoon, Davis, Goerner, and Sampey.

The Board of Trustees and the Executive Committee of the Seminary loyally stood by the Seminary, its president, and the faculty to steer it through the troubled years of the great depression.

Among the special lecturers who appeared on the Norton and Gay Foundations during Sampey's administration we mention but a few: Kenneth Scott Latourette, the missionary-statesman; George W. Truett, the beloved preacher of Dallas and the world; Dr. E. B. Frost, director of the Yerkes Observatory of the University of Chicago; Dr. Toyohiko Kagawa, the man who lived "beyond the deathline" in the slums of Tokyo, evangelist of God's grace in Japan; Dr. William S. Sadler, world renowned expert in psychiatry; Dr. A. H. Compton, eminent physicist; Dr. William Lyon Phelps of Yale University, incomparable teacher of English literature, and the irrepressible Dr. C. Oscar Johnson of St. Louis, Missouri, elder Baptist statesman. Men of this stamp and breadth brought quickening of heart and mind to students, faculty, and alumni in a day that tried men's souls.

No historian's pen can fully or adequately describe what John R. Sampey was and wrought in his long and eventful career: preacher for sixty-seven years; professor of Old Testament at Southern Seminary for sixty years; a loving husband; friend and counselor of thousands of students and pastors. He was truly "a servant of the servants of God." When in 1942 Dr. Sampey resigned his office as president of Southern Baptist Theological Seminary, he left it strong, virile, and poised toward a greater future in the Lord's service.

Ellis A. Fuller, 1942–50

Dr. Ellis A. Fuller, eminent pastor, preacher, schoolman, evangelist, and denominational leader, came to the helm of

Southern Baptist Theological Seminary in 1942, half a year after Pearl Harbor. The eight years of Dr. Fuller's administration were crowded with breath-taking events in the life of the world and of the school he came to lead with such signal success.

President Fuller was a man of large vision, restless energy, and bold, aggressive action. Reared on a humble farm near Cross Hill, South Carolina, he learned "to play, plow, plant, cultivate, and harvest" at an early age. Daily Bible reading and prayers were part of his home training. Converted at eleven, young Fuller united with the Beaver Dam Baptist Church which nine years later he served as pastor at a salary of fifty dollars a year. In 1912 Fuller graduated from Presbyterian College at Clinton, South Carolina. Had it not been for an athletic scholarship he might never have been able to go to college. For five years after his college graduation Fuller ministered in country churches. He also taught high school, and, ever the builder, he led in a building project of a new school at Montville, South Carolina, of which he became principal. Eventually he entered Southern Baptist Seminary, graduated with the Master of Theology degree in 1921, and carried on graduate work, for several years being a fellow with Dr. Robertson in New Testament. Although he passed his doctoral examination, he never was able to finish his thesis. From 1928 to 1942 Dr. Fuller was pastor of the First Baptist Church in Atlanta, Georgia. During his pastorate sixty-five hundred new members were added to the church, one third of whom came into the fold on profession of faith. For fourteen years Dr. Fuller was president of the Home Mission Board of the Southern Baptist Convention, and from 1939 to 1943 he was president of the Georgia Baptist State Convention.

Dr. Fuller thus came well prepared to the leadership of Southern Seminary. Though America was at war, the new president at once discerned the need of enlarging the material facilities of the Seminary. Married students were paying exorbitant rents in often undesirable quarters. Classrooms were at a premium. The Seminary chapel never could hold all who wanted to worship. Dr. Fuller's financial wizardry, his winsome way

217

with people, and the Seminary's invigorated public relations program soon discovered sources from which to finance new projects. In rapid succession the material needs of the Seminary were being met. Eighteen new buildings, at a cost that ran into millions, had been added to the Seminary plant when on October 28, 1950, in far-off San Diego, California, Dr. Ellis A. Fuller was struck down by a heart attack.

Among these new buildings were, first of all, Norton Annex, a valuable addition to the administration building. It furnished sorely needed classrooms, a technical radio studio, student center and cafeteria, post office, seminar rooms, and a book store.

Foster Hall, located on the edge of the campus, provides twelve apartments for younger professors.

Through the generosity of Mr. and Mrs. V. V. Cooke, prominent philanthropists of Louisville, and Mrs. George Neal and Mrs. Ben Clarkson the Seminary came into possession of a lovely campus with two extremely fine buildings for the use of the School of Music. Cooke Hall and Barnard Hall attest Dr. Fuller's dream of creating a School of Music second to none in the United States. It came into being in 1943 and opened its first session in 1944 with twenty students enrolled. Dr. and Mrs. Donald Winters, who had been associated with Dr. Fuller since 1940 at the First Baptist Church of Atlanta, Georgia, did the pioneering work for this school and gave themselves tirelessly to its advancement.

Faculty Center was still another building added in Dr. Fuller's time. It serves as a residence for visiting lecturers. Professor Elmer Homrighausen, Gay Lecturer for 1949, was the first guest in this beautiful building. Faculty meetings are also held here.

Fuller Hall, with ninety-six apartments for married students, was nearly completed when the man for whom it is named died.

But the crowning achievement with regard to new buildings was the Alumni Chapel. A Georgian colonial structure with imposing spire, seating more than 1,700 people, it was financed largely by Seminary alumni. Alumni Chapel was dedicated in the spring of 1950, with Dr. Ellis A. Fuller, who had dreamed it into existence, as the main speaker. Dr. Maurice Trimmer of West Virginia deserves highest credit, as do other alumni, for boldly advancing this project among graduates of Southern Seminary.

Still another acquisition was the Presidential Manse, located in Cherokee Park and given to the Seminary by the late Mrs. George W. Norton.

The Samuels Missionary apartments, given by a consecrated layman of Washington, D. C., furnishes adequate facilities for four missionary families on furlough.

But President Fuller was also deeply concerned about the faculty. When he took the helm of Southern Seminary he was greeted by eleven full-time faculty members. Before he laid down his work for higher labors, fifteen new professors had been engaged as professors of the School of Theology alone.

Of the eleven men that constituted the faculty of Southern Seminary in 1942, Dr. W. O. Carver, who became professor emeritus in 1943, had served with great effectiveness for more then forty-four years. Professors Dobbins, Davis, Johnson, Adams, and Yates had been on the faculty for twenty years or more. Dr. Frank Marion Powell, professor of church history, had served from 1918 to 1941. Dr. Harold W. Tribble had taught since 1925, becoming the successor of Dr. E. Y. Mullins in the field of systematic theology in 1928. Dr. Jesse B. Weatherspoon had joined the faculty in 1929.

When Dr. Fuller's career came to an end in 1950, the composition of the faculty had considerably changed. A large group of younger men, all of them graduates of the school, had been added to the faculty from 1942 to 1950.

Among the older men who greeted Dr. Fuller's coming in 1942, Dr. Gaines S. Dobbins, professor of religious education and church administration had, next to Dr. Carver, made the richest contribution as a writer of more than twenty books. Mr. Erwin L. McDonald has written these words about Dr. Dobbins:

219

For more than thirty years he has risen early and worked late to carry his writing ministry along with his teaching. Pre-eminently the teacher, he has used his flair for writing to implement his work in the classroom. Many of the books he has produced (at the rate of one a summer for the past twenty years) have been used as textbooks in his classes.

One of his books, "Evangelism According to Christ," has been a best-seller in other denominations as well as among Southern Baptists. Seventh Day Adventists made it required reading for their missionaries and bought it by the thousands and a number of colleges and seminaries, including staid Princeton Theological Seminary, have adopted it as a textbook.[1]

The Pastoral Psychology Book Club selected Dr. Dobbins' *Evangelism According to Christ*, published by Broadman Press and Harper & Brothers in 1948, and *Winning the Children*, released in 1953 by Broadman Press, as one of its book-of-the-month choices. One of the best known of Baptist publications, the *Baptist Adult Training Union Quarterly*, was originated by Dr. Dobbins and edited by him for seventeen years. He saw its circulation climb from twenty-five thousand to nearly a million. *The Churchbook*, first published in 1951, is a "treasury of materials and methods for pastoral leadership in church life." With the more than six million words which Dr. Dobbins has written in the course of the past decades in the form of educational quarterlies, magazines, books, and special articles for Baptist weekly newspapers, he deserves this word of praise from one of his former students: "Perhaps no one has made so great an impact upon his denomination for the advancement of Christianity as has Dr. Dobbins, the Southern Baptist teacher and writer par excellence."[2]

In 1956 Dr. Dobbins, retiring as dean of the School of Religious Education at Southern, became distinguished professor of church administration at Golden Gate Baptist Theological Seminary in Berkeley, California. In 1958 he made an extended tour

---

[1] Erwin L. McDonald, "Dr. Dobbins Adds New Book to Baptist Shelf," *The Tie*, XIX (September, 1951), 3.

[2] *Ibid.*, p. 5.

of Europe and the East in the interest of Christian education.

Dr. William Hersey Davis excelled as a teacher of New Testament interpretation. He was an impressive person, with long arms and legs, bushy eyebrows, and searching eyes. His scholarly strength lay not so much in the writing of learned books as in his expert knowledge of lexicography and of ancient papyri and their bearing on the Greek New Testament. His *Beginners' Grammar of the Greek New Testament*, first published in 1923, came out in its fifth edition in 1942 and has gone through many printings. In 1933 he issued *Greek Papyri in the First Century* in honor of his elder colleague, Dr. A. T. Robertson.

Dr. Edward A. McDowell, his former student and later successor, has characterized Dr. Davis' virtues as consisting of a passion to discover truth; a contagious enthusiasm for the subject he was teaching; a method of teaching which challenged the interest of the students; and a love for the student that was personal and sincere.

Some of his graduate students regretted Dr. Davis' lack of appreciation for theology. Under pressure from Dr. McDowell he finally offered a course in the principles of interpretation. Again, Dr. Davis seemed little concerned about current studies in the field of New Testament, according to the testimony of some of his best students. However, that might have been due to his own originality of thought and outlook. He always conveyed to those who heard him a faith tested in the crucible of Christian experience, a faith that unwaveringly was fixed on Jesus Christ, the Son of God.

Dr. James McKee Adams labored long and fruitfully in the field of biblical introduction and archeology. Frequent journeys to Palestine deepened his insights and enlarged his perspectives. Several of his books, such as *Ancient Records of the Bible* and *Biblical Backgrounds*, have been widely used in many theological schools.

Dr. Edward A. McDowell made a singular contribution as a New Testament teacher in revealing a deep appreciation for the profound theological content of its message. He also showed great awareness of the critical problems of the New Testament text and was sensitive to currents of thought among scholars of a persuasion different from his own. He tried seriously to relate the gospel of Christ to the baffling social issues of the day. He perhaps more than any other person on the faculty of Southern in the thirties and forties of this century encouraged a better understanding between the races, actively participating in interracial fellowships in and around Louisville. His books, *Son of God and Suffering Servant* and *The Meaning and Message of Revelation*, demonstrate his exegetical and critical abilities. Together with Dr. W. Hersey Davis, Dr. McDowell published in 1948 *A Source Book of Interbiblical History*.

Dr. Sydnor L. Stealey was the first professor to join the faculty upon Dr. Fuller's coming. He came to the Seminary in 1942 with a large fund of experience in the pastorate and as a denominational leader. Though an avid reader and an able professor of church history with a special love for Baptist history, Dr. Stealey especially endeared himself to many by his natural wit, homespun wisdom, and wise counsel. As president of Southeastern Baptist Theological Seminary at Wake Forest since 1951 he has already made a splendid record as a seminary administrator.

Dr. Olin T. Binkley came to Southern from Wake Forest College in 1944. Equipped with the finest of training, he made Christian ethics alive and relevant to the total scheme of Christian concerns. His sensitivity to the agonizing needs of humankind deeply impressed his students. In faculty discussions Dr. Binkley could always be counted on the side of reason and constructive forward-looking measures.

Southern Baptist Seminary reluctantly released Drs. Stealey, McDowell, and Binkley to Southeastern Baptist Seminary, which since 1951 has risen to numerical and intellectual strength, numbering its students already by more than seven hundred men and women.

Dr. Weatherspoon, now professor emeritus, spans with his teaching experience the Sampey-Fuller-McCall administrations.

Even while he was pastor of Highland Baptist Church of Louisville, from time to time he assisted in teaching in the days of Dr. Mullins. Hardly could one find a finer and more cultured teacher of the art of preaching anywhere. In addition, prior to the establishment of chairs of Christian ethics, Dr. Weatherspoon taught Christian sociology, standing in a worthy succession of men like Dargan and Gardner. We have already referred to his revision of Dr. John A. Broadus' famous treatise on *The Preparation and Delivery of Sermons.* His *Sent Forth to Preach, Studies in Apostolic Preaching* has found appreciative readers in many academic and lay circles. Dr. Weatherspoon's biography of Dr. Theron Rankin, eminent Southern Baptist foreign mission leader, was published in 1958.

As a member of the Social Service Commission of the Southern Baptist Convention, Dr. Weatherspoon has rendered an inestimable service to his brethren. It was he who at the St. Louis Convention of 1954 led the way to the endorsement by the Southern Baptist Convention of the Supreme Court decision on the public school integration. "Lady," his charming wife, has left behind her a rich treasure of devotion and Christian grace.

The work of the professors during this period as in other days was again supplemented by the contributions of visiting speakers and lecturers. Dr. D. F. Fleming of Vanderbilt University spoke on the Gay Foundation in 1942–43, while Dr. George A. Buttrick of New York City delivered the Mullins Lectures on preaching. Dr. John S. Bonnell was Norton lecturer of 1944–45, and Dr. Halford E. Luccock of Yale University thrilled large audiences as he discoursed on "The Preacher and Literature." During the following years Dr. William O. Carver spoke for the second time on the Norton Foundation. Professor Herbert Farmer of Cambridge, England, lectured in 1945–46 on "The Sources and Setting of Preaching." The next year the Seminary welcomed Dr. Edwin Lewis of Drew Theological Seminary and Dr. Nels F. S. Ferré as visiting lecturers. They spoke respectively on "The Philosophy of the Fourth Gospel" and "Pillars of Faith."

It was most fitting that Dr. Charles L. Graham, pastor of Crescent Hill Baptist Church, Louisville, which had so often acted as host to the Seminary at commencement time, should deliver the Mullins Lectures for 1947. Dr. John Mackay of Princeton Seminary spoke challengingly in the same year on "Who Will Win the World?" In 1949 Professor Elmer G. Homrighausen inspired the pastors with his provocative messages on the nature of the Christian gospel.

Dr. Fuller's career came to a sudden end on October 26, 1950. Humanly speaking, he died before his time. Disregarding his own physical condition, after a heart attack shortly before the new Alumni Chapel was dedicated in March of 1950, "he died literally at the front which he always had sought out."

Dr. Ellis A. Fuller loved people, great and small. He had a shrewd insight into the foibles of human nature and freely confessed his own. He believed in democracy because he believed in the judgment of common folk. He loved Southern Baptists and all of God's people with a passionate love. Well did he know their limitations, but he also knew of their greatness. Though eminently successful as pastor and administrator, he never lacked the finer things of the spirit, that is, compassion and mercy. Those who knew and loved him realized that the venom and untruthfulness of some of his critics deeply wounded his heart. Yet never did one hear an evil or impatient word from his lips. He rather prayed for his detractors.

When, after the Copenhagen Baptist Congress of 1947, Dr. Fuller visited with the German Baptist brethren at Kassel and saw their publication house in utter ruins because of the ravages of the war, he wept like a child. But Dr. Fuller did more than weep. Upon his return to America he induced the Foreign Mission Board in Richmond to make available to the brethren in Kassel a substantial sum of money with which to rebuild their plant. Dr. Fuller loved not only in word but in deed. He was ever a man of consecrated action on behalf of the kingdom projects he came to deal with. With him ended a brief but exceedingly fruitful epoch of Southern Seminary history.

Dr. Gaines S. Dobbins became acting president after Dr. Fuller's death and presided wisely over the affairs of the Seminary until the election of the new president in the summer of 1951.

During Dr. Dobbins' term of office a number of productive changes took place in the life of the Seminary. First, the trustees voted that qualified Negro students be admitted to the Seminary. The students of Southern had for years pleaded for this venture into equal opportunity for all races. When at the fall convocation of 1948 the first Negro, Dr. Garland K. Offut, received the Th.D. degree from Southern Baptist Seminary, the student body burst out into enthusiastic applause that lasted several minutes. This step sanctioned by the Board of Trustees was the fulfilment of a dream of many years.

The first summer pastors' conference was inaugurated at this time, with Dr. Roland Bainton of Yale University and Dr. Paul Minear of Andover-Newton Theological School as visiting lecturers.

Extensive remodeling and enlarging of the library took place, the old chapel being transformed into a large reading room. A child care program was set up for the benefit of married students, and the term system was replaced by the semester system. In conjunction with other Southern Baptist seminaries, Dr. Dobbins helped establish an extension department for less educated ministers. Steps were also taken to raise standards for admission to graduate study in the Seminary. All in all, Dr. Dobbins' interim presidency was marked by continued progress. When the new president arrived on the scene, the Seminary was in a healthy condition, ready for new ventures and forward movements.

DUKE K. McCALL, 1951–

Dr. Duke K. McCall was elected president of Southern Baptist Theological Seminary in the summer of 1951. The son of Judge and Mrs. John McCall of Tennessee, the new president graduated from Furman University and received the Doctor of Theology degree in Old Testament from Southern in 1941. For a few years Dr. McCall was pastor of Broadway Baptist Church in

Louisville, Kentucky, then from 1943 to 1946 president of New Orleans Baptist Theological Seminary, and subsequently executive secretary of the Executive Committee of the Southern Baptist Convention. Thus the new leader came to the presidency of Southern with considerable administrative experience, besides being at the same time the youngest president of any of the Southern Baptist theological schools.

Since we are still too close to the past years properly to evaluate all that has been accomplished under Dr. McCall's leadership, a brief chronicle will have to suffice at this point.

From a material vantage point the acquisition of Green Tree Manor, twenty-six buildings with 254 apartments, located a mile northeast from the main campus, has perhaps been of signal significance. This project, now called Seminary Village, "the biggest real estate deal in Louisville in a decade," has been a great boon to the married students, especially those with children, many of whom, despite the erection of Fuller Hall in 1950, were still without proper homes.

The carillon bells of Alumni Chapel, given by Mr. and Mrs. J. Newton Rayzor of Houston, Texas, and Schulmerich Carillon, Inc., in honor of Dr. Ellis A. Fuller, were first played on Sunday, September 23, 1951, by Professor Alexander McCurdy of Curtis Institute in Philadelphia. On that occasion Dr. McCall delivered a brief address of acceptance, paying tribute to the memory of the late President Fuller.

Small and large bequests have come to the Seminary during the past seven years (1951–58): the Dr. George W. Threlkeld Bequest of $45,000 in 1951; the anonymous gift from a Tennessee layman of a hundred shares of common stock of the United States Steel Corporation in 1953; the pledge of Southern alumni at their May, 1957, convention luncheon in Chicago to undergird their alma mater with a gift of $500,000 for the new James P. Boyce Memorial Library; and the $240,000 bequest of March, 1958, by Miss Lizzie Boyce, the daughter of the founder of the Seminary.

In the academic realm many things of an encouraging nature

have happened since Dr. McCall assumed the leadership of the Seminary. We mention but a few constructive changes.

First, the Seminary was organized in 1953 into three distinct though closely interrelated schools: the School of Theology, with President McCall as dean; the School of Religious Education, with Dr. Gaines S. Dobbins as dean; and the School of Music, with Dr. Forrest H. Heeren as dean.

Second, after a two-year study of the curriculum the Bachelor of Divinity course has been considerably strengthened, with larger course requirements in the main fields of theological study.

Third, the graduate program has been tightened in such a manner as to encourage only well-qualified students for advanced courses of study leading toward the Master of Theology and Doctor of Theology degrees.

Fourth, the establishment of a regular eight-week summer school, with Dr. Henry C. Goerner as director, has found wide approval among both the students of the Seminary and returning pastors. Distinguished visiting professors from other schools of learning, among them Dr. Arthur Crabtree from Zürich and Dr. Marcus Barth from the University of Chicago, have enhanced this effort. Enrolment has moved from below two hundred to the four hundred mark.

Fifth, the faculty of the Seminary has been enlarged so that presently some sixty full-time professors and instructors are employed to teach more than thirteen hundred students. At Dr. McCall's coming the Seminary had but one dean; there are now five deans helping to lighten the load of the administration.

Lastly, the School of Church Music has become a graduate school since 1956—that is, it prepares men and women only for advanced degrees in sacred music, including the Doctor of Music degree.

In 1955 the Lizette Kimbrough McCall Foundation for World Evangelism was inaugurated in the week of November 8–11, with Dr. H. Guy Moore of Broadway Baptist Church, Fort Worth, Texas, as the main speaker.

An evening school for the benefit of the wives of students has also been established and a director of women engaged to supervise this needful work and to have the oversight of the young women in the student body.

The faculty has, of course, felt the strain of an ever-increasing student body, the necessity of keeping abreast of the scholarship of the times, and the demands of the most rapidly growing denomination in America. They have been much in demand as evangelists, Bible teachers, religious emphasis speakers, and counselors in many benevolent and Christian organizations.

Through the foresight of the Board of Trustees, regular sabbatical leaves have been granted as in the past, and members of the faculty have studied in England, Scotland, Germany, and Switzerland.

Professor William H. Morton was Fellow of the American School of Oriental Research in 1950–51 and its director 1954–55, directing excavation work at Dhiban, Palestine. In 1956 he was visiting professor at the institute of this society at Jerusalem.

Miss Audrey Nossaman of the School of Music was the recipient of a Fullbright Scholarship for study in Italy, while Acting Dean Henlee Barnette was enabled by the J. Newton Rayzor Fund to travel extensively in Soviet Russia in the summer of 1957, gathering valuable experiences and insights into the theory and practice of communism and the ongoing of the evangelical witness in that vast empire.

Dr. Duke K. McCall, the president of Southern, has circled the globe in the interest of missions and also as a representative of the U. S. Air Force in the Far East and Europe, studying the moral and spiritual problems of men in the armed forces. He has also edited a book, written by a number of Southern professors and associated scholars under the title *What Is the Church?*, a Broadman publication of 1958.

Professors Owens, Edge, Dobbins, Francisco, Weatherspoon, Lumpkin, Rust, and Mueller have written books in their respective fields, and Professors Moody, Price, Ranson, Peacock, Rust, Barnette, Stanfield, Turlington, Smith, Jones, McGlon, and Francisco have written significant articles and contributed to encyclopedias and symposium works. Dr. Wayne E. Oates, who joined the faculty in 1948, has written eight books since 1950, and his contribution to the field of pastoral work received honorable mention in the Niebuhr Report on Theological Education in America.

The faculty owes a debt of gratitude to the Board of Trustees and the administration for constant efforts to create agreeable working conditions for the members of the staff and faculty. Were it not for their initiative, younger faculty members would often be unable to purchase new homes. Subsidies for attendance at professional meetings or participation at state and national Baptist conventions, while not large, are a real help and enable the faculty to keep in touch with the movements of the day.

And what shall we say of all those men and women who through the years have quietly worked behind the scenes in order to make Southern Baptist Seminary a more effective instrument of kingdom service? A Seminary like this could not continue to exist for one hour without the prayers of millions of brethren in and beyond the Southern Baptist Convention. The many generous benefactors of the past and present—the Nortons, Bostwicks, Rockefellers, Brays, Colgates, Chenaults, Leverings, Caldwells, Gays, Pratts, Lawrences, to mention but a few of many; the members of the Board of Trustees; chairmen of the Board of Trustees like Basil Manly, Sr., A. M. Poindexter, J. B. Jeter, J. G. Jones, Joseph Emerson Brown, Joshua Levering, Forrest Feezor, H. I. Hester, and Wade Bryant; or Herbert O. McKinney, for many years assistant to the treasurer of the Seminary (1931–43); B. Presley Smith, who labored among us from 1889 to 1932 in multitudinous capacities—all of these deserve thanks.

The present superintendent of buildings and grounds, T. R. Allen, Jr., has put many in his debt through his kindly services and his efficient management of affairs. P. H. Bufkin, the treasurer, efficiently manages the large financial matters of the Seminary with its budget of over $1,250,000. Librarian Leo T.

Crismon unceasingly watches over the rich treasures of the library, now crowded beyond description, and through his courtesy and patience is a helper to thousands of students, absent-minded professors, and a host of visitors.

The Seminary's greatest asset is in its alumni. Again and again they have come to the aid of the Seminary in times of emergency. Dr. McCall, in one of his editorials in *The Tie*, rightly stated that the fruitage of all that takes place on the Southern campus is in the product, the graduates who minister here and around the world in the name of Christ.

Is the Southern graduate a lover of men? Is he an evangelist, the herald of glad tidings of joy? An ambassador of Jesus Christ, Son of God and Son of man, the only Saviour of men? Does he know how to preach the Word of God effectively? Witness to men and women grappling with temptations and sins as hard as steel? Is he wise, patient, prayerful as he deals with immortal men bound for an eternal destiny? Is he able to forgive and forbear? To lead others and to be led by God's Spirit in the ways of truth? The final appraisal, of course, is with Him who judges the hearts of men!

But Southern Seminary is grateful for every alumnus who at home or on far-off mission fields bears a faithful witness to our Lord Christ.

We are proud of all those who in small or large places of service are engaged in the King's business.

Leaders in evangelism, religious education, sacred music, pastoral counseling, presidents of colleges and institutes, members of the Executive Committee of the Southern Baptist Convention, editors of Broadman Press, the executive secretary of the Sunday School Board in Nashville—all are beholden to Southern whether they graduated from its schools or not. For Southern Baptist Theological Seminary is the mother seminary of the five other theological schools under the control of the Southern Baptist Convention. Many of their professors and five of the six seminary presidents of Southwestern, New Orleans, Golden Gate, Southeastern, Midwestern, and last but not least, Southern Seminary,

230

are graduates of the school established in Greenville, South Carolina, in 1859.

May we covet greater wisdom in guiding the students entrusted to our care through their course of study.

We invoke the divine benedictions of the God of all grace, mercy, and power, the God and Father of our Lord Jesus Christ, that come what may, this Seminary will be faithful to its noble heritage of faith and learning.

Chronology

1764 Founding of College of Rhode Island, now Brown University, first Baptist college in Colonial America.

1788 Virginia Baptists appoint committee of ten to establish a seminary of learning.

1790 Charleston, South Carolina, Baptist Association maintains a theological library for divinity students.

1819 Founding of Hamilton Literary and Theological Institution, later Madison University, now Colgate University.

1825 Newton Theological Seminary, first Baptist seminary in America, now Andover-Newton Theological School, Newton Centre, Massachusetts.

1835 Western Baptist Theological Seminary projected at Cincinnati, Ohio.

1835 Basil Manly, Sr., first advances idea of a central theological school for Southern Baptists.

1845 Western Theological Institute opens at Covington, Kentucky, and collapses in 1847.

1845 Southern Baptist Convention founded at Augusta, Georgia, May 8–12.

1846 Southern Baptist Convention raises $11,735.22 for Foreign Missions and $9,594.60 for Home Missions.

1847 American Baptist Indian Mission meets in Nashville, Tennessee, in October.

1849 Educational Convention meets at Nashville, Tennessee, in May.

1849 Educational Convention at Charleston, South Carolina; Resolution of October 30, 1847, looking toward establishing a central theological seminary for Southern Baptists.

1854 Baptist Education Society in Virginia re-opens question of a central theological seminary for Southern Baptists.

1855 Educational Convention at Montgomery, Alabama, in May.

232

1856 Friends of theological education meet in Augusta, Georgia, in April.

1856 James P. Boyce delivers his Inaugural Address at Furman University, Greenville, South Carolina, on "Three Changes in Theological Education."

1857 Educational Convention meets at Louisville, Kentucky, in May.

1858 Educational Convention meets at Greenville, South Carolina, in May.

1859 First Board of Trustees of Southern Baptist Theological Seminary meets at Richmond, Virginia, in May.

1859 Southern Baptist Theological Seminary opens at Greenville, South Carolina, October 3, with twenty-six students and four professors—Boyce, Broadus, Manly, Williams.

1861 First Commencement at Southern on May 27; Dr. E. T. Winkler, speaker.

1865–1866 First post-war session of Southern Seminary, with seven students enrolled.

1869 Dr. Crawford H. Toy becomes professor of Old Testament.

1870 Dr. John A. Broadus publishes his homiletical classic *A Treatise on the Preparation and Delivery of Sermons.*

1871 Trustees decide to find new location for Seminary.

1872–1877 Dr. J. P. Boyce lives in Louisville, Kentucky, to prepare removal of Seminary to that city and to raise an adequate endowment.

1872 Dr. William H. Whitsitt becomes professor of church history.

1872 President N. K. Davis invites Southern to unite with Bethel College, Russelville, Kentucky, to form the Southern Baptist University.

1873 Financial crash threatens plans to move Seminary.

1873 Southern Baptist Convention meets at Mobile, Alabama; influential Baptist leader tries to thwart removal of Seminary from Greenville, South Carolina, to Louisville.

1874 Dr. John A. Broadus secures $10,000 from Northern Baptist brethren.

233

1874   On January 20 Boyce proposes to Executive Committee of Southern to suspend Seminary until adequate endowment is raised.

1877–1878   First session in Louisville with 89 students enrolled.

1877   On August 30 J. P. Boyce delivers opening address to faculty and students of Southern at new Louisville location.

1879   Professor Crawford H. Toy resigns.

1880   On February 11 Joseph Emerson Brown of Atlanta, Georgia, gives $50,000, the Seminary's first large gift, to Southern.

1880   Joshua Levering joins Board of Trustees and from 1895 to 1935 serves as a far-sighted president of the board.

1882   Graduate theological studies projected.

1885   Dr. John R. Sampey begins his career as teacher of Old Testament and Hebrew.

1886   John D. Rockefeller gives $25.000 to Southern Seminary. Northern Baptist brethren give altogether $60,000 for the erection of New York Hall.

1886   Dr. John A. Broadus brings out his *Commentary on the Gospel of Matthew.*

1886–1888   New York Hall being built and completed for occupancy.

1888   Student-sponsored *Seminary Magazine* established.

1888   In May J. P. Boyce formally made president of the Seminary at Southern Baptist Convention in Richmond, Virginia.

1888   President J. P. Boyce dies at Pau in Southern France, December 28.

1888   Archibald Thomas Robertson begins his career as a teacher of the New Testament and the Greek language.

1888–1889   Student enrollment stands at 164.

1889   The Trustees in their May meeting elect Dr. John A. Broadus president of the Seminary.

1891   The Memorial Library, the gift of Mrs. J. Lawrence Smith of Louisville, is formally opened on May 6th, with President William R. Harper of the University of Chicago as speaker.

1892   Dr. S. C. Dargan joins faculty in the department of homiletics.

1893 Norton Hall, classroom and administration building, dedicated November 1. Cost $60,000.

1894 Dr. William J. McGlothlin elected to faculty, teaching Hebrew and Old Testament.

1894 Student enrollment climbs to 267.

1894 First Doctor of Theology degrees conferred on four candidates in May.

1894 The Gay Lectureship established through gift of $5,000 by Julius Brown Gay of Alabama.

1895 President John A. Broadus dies on March 16 in Louisville, Kentucky.

1895 Dr. William H. Whitsitt is elected president of Southern.

1895 Student body during session of 1895–96 rises to 316.

1895 Dr. William Owen Carver begins his long and fruitful career.

1896 The Whitsitt Controversy rages for three bitter years.

1896 The Joshua Levering Gymnasium erected at cost of $10,000.

1899 President Whitsitt forced to relinquish his post. Trustees reaffirm freedom of research for the faculty.

1899 In June Dr. E. Y. Mullins elected as the fourth president of Southern.

1900 Dr. William Owen Carver pioneers as head of new missions department.

1902 Trustees authorize attendance of women of Seminary classes; by 1904 forty-eight women are enrolled.

1904 The faculty inaugurates *The Baptist Review and Expositor,* a scholarly journal.

1904 Professor A. T. Robertson advances the idea of a Baptist World Congress in London, England.

1906 New chair in Sunday School pedagogy established jointly by Seminary and Southern Baptist Convention Sunday School Board with Dr. B. H. Dement as first incumbent.

1907 Dr. Burrows and Dr. Whitsitt deliver the first Founders' Day addresses on January 11 on Boyce and Broadus.

1909　The Twentieth Century Endowment Jubilee Campaign, started in 1902, raises Seminary endowment to $600,000.

1911　Norton Lectureship established.

1911　W. O. Carver publishes his *Missions in the Plan of the Ages*.

1914　Professor A. T. Robertson issues his *A Grammar of the Greek New Testament in the Light of Historical Research*.

1920　In twenties professors Davis, Dobbins, Powell, Yates, Adams, and Tribble join faculty.

1923　Dr. E. Y. Mullins is elected president of the Baptist World Alliance in Stockholm, Sweden.

1923　Cornerstone laying of new campus in Crescent Hill section of Louisville on November 5.

1926　Seminary moves from downtown Louisville to the "Beeches" at 2825 Lexington Road, March 26–27.

1928　President Edgar Young Mullins dies November 23.

1928　Ph.D. program instituted in lieu of Th. D. degree.

1929　Dr. Jesse B. Weatherspoon joins faculty as professor of preaching and Christian ethics.

1929　Dr. John R. Sampey assumes the presidency of Southern. Student enrollment totals 435.

1932　Student body totals 391.

1933　Professor Gaines S. Dobbins elected treasurer of the Seminary.

1934　Student body falls to 353.

1935–1936　Student enrollment rises to 389.

1937　Louisville stricken by the Great Flood. Seminary buildings shelter flood victims.

1941–1942　Student enrollment reaches 520.

1942　President John R. Sampey resigns.

1942　At San Antonio, Texas, Dr. Ellis A. Fuller of Atlanta elected president of Southern Seminary.

1943 School of Music established with Dr. Donald Winters as its first director. Trustee V. V. Cooke donates Cooke Hall to the new school.

1948 Six new professors added to faculty at fall opening. Garland K. Offut is first Negro to receive the Th.D. degree.

1950 Alumni Chapel completed and dedicated in March.

1950 President Ellis A. Fuller, after eight years as president of Southern, dies of a heart attack at San Diego, California, October 20.

1950 Dr. Gaines S. Dobbins becomes interim president.

1951 Dr. Duke K. McCall elected seventh president of Southern Seminary.

1953 Green Tree Manor, 265-apartment project, now Seminary Village, acquired by Seminary.

1953 Three new deans elected: Forest Heeren, School of Music; Gaines S. Dobbins, School of Religious Education; and Hugh R. Peterson, Dean of Students.

1953 School of Religious Education established with seven full faculty members.

1954 First summer school session starts June 8, Dr. H. C. Goerner, director.

1956 First Layman's Leadership Institute on Southern's campus, January 12–14.

1956 Enrollment in the ninety-eighth year of Seminary rises to 1767 students. Eight new professors added to faculty.

1956 Dr. Allen Graves inaugurated as Dean of School of Religious Education on September 18.

1957 Librarian Dr. Leo Crismon turns a spade of dirt at ground-breaking ceremonies for the James P. Boyce Memorial Library, May 24.

1957 Professor Ernest Loessner elected by Southern alumni in Chicago as director of $500,000 alumni campaign for the J. P. Boyce Library.

1957 Dr. William Peyton Thurman of Hopkinsville, Kentucky, elected dean of students.

Abstract of Principles

The following is an excerpt from the Fundamental Laws of the Seminary written into its charter on April 30, 1858: "9. Every Professor of the Institution shall be a member of a regular Baptist Church; and all persons accepting Professorships in this Seminary, shall be considered by such acceptance, as engaging to teach in accordance with, and not contrary to, the Abstract of Principles hereinafter laid down."

I. The Scriptures

The Scriptures of the Old and New Testaments were given by inspiration of God, and are the only sufficient, certain and authoritative rule of all saving knowledge, faith and obedience.

II. God

There is but one God, the Maker, Preserver and Ruler of all things, having in and of himself, all perfections, and being infinite in them all; and to Him all creatures owe the highest love, reverence and obedience.

III. The Trinity

God is revealed to us as Father, Son and Holy Spirit each with distinct personal attributes, but without division of nature, essence or being.

IV. Providence

God from eternity, decrees or permits all things that come to pass, and perpetually upholds, directs and governs all creatures and all events; yet so as not in any wise to be the author or approver of sin nor to destroy the free will and responsibility of intelligent creatures.

V. Election

Election is God's eternal choice of some persons unto everlasting life— not because of foreseen merit in them, but of his mere mercy in Christ —in consequence of which choice they are called, justified and glorified.

VI. The Fall of Man

God originally created man in His own image, and free from sin; but, through the temptation of Satan, he transgressed the command of God, and fell from his original holiness and righteousness; whereby his posterity inherit a nature corrupt and wholly opposed to God and His law, are under condemnation, and as soon as they are capable of moral action, become actual transgressors.

VII. The Mediator

Jesus Christ, the only begotten Son of God, is the divinely appointed mediator between God and man. Having taken upon Himself human nature, yet without sin, He perfectly fulfilled the law, suffered and died upon the cross for the salvation of sinners. He was buried, and rose again the third day, and ascended to His Father, at whose right hand He ever liveth to make intercession for His people. He is the only Mediator, the Prophet, Priest and King of the Church, and Sovereign of the Universe.

VIII. Regeneration

Regeneration is a change of heart, wrought by the Holy Spirit, who quickeneth the dead in trespasses and sins, enlightening their minds spiritually and savingly to understand the Word of God, and renewing their whole nature, so that they love and practice holiness. It is a work of God's free and special grace alone.

IX. Repentance

Repentance is an evangelical grace, wherein a person being, by the Holy Spirit, made sensible of the manifold evil of his sin, humbleth himself for it, with godly sorrow, detestation of it, and self-abhorrence, with a purpose and endeavor to walk before God so as to please Him in all things.

X. Faith

Saving faith is the belief, on God's authority, of whatsoever is revealed in His Word concerning Christ; accepting and resting upon Him alone for justification and eternal life. It is wrought in the heart by the Holy Spirit, and is accompanied by all other saving graces, and leads to a life of holiness.

XI. Justification

Justification is God's gracious and full acquittal of sinners, who believe in Christ, from all sin, through the satisfaction that Christ has made; not for anything wrought in them or done by them; but on account of the obedience and satisfaction of Christ, they receiving and resting on Him and His righteousness by faith.

XII. Santification

Those who have been regenerated are also sanctified, by God's word and Spirit dwelling in them. This sanctification is progressive through the supply of Divine strength, which all saints seek to obtain, pressing after a heavenly life in cordial obedience to all Christ's commands.

XIII. Perseverance of the Saints

Those whom God hath accepted in the Beloved, and sanctified by His Spirit, will never totally nor finally fall away from the state of grace, but shall certainly persevere to the end; and though they may fall, through neglect and temptation, into sin, whereby they grieve the Spirit, impair their graces and comforts, bring reproach on the Church, and temporal judgments on themselves, yet they shall be renewed again unto repentance, and be kept by the power of God through faith unto salvation.

XIV. The Church

The Lord Jesus is the Head of the church, which is composed of all his true disciples, and in Him is invested supremely all power for its government. According to his commandment, Christians are to associate themselves into particular societies or churches; and to each of these churches he hath given needful authority for administering that order, discipline and worship which he hath appointed. The regular officers of a Church are Bishops or Elders, and Deacons.

XV. Baptism

Baptism is an ordinance of the Lord Jesus, obligatory upon every believer, wherein he is immersed in water in the name of the Father, and of the Son, and of the Holy Spirit, as a sign of his fellowship with the death and resurrection of Christ, of remission of sins, and of his giving himself up to God, to live and walk in newness of life. It is prerequisite to church fellowship, and to participation in the Lord's Supper.

XVI. The Lord's Supper

The Lord's Supper is an ordinance of Jesus Christ, to be administered with the elements of bread and wine, and to be observed by his churches till the end of the world. It is in no sense a sacrifice, but is designed to commemorate his death, to confirm the faith and other graces of Christians, and to be a bond, pledge and renewal of their communion with him, and of their church fellowship.

XVII. The Lord's Day

The Lord's day is a Christian institution for regular observance, and should be employed in exercises of worship and spiritual devotion, both public and private, resting from worldly employments and amusements, works of necessity and mercy only expected.

XVIII. Liberty of Conscience

God alone is Lord of the conscience; and He hath left it free from the doctrines and commandments of men, which are in anything contrary to

His word, or not contained in it. Civil magistrates being ordained of God, subjection in all lawful things commanded by them ought to be yielded by us in the Lord, not only for wrath, but also for conscience sake.

XIX. The Resurrection

The bodies of men after death return to dust, but their spirits return immediately to God—the righteous to rest with Him; the wicked, to be reserved under darkness to the judgment. At the last day, the bodies of all the dead, both just and unjust, will be raised.

XX. The Judgment

God hath appointed a day, wherein he will judge the world by Jesus Christ, when everyone shall receive according to his deeds: the wicked shall go into everlasting punishment; the righteous, into everlasting life.

Faculty

Those who have served on the faculty of the Seminary, named in the order of their election to the faculty by the Board of Trustees, are as follows:

Boyce, James Petigru (1827–1888), 1859–1888
Broadus, John Albert (1827–1895), 1859–1895
Manly, Basil, Jr. (1825–1892), 1859–1871; 1879–1892
Williams, William (1821–1877), 1859–1877
Toy, Crawford Howell (1836–1919), 1869–1879
Whitsitt, William Heth (1841–1911), 1872–1899
Riggan, George Washington (1855–1885), 1883–1885
Sampey, John Richard (1863–1946), 1887–1942
Kerfoot, Franklin Howard (1847–1901), 1887–1899
Robertson, Archibald Thomas (1863–1934), 1890–1934
Dargan, Edwin Charles (1852–1930), 1892–1907
Harris, Henry Herbert (1837–1897), 1896–1897
McGlothlin, William Joseph (1867–1933), 1896–1919
Carver, William Owen (1868–1954), 1898–1943
Mullins, Edgar Young (1860–1928), 1899–1928
Eager, George Boardman (1847–1929), 1900–1920
Dement, Byron Hoover (1863–1933), 1906–1914
Gardner, Charles Spurgeon (1859–1948), 1907–1929
Wayman, Harry Clifford (1881–   ), 1915–1923
Leavell, Landrum Pinson (1874–1929), 1915–1920
Powell, Frank Marion (1886–   ), 1918–1941
Dobbins, Gaines Stanley (1886–   ), 1920–1956
Davis, William Hersey (1887–1950), 1920–1950
Adams, James McKee (1886–1945), 1921–1945
Yates, Kyle Monroe (1895–   ), 1922–1942
Tribble, Harold Wayland (1899–   ), 1925–1947
Weatherspoon, Jesse Burton (1886–   ), 1929–
McDowell, Edward Allison, Jr. (1898–   ), 1937–1952
Johnson, Robert Inman (1895–   ), 1938–
Goerner, Henry Cornell (1908–   ), 1938–1957
Green, James Leo (1912–   ), 1941–1948
Stealey, Sydnor Lorenzo (1897–   ), 1942–1951
Fuller, Ellis Adams (1891–1950), 1942–1950

242

Peterson, Hugh Raymond (1903–   ), 1943–
Binkley, Olin Trivette (1908–   ), 1944–1952
McGlon, Charles Addis (1910–   ), 1944–
Almand, Claude Marion (1915–   ), 1944–1953
Winters, Mrs. Frances Weaver (1908–   ), 1944–1952
Cook, W. Lawrence (–), 1944–1947
Walker, Helen Smith (–), 1946–1947
Winters, Donald (1910–   ), 1946–1952
Francisco, Clyde Taylor (1916–   ), 1947–
Edge, Findley Bartow (1916–   ), 1947–
Nossaman, Audrey M. (1923–   ), 1947–1954
Packard, Donald Wheeler (1914–   ), 1947–1957
Pool, Frank Kenneth (1925–   ), 1947–1954
Owens, John Joseph (1918–   ), 1948–
Moody, Dale (1915–   ), 1948–
Morton, William Hardy (1915–   ), 1948–1958
Oates, Wayne Edward (1917–   ), 1948–
Mueller, William Arthur (1902–   ), 1948–
Price, Theron Douglas (1916–   ), 1948–1958
Turlington, Henry Eugene (1918–   ), 1949–1958
Stanfield, Vernon Latrelle (1920–   ), 1949–
Frenz, Mary Lou (1927–   ), 1949–1951
McElrath, Hugh Thomas (1921–   ), 1949–
Smith, Taylor Clarence (1915–   ), 1950–1958
Barnette, Henlee Hulix (1911–   ), 1951–
Jones, John Estill (1921–   ), 1951–1958
McCall, Duke Kimbrough (1914–   ), 1951–
Eddleman, Henry Leo (1911–   ), 1952–1954
Ranson, Guy Harvey (1916–   ), 1952–1958
Coker, Denton Reuben (1920–   ), 1952–1954
Heeren, Forrest Henry (1915–   ), 1952–
Ward, Wayne Eugene (1921–   ), 1953–
Landry, Sabin Paul (1917–   ), 1953–
Dahlin, Walter O. (1921–   ), 1953–1956
Stephens, Farrold (1919–   ), 1953–1957
Loessner, Ernest Joseph (1907–   ), 1953–
Rust, Eric Charles (1910–   ), 1953–
Adams, William Walter (1892–   ), 1954–
Hargis, Pauline (1916–   ), 1954–1958
Lumpkin, William Latane (1916–   ), 1954–1958
Jackson, Herbert Cross (1917–   ), 1954–
Jenkins, Paul Rogers (1929–   ), 1954–1956

Wood, James Henry (1921–   ), 1954–1958
Ashcraft, Jesse Morris (1922–   ), 1955–1958
Proctor, Robert Allen (1920–   ), 1955–
Graves, Allen Willis (1915–   ), 1955–
Elliott, Ralph Harrison (1925–   ), 1956–1958
Hall, Thomas Oscar, Jr. (1923–   ), 1956–1958
Lewis, John Moore (1921–   ), 1956–1958
McClanahan, John Howard (1929–   ), 1956–1957
Peacock, Heber Fletcher (1918–   ), 1956–1958
Wamble, Gaston Hugh (1923–   ), 1956–1958
Warkentin, Mabel (1926–   ), 1956–
Crismon, Leo Taylor (1906–   ), 1956–
Stiles, Joseph (1903–   ), 1956–
Howington, Nolan P. (1917–   ), 1957–
Hinson, Maurice C. (1930–   ), 1957–
Ferguson, Ray (–   ), 1957–58
Bushnell, William C. (1922–   ), 1957–
Hammar, Russell A. (1920–   ), 1957–
Thurman, William Peyton (1913–   ), 1957–
Southard, Samuel (1924–   ), 1958–
Sims, John Norman (1928–   ), 1958–
Russell, Allyn (1920–   ), 1958–
Hutchens, Elizabeth (1924–   ), 1958–
Callaway, Joseph (1920–   ), 1958–
Vardaman, E. J. (1927–   ), 1958–
Ellis, E. Earle (1926–   ), 1958–
Hull, William E. (1930–   ), 1958–

Bibliography

General Articles Chronologically Arranged

STRONG, AUGUST H. "Recent Tendencies in Theological Thought," *The American Journal of Religion*, (January, 1897).

DONOVAN, W. N. "Forty Years Among Students for the Baptist Ministry," *The Crozer Quarterly*, (July, 1943).

MOFFAT, JAMES. "The Limits of Historical Method," *Contemporary Thinking About Jesus*. Compiled by Thomas S. Kepler. (Nashville: Abingdon-Cokesbury Press, 1944).

McCRACKEN, R. J. "Let the Preacher Preach the Word," *Theology Today*, (October, 1946).

TILLICH, PAUL. "The Problem of Theological Method: A Conversation," *The Journal of Religion*, (January, 1947).

HERRIOTT, FRANK W. "Theology and Method for Ministers," *Union Seminary Quarterly Review*, (March, 1949).

PIPER, OTTO A. "The Authority of the Bible," *Theology Today*, (July, 1949).

NASH, ARNOLD S. "The Totalitarian University and Christian Higher Education," *Theology Today*, (October, 1949).

LITTELL, FRANKLIN H. "American Thoughts about the Church," *Union Seminary Quarterly Review*, (March, 1950).

RENDTORFF, HEINRICH. "Warum Theologische Wissenschaft," *Theologische Literaturzeitung*, No. 6, 75, Jhg., (June, 1950).

HAHN, WILHELM. "Zur Frage des Theologischen Studiums," *Theologische Literaturzeitung*, No. 10, 77, Jhg., (October, 1952).

SCHMIDT, KARL LUDWIG. "The Church," *Theology Today*, (April, 1952).

MACKAY, JOHN A. "Church Order: Its Meaning and Implications," *Theology Today*, (January, 1953).

JOHNSON, ROBERT C. "The Jesus of History and the Christian Faith," *Theology Today*, (July, 1953).

245

RUST, ERIC C. "Time and Eternity in Biblical Thought," *Theology Today*, (October, 1953).

BOWMAN, JOHN WICK. "From Schweitzer to Bultmann," *Theology Today*, (July, 1954).

ECKARDT, A. ROY. "Racial Prejudice and Discrimination: Civil and Christian Approaches," *Theology Today*, (October, 1954).

NIEBUHR, H. RICHARD *et al.* "The Main Issues in Theological Education," *Theology Today*, (January, 1955).

BENNETT, JOHN C. "Are There Tests of Revelation?" *Theology Today*, (April, 1955).

HOON, PAUL W. "The Relation of Theology and Music in Worship," *Union Seminary Quarterly Review*, (January, 1956).

BLIZZARD, SAMUEL W. "The Training of the Parish Minister," *Union Seminary Quarterly Review*, (January, 1956).

SCHNEIDER, JOHANNES. "Verkündigung und Theologie," *Wort und Tat*, (May–June, 1956).

FARBER, BENJAMIN F. "The Seminary Student Yesterday and Today," *Theology Today*, (July, 1956).

BAILLIE, JOHN. "Some Reflections on the Changing Theological Scene," *Union Seminary Quarterly Review*, (January, 1957).

GLEN, STANLEY. "Psychological Therapy and Christian Salvation," *Theology Today*, (January, 1958).

RAMM, BERNARD. "Baptists and Sources of Authority," *Foundations*, (July, 1958).

MARING, NORMAN H. "Baptists and Changing Views of the Bible, 1865–1918," *Foundations*, (July, 1958).

———. "Baptists and Changing Views of the Bible, 1865–1918," part II, *Foundations*, (October, 1958).

FERRÉ, NELS F. S. "Contemporary Theology in the Light of 100 Years," *Theology Today*, (October, 1958).

CRISMON, LEO T. "Theological Education," *Encyclopedia of Southern Baptists*, (Nashville: Broadman Press, 1958).

MUELLER, WILLIAM A. "Theological Education," *The Encyclopedia Americana*, (New York: Americana Corporation, 1958).

Books

BAINTON, ROLAND H. *Yale and the Ministry*. New York: Harper & Brothers, 1957.

BARNES, W. W. *The Southern Baptist Convention, 1845–1953*. Nashville: Broadman Press, 1954.

BARTH, KARL. Der Christ als Zeuge [Theologische Existenz Heute, Heft 12]. Munich: Chr. Kaiser Verlag, 1934.

BAKER, ROBERT A. *Relations Between Northern and Southern Baptists*. n.p. 1948.

BAUR, F. C. *Geschichte der christlichen Kirche*. Tübingen, L. Fr. Fues 1863.

BOYCE, JAMES P. *Three Changes in Theological Education*. Greenville, South Carolina: C. J. Elford, 1956.

————. *Abstract of Systematic Theology*. Philadelphia: American Baptist Publication Society, 1899.

BROADUS, JOHN A. *Commentary on the Gospel of Matthew (An American Commentary on the New Testament*, ed. Alvah Hovey). Philadelphia: American Baptist Publication Society, 1886.

————. *Jesus of Nazareth*. New York: A. C. Armstrong & Son, 1890.

————. *Memoir of James Petigru Boyce*. New York: A. C. Armstrong & Son, 1893.

————. *Sermons and Addresses*. Baltimore: H. M. Wharton and Company, 1886.

————. *Addresses, Essays, and Lectures*. Philadelphia: American Baptist Publication Society, 1883.

BROWN, WILLIAM A., ed. *The Education of the American Minister*. New York: New York Institute of Social and Religious Research, 1934.

————. *The Case for Theology in the University*. Chicago: The University of Chicago Press, 1938.

BURROUGHS, P. E. *Fifty Fruitful Years*. Nashville: Broadman Press, 1941.

CARVER, W. O. *Missions and Modern Thought*. New York: The Macmillan Company, 1910.

————. *Christian Missions in Today's World*. New York: Harper & Brothers, Publishers, 1942.

————. *Out of His Treasure*. Nashville: Broadman Press, 1956.

CATHCART, JOHN A. *The Baptist Encyclopedia*. Philadelphia: Louis H. Everts, 1881.

CUTHBERT, JAMES HAZZARD. *Life of Richard Fuller*. New York: Sheldon and Company, 1879.

DANIEL, ROBERT NORMAN. *Furman University*. Greenville, South Carolina: Hiott Press, 1951.

DE BLOIS, AUSTEN KENNEDY. *Fighters for Freedom*. Philadelphia: Judson Press, 1929.

FABER, HERMANN. *Neue Wege der Pfarrerausbildung*. Tübingen: J. C. B. Mohn (Paul Siebeck), 1934.

FOSTER, HENRY B. *History of the Tuscaloosa County Baptist Association, 1834–1934*. Tuscaloosa, Alabama: Weatherford Printing Company, 1934.

GAMBRELL, MARY L. "Ministerial Education in Eighteenth Century New England." (Unpublished Ph.D. dissertation, Columbia University, New York, 1937).

GILL, EVERETT. *A. T. Robertson, A Bibliography*. New York: The Macmillan Company, 1943.

HARTSHORNE, HUGH, AND FROYD, MILTON C. *Theological Education in the Northern Baptist Convention*. Philadelphia: Judson Press, 1945.

HENRY, CARL F., ed. *Contemporary Evangelical Thought*. New York: Channel Press, 1947.

HENRY, ROBERT S. *The Story of Reconstruction*. New York: Peter Smith, 1951.

———. *The Story of the Confederacy*. New York: Grosset and Dunlap, 1936.

HERRICK, EVERETT CARLTON, *Turns Again Home*. Boston: Pilgrim Press, 1949.

HEWITT, ARTHUR WENTWORTH. *High Shepherds: A Book of the Rural Pastorate*. Chicago: Willet, Clark & Company, 1939.

HUDSON, WINTHROP S. *The Great Tradition of the American Churches*. New York: Harper & Brothers, 1953.

JAMES, W. C. *A History of the Western Baptist Theological Seminary*. Louisville: Baptist World Publishing Co., 1905.

JOHNSTON, J. STODDARD, ed. *Memorial History of Louisville*. Chicago: American Biographical Company, 1896.

KELLY, ROBERT L. *Theological Education in America.* New York: George H. Doran Company, 1924.

KIMBROUGH, B. T. *The History of the Walnut Street Baptist Church.* Louisville: Western Recorder Press, 1949.

LEWIS, A. FAYETTE. *History of Higher Education in Kentucky.* Washington, D. C.: United States Government Printing Office, 1899.

LITTLEJOHN, CARRIE U. *History of Carver School of Missions and Social Work.* Nashville: Broadman Press, 1958.

LORD, F. TOWNLEY. *Baptist World Fellowship.* Nashville: Broadman Press, 1955.

MANLY, BASIL, JR. *The Bible Doctrine of Inspiration.* New York: A. C. Armstrong and Son, 1888.

MANLY, LOUISE, compiler. *The Manly Family.* Greenville, South Carolina: n.p., 1930.

McGLOTHLIN, W. J. *Baptist Beginnings in Education.* Nashville: Sunday School Board of the Southern Baptist Convention, 1926.

McGLON, CHARLES A. "Speech Education in Baptist Theological Seminaries, 1819–1943." (Unpublished Ph.D. dissertation, Columbia University, 1943).

McNEILL, JOHN THOMAS. *A History of the Cure of Souls.* New York: Harper & Brothers, 1951.

MULLINS, ISLA MAY. *Edgar Young Mullins.* Nashville: Sunday School Board of the Southern Baptist Convention, 1929.

NEWMAN, A. H. *History of the Baptists in the United States.* Philadelphia: American Baptist Publication Society, 1895.

NIEBUHR, H. RICHARD. *The Purpose of the Ministry.* New York: Harper & Brothers, 1956.

NIEBUHR, H. RICHARD *et al. The Ministry in Historical Perspective* (New York: Harper & Brothers, 1956).

——. *The Advancement of Theological Education.* New York: Harper & Brothers, 1957.

ROBERTSON, A. T. *Life and Letters of John Albert Broadus.* Philadelphia: American Baptist Publication Society, 1901.

SAMPEY, JOHN R. *Southern Baptist Theological Seminary, The First Thirty Years.* Baltimore: Wharton, Barron and Company, 1890.

SAMPEY, JOHN R. *Memoirs of John R. Sampey*. Nashville: Broadman Press, 1947.

SCHLATTER, ADOLF. *Das christliche Dogma*. Stuttgart: Calver Verlag, 1923.

TORBET, ROBERT G. *A History of the Baptists*. Philadelphia: Judson Press, 1950.

WELCH, CLAUDE. *The Reality of the Church*. New York: Charles Scribner's Sons, 1958.

WILKINSON, WILLIAM CLEAVER. *Modern Masters of Pulpit Discourse*. New York: Funk & Wagnalls Co., 1905.

WILLIAMS, GEORGE H., ed. *The Harvard Divinity School*. Boston: Beacon Press, 1954.

Index

Adams, J. McKee, 207, 216, 219, 221
Adams, Theodore F., 189
Adams, W. W., 32, 203
Alien immersion, 105
Allen, T. R., Jr., 229
Allmond, Marcus B., 51
Almond, A. D., 154
Alumni Chapel, 218–19, 226
American Association of Theological Schools, 215
American Baptist Home Mission Society, 41, 107
American Baptist Indian Mission Association, 10
American Baptist Missionary Union, 8, 106
American Baptist Publication Society, 93, 108
Apostolic polity, 108–9
Archeology, 81, 90, 120, 228
Arminianism, 29, 58, 121
Arnold, Matthew, 76
Ashmore, William, 9
Athanasius, 70
Augusta (Ga.), 2, 13

Bainton, Roland H., 18, 225
Baptists, Northern, 6, 8, 9, 32, 38, 41, 65, 88, 156
  aid of, 38, 41, 48, 49, 94
Baptists, Southern, viii, 2, 5, 8, 12, 28, 32, 40, 65, 105, 110, 165
  Baptist origins, 155 ff., 158 ff., 162–63
  Convention, 2, 9, 11, 12, 40, 41, 43, 45, 49, 51, 65, 93, 98, 106, 107, 123, 156, 162, 168, 171, 205, 212, 213
  Domestic Board of Missions, 3

Baptists, Southern (*Continued*)
  Foreign Mission Board, 3, 107, 123
  Home Mission Board, 182, 217
  Sunday School Board, 66, 92, 93, 110, 130, 170, 186, 230
  Sunday School lectures, 187
Baptist World Alliance, 187–89, 209–10, 212
Baptism, 155, 157–58, 163
Barnes, W. W., 12, 16, 156, 179
Barnette, Henley, 228
Barth, Karl, 147
Barth, Marcus, 227
Baur, Ferdinand Christian, 76, 78–79
Baylor University, 9, 170, 208
Berlin University, 144, 195, 199
Bible, 70, 71, 80, 96, 97, 122, 137
  Geneva Bible, 70
  Old Latin Bible, 70
Biblical Criticism, 1, 27, 58, 64, 69, 90, 96, 100, 133, 138, 149
Biblical Recorder, 160
Binkley, Olin T., 222
Bonnell, John S., 223
Bostwick, J. A., 48
Bowen, C. C., 65
Bowen, T. J., 1
Boyce, James P., viii, 1, 2, 10–52, 55–61, 64–65, 84, 89, 93, 99, 102–5, 110, 119, 123, 126, 132 ff., 135, 139, 189, 213
Boyce, Ker, 16, 20–21
Brantley, W. T., 17
Bray, Mellen, 190
Briggs, C. Augustus, 62
Broaddus, Andrew, 4, 25
Broadman Press, 6, 111, 230

251

Broadus, John A., 2, 11, 13–14, 21–22, 35–37, 40–52, 61–83, 93, 95, 99, 100, 102, 104–5, 110, 114, 123–24, 130, 139–40, 144–45, 150, 153–54, 186, 189, 197, 213, 223
Broadway Baptist Church (Louisville, Ky.), 48, 225, 226
Brooks, Phillips, 67
Brown, Joseph Emerson, 46, 128, 229
Brown University, 3, 7, 17–19, 21–22, 43, 52, 63
Bryant, Wade, 229
Budde, Karl, 140
Buddhism, 76
Bunyan, John, 25, 70, 122
Burleson, Rufus C., 9
Burrows, J. L., 189
Bushnell, Horace, 61, 134
Buttrick, George A., 223

Cadbury, Henry J., 204
Calvin, John, 79, 132–33
Calvinism, 32, 54, 57–58, 89, 121
Campbell, Alexander, 29, 30, 157
Carley, Ann Tarleton, 127
Carroll, B. H., 123, 160, 165–66, 170–71, 174, 176
Carver School of Missions and Social Work, 192, 208
Carver, William Owen, 3, 9, 31, 49, 57, 61, 67, 82, 98, 101, 142, 146, 150–51, 153–54, 162, 164, 181–82, 188, 192, 195–203, 213, 216, 219
Charleston (S. C.), 5, 11, 16, 17, 20, 35, 84
 association, 5, 21
 First Baptist Church, 18, 84
Charlottesville (Va.), 62, 68
Christian Index, 19, 46, 160
Chrysostom, 108
Church, 9, 18, 29, 30–31, 59, 63, 108, 147, 149, 166
Church Fathers, 31, 70
Church history, 143–50
Civil War, vii, 15, 34, 43, 64
Clarke, John, 3
Clarke, William Newton, 177
Cocke, General J. H., 62
Compton, A. H., 216
Colonial America, 3
Confederacy, 34–35, 37, 103

Cooke, V. V., 218
Cox, Joseph P., 84 ff.
Cox, Norman W., 195
Crabtree, Arthur, 227
Crismon, Leo T., 154, 215, 229
Crozer Theological Seminary, 43, 63, 148
Curry, J. L. M., 51, 66, 123, 129
Cutting, S. S., 41
Cyprian, 108

Dargan, C. E., 67, 127, 153, 162, 164, 168, 181, 192–93, 198
Dargan, J. O. B., 40
Darwin, Charles, 1, 76, 137, 138
David, Robert U., 39
Davis, Hersey W., 207, 216, 219–20, 222
Davis, Jefferson, 34
Dayton, A. C., 159
DeBlois, A. K. de, 19, 186
Deissmann, Adolf, 203
Dement, B. H., 187
Denison University, 7
Didache, 120, 122
Dillard, R. T., 8
Dobbins, Gaines S., 187, 209, 214, 219, 220, 225, 227, 228

Eager, George B., 191, 192
Eaton, T. T., 100, 160, 161, 165
Edge, Finley, 228
Education, 5, 10, 11, 13, 22, 24, 114, 117, 164, 186,
Edwards, Jonathan, 85
Ecclesiology, 108, 158–64, 193, 202
Elford, C. J., 93
Evening School, 227
Evolution, 1

Faculty Center, 218
Feezor, Forrest, 229
Ferré, Nels F. S., 223
Fisher, George Park, 18
Fleming, D. F., 223
Founders' Day, 189–90, 207, 235
Francisco, Clyde, 228
Frost, E. B., 216
Fuller, Ellis A., 216–19, 222, 224, 226
Fuller, Richard, 18, 41
Furman, James C., 34, 39–40

Furman, Richard, 5
Furman University, 13, 19, 21–22, 34, 39, 126

Gamaliel, 83
Gano, John, 25
Gardner, C. S., 173, 174, 207
Garrison, W. E., 202
Gay Foundation, 153
Georgetown College (Ky.), 7, 8, 92, 95, 96, 97, 103, 144
Georgia, 6, 14, 35, 36, 46, 102
    University of, 102
Gezork, Herbert, 207
Goerner, C. H., 216, 221
Goethe, Wolfgang von, 132
Going, Ezra, 7
Goodspeed, Edgar J., 203
Graves, Allen W., 128
Graves, J. R., 10, 12, 171, 197
Great Awakening, 3
Greene, J. P., 176
Green, W. H., 89
Green Tree Manor (Seminary Village), 226
Greenville (S. C.), vii, 12, 15, 33–35, 37, 42, 64, 110, 126

Halle University, 21, 199
Hamilton Literary and Theological Institution, 3, 9, 177
    Colgate University, 3
    Madison University, 20, 23
Harper, William Rainy, 64, 83, 114, 132, 212
Harris, Herbert H., 144, 154, 162, 164
Harris, Theodore, 42, 48, 190
Hart, Oliver, 5
Harrison, Gessner, 62
Harrison, J. Frank, Chair of New Testament Interpretation, 215
Harnack, Adolf von, 194
Harvard University, 52, 64, 69, 77, 99, 102, 139, 141–42
Hatcher, H. E., 118, 122
Hatcher, W. E., 165–66, 174, 176, 187
Hegel, W. G. F., 200
Hermeneutics, 26–27, 58, 72, 74–75, 80, 97, 136–37, 150
Herrick, C. Everett, 87
Hester, H. I., 229

History, 5, 9, 108, 121, 131, 160, 216
Hodge, Charles, 20, 56, 89, 134
Homrighausen, Elmer, 218, 224
Hopewell Academy, 3
Hopkins, Mark, 61
Houston, Sam, 9
Hovey, Alvah, 69
Hudson, Winthrop S., 60, 61
Humboldt, Alexander von, 132
Humphrey, Judge Alexander, 511

Ibsen, Henrik, 76
Individualism, 2

Jackson, Andrew, 2
James, William, 192
James, W. C., 7
Jesus Christ, 30–31, 44, 54, 56, 63–64, 75 ff., 86, 92, 104, 205
    resurrection of, 78–79
Jesus of Nazareth, 75–78
Jeremias, Alfred, 141
Jeter, J. B., 11
Jewish Encyclopedia, 141
Johns Hopkins University, 64, 75
Johnson, Inman, 207, 219
Johnson, C. Oscar, 189, 216
Johnson, W. B., 11–12
Johnson's Universal Cyclopedia, 155, 166, 168
Jones, T. G., 39
Jones, John E., 228, 243
Judson, Edward, 48

Kagawa, Toyohiko, 216
Kalamazoo College, 65
Keble, John, 132
Kentucky Baptists, 95
Kerfoot, F. H., 57, 153–54, 162, 164, 175–76, 181, 182
Kierkegaard, Soren, 5
Kind Words, 65, 93
Koehler, Walther, 5
Koran, 28

Lumpkin, William, 228
Landmarkers, 12, 105, 120, 156, 158–59, 197
Languages, 24, 70, 90, 98, 113 ff., 203–4
Latourette, Kenneth S., 216

Leipzig University, 144
Lee, General Robert E., 36, 196
Levering Gymnasium, 152
Levering, Joshua, 152, 167, 173, 174, 229
Lewis, Edwin, 223
Lewis, Walter O., 189
Lightfoot, J. B., 64, 70
Lincoln, Abraham, 34
Livingstone, David, 1
Locke, John, 132, 134
Lord's Prayer, 74
Lord's Supper, 73, 159
Louisville (Ky.), 39, 40–46, 50, 95, 139, 177
Luccock, Halford E., 223
Luther, Martin, 5, 16, 18, 70, 73, 79, 132
Lyman Beecher Lectures, 63
Lyon, David Gordon, 136, 137

Mackay, John, 224
MacMurray, John, 5
Manly, Basil, Sr., 2, 6, 10, 17, 84, 85–86, 92, 127
Manly, Basil, Jr., 2, 10–11, 14, 32, 37, 47, 51, 66, 84–102, 126–27, 130–31, 144, 186
Manly, Basil, Chair of Religious Education, 187
Marx, Karl, 1
Mather, Cotton, 134
Mather, Increase, 134
Maurice, Frederick D., 132
McCall, Duke K., 2, 156, 222, 225–26, 228
McCall, Lizette Kimbrough, Foundation for World Evangelism, 227
McDonald, Erwin L., 219–20
McDowell, Edward A., 216, 221–22
McFerran, J. B., 42
McFerran, J. C., 42
McGlon, Charles A., 5, 68
McGlothlin, W. J., 164, 181–82, 192, 194–96
McGuffey, W. H., 62, 64
Melanchthon, Philipp, 5, 203
Mercer, Jesse, 4, 19, 25
Mercer University, 14, 102
Methodists, 45, 60, 152
Mill, John Stuart, 76

Milton, John, 70
Minear, Paul, 225
Ministry, 3, 4, 22–25, 29, 35, 45, 71
Missions, 9, 24, 28, 64, 120, 135, 153, 198, 201–2
  Missionary Day, 123
Moffat, Robert, 1
Moody, Dale, 202
Moody, Dwight L., 1, 63
Moore, George Foote, 140
Moore, H. Guy, 227
Mormanism, 146
Morton, William H., 228
Moses, Rabbi, 51
Moulton, W. F., 64
Müller, Max, 74
Mullins, E. Y., 57, 132, 176–92, 198, 208–10, 213, 219
Music, School of, 218, 227, 228, 230, 231

Nash, Arnold, 99
Newman, A. H., 160
Newman, John Henry, 16
New Testament, 29, 30, 63, 69, 71, 79, 94, 108, 109, 113 ff., 128, 156, 158, 198, 204
Newton, Louie D., 188
Newton, Theological Institution (Andover-Newton), 3, 9, 23, 52, 63–64, 69, 87, 94, 100, 148, 176, 207, 208
New York Hall, 49–50
Northen, W. J., 167
Norton, George W., 42, 47, 153, 229
Norton, Mrs. George W., 219, 229
Norton, W. F., 42, 47, 229
Nossaman, Audrey, 228

Oates, Wayne E., 228–29
Old Testament, 90–91, 96, 99, 100, 113 ff., 130, 138, 142, 211, 212
Oncken, Johann Gerhard, 251
Orthodoxy, 30, 81, 119
Owens, Joseph J., 228

Parker, Theodore, 24
Particular Baptists, 31
Pastoral Care, 26, 144, 228, 229
Patterson, W. Morgan, 159
Paul, the apostle, 43, 122
Peacock, Heber F., 228

Peck, John Mason, 7
Pendleton, J. M., 10, 159
Peter, Arthur, 42
Phelps, William Lyon, 216
Philosophy, 18, 24, 55, 59, 148, 200
    theology and philosophy, 148–49
Plato, 18, 134
Poindexter, A. M., 10–13, 20, 68, 229
Poteat, E. M., 160
Powell, Frank K., 207, 219
Preaching, 3, 35, 150, 223
Presbyterians, 17, 20, 58, 63, 108, 121
Price, Theron D., 228
Princeton Theological Seminary, 8, 20, 89, 101, 120, 135
Puritanism, 61

Ramsey, David M., 83
Ranke, Leopold von, 132
Rankin, Theron, 223
Ranson, Guy H., 228
Rauschenbusch, Walter, 206, 207, 222
Rayzor, Mr. & Mrs. J. Newton, 226, 228
Reformation, 16, 71, 79
Renan, Ernest, 71, 78
Religious Education, 184, 186, 187, 197, 209, 212, 215, 219–20, 227–28, 230, 237
Religious Herald, 12, 160, 188
Revelation, 81, 207
Review and Expositor, 185 ff.
Righteousness, 73
Robertson, A. T., 1, 4, 44, 65, 67, 124, 126, 153, 162, 164, 167, 174, 181, 187, 188, 192, 198–99, 203–6, 216–17
Robinson, Ezekiel G., 8
Rochester Theological Seminary, 9, 23
Rust, Eric, 228

Sadler, William, 216
St. Bernard, 70
Sampey, John R., 21–22, 64, 126, 128–30, 144, 154, 161–64, 168–69, 173, 192, 209, 211–14, 216, 222
Schaff, Philip, 64
Schlatter, Adolf, 53
Schleiermacher, Friedrich W., 85, 192
Sears, Barnas, 94
Seminary Magazine, 49, 99, 119, 123, 125

Shakespeare, J. S., 188
Slavery, 2, 8, 34, 93
Smith, Mrs. J. Lawrence, 41, 84, 131
Smith, Presley B., 229
Smith, Samuel, 88
Smith, Taylor C., 228
Smyth, John, 31
Soul liberty, 104, 163–71, 179, 182, 185
South Carolina, 6, 13, 14, 15, 33, 34, 84, 93
Southeastern Baptist Theological Seminary, 222
Southern Baptist, 19
Southern Baptist Theological Seminary
    Abstract of Principles, 22, 29–31, 89, 166
    board of trustees, 14, 38, 39, 42–43, 49, 51, 117, 129, 135, 139, 142, 165 ff., 173, 229
    James P. Boyce Memorial Library, 226
    buildings, 15, 47
    confessional standards, 29–31
    curriculum, 22, 45, 90–91, 111
    endowment, 13, 15, 37, 38, 40–42, 46–48, 142
    establishment, 13–14, 16, 21, 31, 51, 63, 84, 89, 102
    faculty, 14–15, 33, 38–39, 42–43, 51–52 ff., 103, 124, 162 ff., 181, 183, 228
    finances, 13, 33, 35, 38, 40, 43, 63
    graduate studies, 27, 28, 31, 116
    library, 126–29, 132
    location, 39–40, 44–45, 95, 208
    Memorial Library, 131, 153, 209
    plan of organization, 14, 89, 102
    seminary hymn, 92
    student aid fund, 38, 94, 99
    student discipline, 124–25, 154
    students, 15, 20, 22, 31, 34, 37, 42, 57
        enrolment, 37, 45, 47, 152, 168, 215
Southwestern Baptist Theological Seminary, 170
Spalding, Mrs. John S., 128
Spencer, Herbert, 1, 134
Spurgeon, Charles H., 1, 67, 122
Stanfield, Vernon L., 68
Stealey, Sydnor L., 222
Stevens, J., 7

Strauss, David Friedrich, 71, 76
Summer school, 227

Talmud, 70
Tennessee Baptist, 160
Thayer, J. H., 64, 69
Theology, 55, 56, 147 ff.
 systematic theology, 26, 54–59, 103, 105, 113, 119, 149, 150
 theological education, 3–8, 87–89, 96, 97, 112, 114, 119, 125, 131, 151
 theological encyclopedia, 53–56
Tischendorf, Kenrad, 1, 132, 144
Toy, Crawford H., 1, 42, 63–64, 69, 81, 93, 96, 99, 110–11, 118, 126, 135–42, 154
Tribble, Harold W., 57, 207–8, 219
Triennial Convention, 7, 10
Trimmer, Maurice, 219
Truett, George W., 189, 210, 216
Tupper, H. A., 20, 34
Turlington, Henry E., 228
Tuscaloosa (Ala.), 86
Twentieth Century Endowment Campaign, 190–191

Union Theological Seminary, 135
Union University, 143

Van Ness, I. J., 174
Vedder, Henry, 171
Virginia, 5, 7, 8, 62, 82, 136
 Baptist Education Society, 12

University of Virginia, 8, 52, 61, 63, 112, 136, 144

Waller, J. L., 10
Walnut Street Baptist Church (Louisville, Ky.), 20, 180–81
Warden, Joseph W., 20, 174
Warfield, B. B., 64
Warneck, Gustav, 199
Wayland, Francis, 18, 19, 22, 24–25, 88
Weatherspoon, Jesse B., 67, 207, 216, 219, 222–23, 228
Weiss, Bernhard, 70
Wellhausen, Julius, 137, 142
Western Baptist Institute, 7–8, 9
Westcott, B. F., 64, 69
Westin, Gunnar, 186
Western Recorder, 160–61, 168
Whitley, W. T., 198
Whitsitt, W. H., 2, 42, 51, 81–82, 99–100, 126–27, 143–79, 189, 213
Wilkinson, W. C., 67
Williams, Roger, 3, 121, 155, 168
Williams, William, 2, 14, 52, 102–6, 126, 128, 159
Winkler, E. T., 14, 35, 102
Woman's Missionary Training School, 183–84, 191, 202

Yale University, 18, 63, 114, 204, 225
Yates, Kyle M., 207, 208, 243

Date Due

Ind.			
OC17 '68			